This book is about practical, ethical, and compassionate a
beautifully crafted common sense. It is an inspirational gif
you. It can shake you up, wake you up, and raise your consci
do the best for ourselves, our families, our animals, and our p
Here is help. After reading this book I didn't just think, yes

.... ZEPHANIAH
Poet, writer, lyricist, musician and trouble maker

Long time permaculture practitioner and activist Graham Burnett has written a very
practical guide to living lightly using permaculture design within the ethical constraints
and opportunities of a vegan diet. Based on lived experience rather than ideology, the
strong focus on food, complete with recipes, helps vegans and omnivores alike make better
use of the diversity of plant based ingredients in cool temperate climates. For vegans
wanting to reduce their ecological footprint, maintain nutritional balance and increase their
autonomy and resilience in a rapidly changing world, this book is the ideal introduction to
permaculture living and land use.

DAVID HOLMGREN
Co-originator of the Permaculture concept

Hugely inspiring and fantastically useful. I love the mix of Graham's cheerful tone, quirky
pictures and hard-won experience. This book will interest anyone seeking to live more
enjoyably and with greater autonomy whether vegan or not.

TOM HODGKINSON
Author of *How To Be Free* and founder of The Idler Academy

In his inimitable maverick fashion, Graham Burnett has jumbled together the pragmatism
of Permaculture with the DIY ethos of punk, and come up with an essential and practical
guidebook for anyone even remotely interested in the true nature of cultural (r)evolution.

PENNY RIMBAUD
Performer, philosopher, writer, and founder of the band/collective, Crass

This wonderful book is full of fascinating new things to learn and old things to remember.
Wherever you live, even in cities, nature is there breaking through, and with a little nurture
will thrive and provide beauty, food, a sense of joy and some hard manual work!

EVE LIBERTINE
Crass vocalist and co-founder of Butterfields Green Community Orchard

Wanting to create ways of living that respect, protect and enrich the awe-inspiring diversity
of life and culture on Earth is one thing; actually setting about doing it is quite another.
In *The Vegan Book of Permaculture*, Graham Burnett gives you many of the practical tools
you need to live in a healthy, connected relationship with both the human and non-human
world around you.

MARK BOYLE
Author of *The Moneyless Manifesto*

Graham has put together a wise, concise and accessible guide useful for both experienced
and those fresh to permaculture and veganism. The recipes are so vibrant you can almost
taste them on the pages!

LOOBY MACNAMARA
Permaculture teacher and author of *People and Permaculture* and *7 Ways to Think Differently*

Graham Burnett is indubitably the Godfather of London Permaculture.

STEFAN GEYER

Chair of Permaculture Association and host of 21st Century Permaculture Radio Show

This book brings permaculture and veganism together into one volume designed to motivate and inspire the compassionate, creative activist inside all of us. Chock full of useful information, it is more than design concepts and practical techniques, it also gives a view of a just, abundant and joyful world, waiting to be.

WILLIAM FAITH

Permaculture designer/teacher, musician and co-founder Black Rose Arts Collective

Graham's much awaited book is far more than just being about permaculture for vegans. Within you'll find in-depth information about creating an ecological and abundant lifestyle that applies to us all. Woven in between the diverse topics are a multitude of tasty vegan recipes that Graham has fine-tuned over the years. As a 30-year vegan myself, I'm looking forward to trying them out and delighted to finally see this long-vacant niche being filled so well. Great job, Graham!

ARANYA

Permaculture teacher and author of Permaculture Design: A Step-by-Step Guide

Whether you're a vegan, or someone just seeking to eat a lot less meat, this book will be just right for you. He shows how ecological thinking and action is good for us, good for the planet, and tastes great too!

ANDY GOLDRING

CEO Permaculture Association (Britain)

The Vegan Book of Permaculture offers a clear and accessible pathway through the garden of ethical food, from design and cultivation to nutrition and cooking, all aspects of why and how to take up growing and feed ourselves are there for the picking!

CLAIRE WHITE

Permaculture teacher and forest gardener

A refreshing, radical approach to sustainable living, it is absolutely bursting with interesting, inspiring and engaging snippets.

BRENDA DAVIS and VESANTO MELINA

Authors of Becoming Vegan: Express Edition and Becoming Vegan: Comprehensive Edition

Graham has pioneered vegan permaculture and this book is testament to his knowledge and passion. Graham integrates a desire for social justice for non-humans with the ethics, principles and practices of permaculture in a beautiful and accessible way. Its applications worldwide for social change are clear and I hope this book inspires a movement to change our landscapes and society to radically change how we interact with animals and each other.

NICOLE VOSPER

Permaculture designer, gardener and community organiser

The Vegan Book
of Permaculture

GRAHAM BURNETT

Permanent Publications

Published by
Permanent Publications
Hyden House Ltd
The Sustainability Centre
East Meon
Hampshire GU32 1HR
United Kingdom
Tel: 0844 846 846 4824 (local rate UK only)
        or +44 (0)1730 823 311
Fax: 01730 823 322
Email: enquiries@permaculture.co.uk
Web: www.permanentpublications.co.uk

Distributed in the USA by
Chelsea Green Publishing Company, PO Box 428, White River Junction, VT 05001
www.chelseagreen.com

Designed and typeset by Emma Postill

Cover image by Graham Burnett
Cover design concept Tibor Miklos

Printed in the UK by CPI Antony Rowe, Chippenham, Wiltshire

All paper from FSC certified mixed sources

The Forest Stewardship Council (FSC) is a non-profit international
organisation established to promote the responsible management of
the world's forests. Products carrying the FSC label are independently
certified to assure consumers that they come from forests that are
managed to meet the social, economic and ecological needs of present
and future generations.

British Library Cataloguing-in-Publication Data
A catalogue record for this book is available from the British Library
ISBN 978 1 85623 201 2

Contents

Recipe Index

Introduction

Permaculture can be summed up as using ethical design to create abundant yet sustainable ways of living for all Earth Citizens. It stresses patterns of co-operation rather than competition in order to achieve goals that are both ecologically sound and economically viable. The principles of permaculture can be applied to gardening, agriculture, building, 'green' economics, transport, waste treatment, health care, creating a livelihood and community development. Or to as basic, yet important, an activity as preparing a meal.

How we eat is such a fundamental part of what we are; yet in our industrialised culture it has so often become just another symptom of alienation and disempowerment. Pre-packaged, processed 'fast' foods relegate the acts of cooking and eating to a mere inconvenience, to be dispensed with as quickly as possible in our stressful busy lives. Our leisure time too is at a premium, so who wants to waste it in the kitchen when we could be consuming the cheeky wit or glamorous sophistication of the latest celebrity TV chef? Forget the food miles, factory farms, exploited labourers, eroded soils, polluted water ground water, GMOs and pesticides: just keep spectating...

But it doesn't have to be this way. If nothing else, permaculture gives us the tools and confidence to take responsibility for our lives and actions. Creating a good meal, either for us or to share with friends or family, taking time to prepare fresh, wholesome ingredients with care and respect, can be a deeply liberating experience. It's also a way of taking back some control from the advertising agencies and multinational corporations and making a very real difference in both personal and planetary terms.

The recipes featured in this book are not only delicious, healthy and wholesome; they have also been chosen to be relatively 'low impact'. They use a minimum of packaged or processed ingredients, and the preparation required is uncomplicated. Furthermore, they all emphasise the usage of animal-free, plant based ingredients that, in theory at least, can be grown at home or within a cool temperate climate zone such as the UK, thus reducing both 'food mile' impacts and the 'ecological footprints' caused by large-scale animal-centred agriculture.

Note that this isn't intended to be used as a 'rulebook'. Instead think of the recipes and information in here as broad guidelines and ideas. Some elements and ingredients that work well together as 'patterns' can be adapted to your own preferences, tastes and circumstances. For this reason most of them aren't written down in terms of accurate measurements, but instead encourage you to experiment and get a 'feel' for what is right: what vegetables and grains complement each other? What proportions of herbs and spices will add flavour without dominating? What textures, tastes and colours are aesthetically pleasing to the eye as well as the palate?

Personally I seldom follow the recipes or gardening tips that I find written down in books. Instead I use them as springboards for my own creativity, and I'd encourage you to do the same. My garden is not the same size or shape as yours, neither are my taste buds or ideas about what 'serves 4' means. Don't like carrots? Substitute an apple! Your design proposal to the local council for a forest garden in the grounds of a day centre for people with special needs has been rejected? Rename it an 'edible sensory fruit maze' and resubmit it – it worked for me once! As with the best permaculture designs so with cooking – observation, adaptation and experimentation are the keys!

Recipes are credited throughout to those who have submitted them, even if I have ended up adapting them a bit. Unaccredited recipes are my responsibility (although how they are used is yours!), either my own creations or adapted from sources long forgotten.

CHAPTER 1

Permaculture and Veganism - The Basics

"Permaculture offers a radical approach to food production and urban renewal, water, energy and pollution. It integrates ecology, landscape, organic gardening, architecture and agro-forestry in creating a rich and sustainable way of living. It uses appropriate technology giving high yields for low energy inputs, achieving a resource of great diversity and stability. The design principles are equally applicable to both urban and rural dwellers."

Bill Mollison

So What Is Permaculture Anyway?

'Permaculture' is a combination of the words PERMAnent and agriCULTURE (or latterly PERMAnent CULTURE, for no culture can survive for long without a sustainable agricultural base or land use ethic at its heart). The original ideas were developed in the late 1970s by two Australians, David Holmgren and Bill Mollison, as a response to what they recognised as serious ecological threats to the survival of all of us. It's a holistic design system – a way of making links and connections and seeing how elements are placed in relation to each other. In this way we can create regenerative, self maintaining, low input/high output, non-exploiting systems that will help us to thrive and live abundantly in ways that will meet the needs of future generations as well as our own. Permaculture now probably has as many definitions as there are practitioners, but one that is particularly useful might be: "creating sustainable human habitats by following nature's patterns".

Permaculture isn't about having to get your head around untold facts, figures, Latin names and complicated techniques, rather it is about recognising universal patterns and principles, and learning to apply these 'ecological truisms' to our own gardens and life situations. We can identify the underlying forms that recur throughout the natural world and learn to understand and utilise them in designed ecologies.

At the heart of the permaculture concept is a set of ethics, or 'core values', that are embedded into and inform all of our actions or design decisions:

'Earthcare' (we recognise that our Earth, Gaia, is the source of all life and respect her accordingly).

'Peoplecare' (we support and help each other to change to ways of living that are not harming ourselves or the planet – we realise that we are a part of the Earth, not apart from it).

'Fair Shares' (we ensure that the Earth's limited resources are utilised in ways that are equitable and wise, and that we share our surpluses rather than accumulate them – there's enough for all our needs but not for all our greed).

Influenced by 'Systems Thinkers' such as Howard T. Odum and Donella Meadows, permaculture design principles are a set of guidelines derived from the study of both the natural world and what has worked for non-industrialised sustainable societies, often for many millennia. As peak oil, climate change and the precarious nature of our current financial systems become increasingly difficult to ignore, we can apply these to a variety of circumstances and situations in order to help us transition towards what is likely to be a low energy, low carbon future. Such principles are often about our attitude to situations, and can be clearly demonstrated when applied to our kitchens, gardens, allotments, fields, forests, orchards and cities.

Work with Nature, Not Against Her

Francis Bacon's assertion in the early 1600s that we must 'bend nature to our will' has informed our species' relationship with this fragile planet for much of the modern era. Now in these days of desertification, flooding, global warming and mass extinction, we are seeing just how futile and plain wrong-headed such a philosophy truly is. Putting massive efforts into attempting to 'tame nature', such as by creating and maintaining bare soil by plough, is not only energy consuming, unsustainable and destructive, it is also unnecessary when we can meet the needs of people and the environment by working in harmony with natural systems.

Observation Is the Key

In contrast to our prevailing 'fast food and quick fix' culture, permaculture is about practising protracted and thoughtful observation instead of looking for instant solutions that in the long run often cause even more damage to a situation. Rather than rushing to address what are often superficial symptoms, the first question a permaculture designer will ask is, "What is really going on here?" Are persistent aphid attacks on your runner beans due to a lack of the correct pesticides being applied, or is this a manifestation of more fundamental imbalances within the wider ecology of your garden? Are high levels of crime in your locality best tackled by installing more CCTV cameras in the street, or by addressing deeper social malaises such as inequality, poverty and social alienation? Good observation is about seeing holistically, looking at all the functions and characteristics of the plants, animals and humans in an environment and how they interact with each other, often over extended periods of time. Learn to develop and practise the skills of observation by taking time to sit back, ground yourself and watch, listen, smell, taste, feel and contemplate.

Design from Pattern to Detail

Both in nature and in human communities, patterns in time and space recur on an almost infinite number of levels. Branching patterns can be observed in the form and structure of a tree's growth, as well as in river deltas and the central nervous and circulatory systems of vertebrates. The spiral is a mathematically derived pattern that can be seen on scales ranging from sub-atomic particles to galaxies, or from continental storm fronts to the arrangement of seeds in a sunflower head. The movement of the sun through the sky in summer and winter governs day length and the patterns of plant growth and seasonal activity. We can also determine social and human patterns that are basically unchanged since prehistoric times. These include our need for rituals and festivals that mark special occasions or the cycles of the year, or the importance we almost subconsciously place on the stories and myths that transmit intergenerational knowledge and cultural values.

In a sense patterns are a set of rules and constants that broadly define form, function and behaviour, yet at the same time allow for an infinite variation of detail when made manifest. For example, most of us know an oak tree when we see one; we instantly recognise its distinctive lobed leaves, grey-fissured bark and the typical shape of its trunk and canopy at various life stages from seedling to maturity. Yet no two oak trees are exactly alike. Each individual's specific location, environment and genetic peculiarities cause a myriad of variations in how the basic patterns encoded in the oak's DNA are implemented. So too the permaculture design tool of 'zone and sector planning' (see page 14) is a pattern for predicting and working with human and natural energy flows that has an unlimited number of applications in the real world.

Being able to recognise, understand and utilise the properties of pattern – in other words working with 'pattern language' – is a fundamental prerequisite to developing good design skills in a multitude of contexts that might range from creating location-suitable productive gardens to successfully managing a complex community development project.

Everything Gardens, or Modifies, Its Environment

When we mindfully observe nature, we can see that animals and plants are often carrying out many of the tasks that we consider gardening chores as they go about their daily business of finding sustenance or adapting their habitats to meet their own needs. Worms dig and aerate the land; leaf fall mulches bare soil, adds nutrients and improves its structure; fast spreading wild annual plants ('weeds') such as chickweed provide overwintering ground cover; slugs devour dead plant matter and begin the composting process that is continued by bacteria, fungi and other micro organisms; bees pollinate our fruit bushes and the droppings of birds sew and spread seeds and add fertiliser.

So instead of whipping out the Bug Gun at the first sign of pest damage, why not encourage predators such as ladybirds and hoverflies to do our work for us by planting attractant flowers such as limnanthes (poached egg plant), nigella (love in a mist) or buckwheat? Instead of damaging the soil's structure and straining our backs with constant digging, why not add compost directly to the soil as a surface mulch and utilise the worms' free labour inputs, whilst at the same time suppressing weeds and providing protection from the elements?

The Problem Is the Solution

Or, as Bill Mollison didn't quite say, "You haven't got an excess of slugs, you've got a frog deficiency..." In other words, it is how we look at things that makes them advantageous or not. Sometimes a simple change of perspective can help us to see that what at first appears to be a difficulty or a challenge can in fact be a gift... As another example, the arrival of wild plants on our plots is inevitable; what we do have a choice about is our approach to them. Are they 'weeds', against which a constant yet futile war of attrition is waged, or are they a resource, valuable in at least parts of the garden even if we don't allow them to dominate in our productive areas? Such plants increase biodiversity, act as 'dynamic accumulators' (that is, they mine the subsoil with their roots to bring up minerals that may be deficient on the surface), attract beneficial wildlife and can be harvested for compost or mulch material. Many are even edible or medicinal, or have a host of other uses and properties that are now largely forgotten.

There are also many situations in life that can be transformed from adversity to opportunity when viewed from a fresh angle. For example, being made redundant from a highly paid but under stimulating or ethically compromised job could actually provide a chance for a person to think about 'downsizing' their lifestyle in ways they might not otherwise have considered. Maybe they could free up time for reskilling or become more self-reliant in the quantities of fresh food they are able to grow rather than commuting to the office, or could find other ways of making a living that are more in accord with their interests and passions.

We all have a multitude of skills and abilities – why not think about ways of creating
polycultural livelihoods for ourselves so that we can live by our enjoyment?

Maximise Diversity

In the 21st century the world largely relies on some 20 or so staple crops. Yet the
Cornwall based permaculture growing and research project Plants For A Future[1]
lists over 7,000 species of plants that are edible or otherwise useful to peoplekind
that we can grow in the UK alone.

In a permaculture growing system each function should be supported by many
elements. In other words, nothing should be indispensable as its loss or failure can
be disastrous. A person who has had only one well paid but highly specialised job
throughout their working life would be less able to cope with redundancy than
somebody who has several small incomes earned from a variety of sources. In the
same way, the farmer who grows as wide and diverse a range of edible and useful
plants as possible, for example fruit and nut trees, vegetables, salads, grains and
cereals, and fungi (a polyculture), still gets to eat if some of them don't make it to
harvest. On the other hand, their neighbour who gives all of the same area of land
over to a single crop of wheat (a monoculture) starves if it fails.

The other side of the coin is that every element in the system
should have many uses. Permaculture people tend to spend a
lot of time emphasising the importance of planting trees. This
is because of the multiplicity of their yields and functions.
Not only do they provide food crops in
the form of fruit, nuts, berries, beans and

leaf protein, they also supply bio-fuels, timber, coppice, medicines and fibre as well as a myriad of beneficial effects for wildlife and for planet-wide systems. These include soil building, maintaining fertility, checking erosion, driving global water and air cycles, regulating temperature to name but a few.

Everything Is Part of a Cycle

In the natural world, there is no such thing as 'pollution'. Within an ecosystem, every 'waste product' is useful elsewhere within that system. Examples include the nitrogen, carbon and hydrological cycles. Powered and regulated by the life processes of living trees and forests, for millions of years these have pumped massive amounts of energy around the globe in constantly changing forms. Modern living, however, seems to be all about breaking nature's perpetual cycles, perhaps best symbolised by our practice of flushing our bodily 'wastes' out to sea rather than returning this fertility to the soil. We then need to build high maintenance sewage treatment plants in order to manage and make safe these massive toxic outputs, whilst at the same time adding artificial fertilisers to nutrient deficient agricultural land. Using composting toilets to harvest our faeces that, when thoroughly broken down over a year or so, can then be applied to fruit trees and other edible crops as 'humanure', is an elegant, low effort way of restoring the 'food to fertility to food' loop.

We have also broken the cycle of *time* by changing to a linear perception of its passage. For our ancestors, events were not singular but recurrent, governed by the movements of sun and moon, the passing of the seasons, of sowing and harvest, summer abundance and winter scarcity. Nowadays we see no reason why we shouldn't have spring lamb and fresh strawberries in December, but even though our calendars might run in straight lines, our bodies are still attuned to respond to nature's patterns. Winter Solstice (Christmas) feasting was originally about stocking up our bodies with the last of the previous season's harvest in preparation for the lean months ahead. Is it then coincidence that goosegrass, one of the first plants to appear the following spring, acts as a natural tonic when drunk as a tea, flushing out the body toxins that build up over the winter? Returning to eating what is locally and seasonally available repairs another cycle and puts us in touch with the earth again.

Everything cycles.

Keyhole beds maximise edge and increase the amount of available growing space as well as adding visual interest to the garden.

Yields Are Limited Only by Imagination

'Yield' is usually thought of as the quantity of material output obtained (e.g. amounts of potatoes, grain etc.) calculated against resources or effort put in. But there's no reason why we can't widen our definition. Yields from a system might also include information, lessons learned, experience, the health benefits of exercise and being outdoors, or even just plain fun...

Permaculture designers are like the best cooks and gardeners, constantly trying out fresh ideas, learning new techniques, finding new niches to utilise, seeking new beneficial relationships between elements and gathering knowledge. By comprehending and copying natural systems, we can develop techniques in order to multiply such opportunities, including strategies such as maximising edge. In ecology, it is recognised that the 'edge' or ecotone is basically where the action happens – where a high exchange of materials and energy takes place. The edge is the place where two ecosystems meet, for example, the interface between the sea and the land, or where woodland meets grassland. Such an environment tends to be more synergistic, supporting biological activity from either side of these boundaries, as well as species particular to those conditions, thus making it a highly productive region. Permaculture design seeks to increase edge and its beneficial effects as much as possible, including between people and ideas.

The Vegan Way

Permaculture is an approach rather than a belief system, a useful framework for positive action whatever our lifestyle choices. So whilst adopting an animal-free diet and permaculture may not necessarily be the same thing, for me the ethical underpinning of all permaculture design – Earthcare, Peoplecare and Fair Shares – doesn't seem so very different from the compassionate concern for 'Animals, People and Environment' spelled out on the Vegan Society sticker in my front room window. I became vegetarian when I left school in 1977, and stopped eating animal products altogether in 1984 for a mixture of ethical and spiritual reasons. These can basically be summed up as a desire to strive to survive causing the least suffering possible.

In the UK alone each year, approximately 2.8 million cattle, 8.5 million pigs, 15 million sheep and lambs, 80 million fish and 950 million birds are slaughtered for human consumption.[2] The majority of industrially farmed animals spend their lives trapped in cramped, squalid cages, never once seeing the light of day, and unable to satisfy the natural desires of all creatures for movement or contact with their own kind. For those bred purely for their flesh ('meat') the suffering is relatively limited, for they are slaughtered as soon as they are of an optimum age. Not so for dairy animals however, those creatures imprisoned for the products that they yield. Cows which are subjected artificially to yearly pregnancies, and whose calves are snatched away for veal or to intensive beef units so that we can enjoy

their milk. The hens that are crammed into flocks of up to 30,000 birds at a rate of 19 to the square metre,[3] often de-beaked and force-fed on steroids and protein concentrates in order to produce 'fresh farm eggs'. For these pathetic creatures the luxury of death is found only when they cease to be productive, slaughtered for 'low grade' meat products such as soup or pie ingredients or pet foods.

Personally I don't see a need for my sustenance to be dependent on the suffering and death of other sentient beings. For me, what and how I eat is a celebration of life, so shouldn't have to involve its negation. But there are also strong environmental arguments why those who seek more earth right ways of living might also consider eating less meat and dairy products.

Vegan for the Land

A vegan diet using locally grown organic produce is amongst the most sustainable. A plant based diet requires far less land than that needed to maintain a typical western diet. Farmed animals consume much greater amounts of protein and calories than they are able to convert into produce, so far larger quantities of crops are needed to feed humans with animal products than are needed to feed people directly. Globally the world's forests are being destroyed to make ever more room for cattle ranching or for the production of crops like soya for animal feed. These forests play a vital role in maintaining the ecological balances of the planet, regulating oxygen and carbon dioxide levels in the atmosphere, providing habitat for innumerable species of plants and animals, controlling water cycles and preventing soil erosion and the spread of deserts.

In the UK animal farming accounts for some 85% of agricultural land use, either directly for grazing or for the production of fodder crops, with two-thirds of the British cereal crop being fed to livestock annually. Yet it has been estimated that a future vegan Britain, using permaculture design and methods to increase integration of lifestyle with natural and renewable cycles, could be self-reliant in food, fertility, fibre and fuel on around one third to a half of the agricultural land currently available, especially if home gardens and public urban spaces were used for food growing, and land currently considered 'marginal' or suitable only for rough grazing was made directly productive by planting high protein edible or otherwise useful tree crops.[4] This abundance could greatly reduce the need for food imports, often from so-called 'Third World' countries that would then be free to utilise land to feed their own populations. Millions of acres could also be given over to uses such as recreation, wildlife habitat and, most importantly, reforestation projects, making a significant contribution to the reversal of the 'greenhouse effect'.

Cattle, sheep and other ruminants are a significant source of methane, a powerful greenhouse gas. Reducing livestock farming, whilst at the same time launching massive reforestation projects, could potentially not only help to lock up the carbon released by centuries of fossil fuel burning and land clearances, but also be a step towards cutting methane emissions. Thus climate change could be tackled on two fronts simultaneously.

There is also the question of water as a global resource. Agriculture accounts for some 70% of fresh water usage worldwide, including the production of grain, 40% of which is fed to livestock to produce the meat-rich diet of the north. The extraction of water from aquifers in India (where nearly all water is used in agriculture) exceeds recharge by a factor of two or more. Furthermore, dry-lands and desertification are spreading as forests are cut down, at least partly as a consequence of increasing pressures placed upon the land by mass-scale animal farming and feed production.

Vegan for Health

Moving towards a more plant based diet is not only better for planetary health; it also makes sense for our own well-being. Excessive animal products tend to clog and acidify the body system, and have been linked to many diseases including cancer, diabetes, high blood pressure, heart problems, constipation, obesity and allergies. By contrast, studies have shown that a well-planned vegan wholefood based diet can not only reduce the incidence of these illnesses, but also greatly improve general health.

Poor husbandry practices engendered by mass-scale animal farming have been linked to potentially devastating diseases of humankind such as BSE, E. coli, salmonella poisoning and bird flu. The indiscriminate use of antibiotics in animal feed poses yet another risk to human health. Half of all antibiotics produced are fed to farm animals, both to combat disease and promote faster growth. The result is that many diseases, including meningitis, enteric fever and septicaemia, can develop antibiotic resistance and become 'superbugs'. Furthermore, such antibiotics can also find their way onto our plates via the animal products based food chain and in turn weaken our own immune systems.

In short, western expectations for meat and dairy to be available on the table three times a day, seven days a week, 52 weeks a year are globally unsustainable by any standards. The vegan way might not be the solution for everybody, but I believe we will all need to at least think about lifestyles and diets that are less dependent on animal products and the inputs these entail if all Earth Citizens are to live and eat well in a sustainable future.

Of course, only the individual can decide where they should draw the line between their own ideals, and how far they can acceptably compromise with global systems that are unjust, environmentally destructive and exploitive of people, animals and planet. Permaculture is about personal accountability and paying attention to energy flows and cycles, and it's as easy to lead an unsustainable, unaccountable vegan lifestyle based on imported, fossil fuel hungry, monoculturally grown and over-processed soya based convenience foods as it is to live as an unsustainable and unaccountable omnivore. What is important is that we all develop an awareness of our own 'energy budgets' and the 'ecological footprints' of how we live, and begin to work to steadily reduce these. In the longer term we need to meet a far greater percentage of our needs from home, market and forest gardens, as well as from the yields of trees.

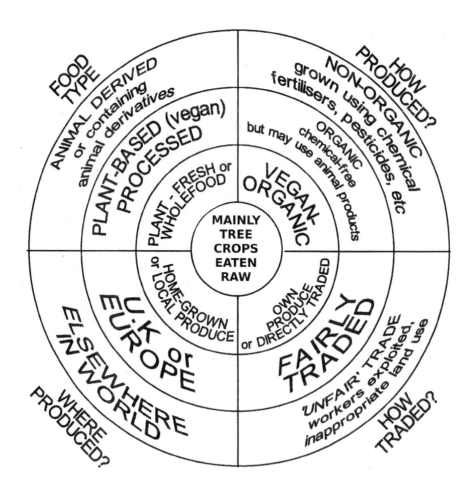

The Food Wheel developed by Alan and Elaine Garrett of
the Movement for Compassionate Living. [5] For a more compassionate diet,
choose foods that are as close to the centre of the wheel as possible.

Permaculture Without Animals?

Not all permaculturists or permaculture projects are vegan, and I've often been asked whether a completely animal-free permaculture is even actually possible. My response is, of course not, and neither would it be desirable. For example, how would we fence out the earthworms that build our soil and maintain its fertility, or the bees that pollinate our fruit trees and vegetables, and why ever would we wish to? In fact, we actively design in features that are intended to attract wildlife: ponds for frogs, toads and dragonflies, and flowering plants to bring in the ladybirds and hoverflies that keep populations of potential pests like slugs and aphids in check, and are essential to maintaining healthy productive ecosystems. What we don't include are those 'system components' that we believe perpetuate exploitative relationships with our non-human Earth co-citizens, such as pigs, goats and chickens, whose primary function is the production of meat, milk and eggs.

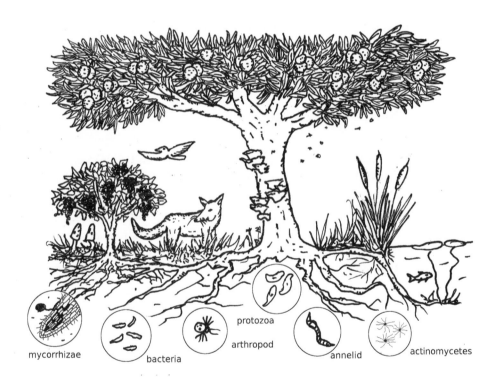

Many kingdoms of life interact in the forest garden.

The Naturewise forest garden in north London[6] is one example of an edible landscape that is ostensibly 'stock free', although in actuality members of several of the Kingdoms of Nature work together here for mutual benefit. Deep rooted comfrey plants mine nutrients like nitrogen, potassium and phosphorous from the subsoil, making them available to fruit trees and bushes. Birds and bees buzz around the canopy layer, whilst insects and arthropods patrol the undergrowth and leaf litter, checking and balancing pest populations and playing their role in the cycles of growth and decay. Fungi and bacteria continue the process. These break down dead matter into rich humus and minerals that are exchanged with plant roots via associations with mycorrhizal soil networks in return for sugars and carbohydrates manufactured by photosynthesis. Based on the structure of natural woodland, the forest garden is a complex web of which humans too are an integral part. Aside from a bounty of apples, pears, figs, grapes, strawberries, currants and edible leaves, one of the most important yields of this mini-woodland is the sense of community that the space offers to the volunteers that spend time here. And being situated in a school playground it also acts as an open air classroom where children of many ethnic and cultural backgrounds are able to interact with nature, an opportunity that is often all too rare in the inner city.

Understanding 'Zones'

Good design is about maximising the beneficial connections between elements, in other words, putting things in the right place. This is about efficiently utilising our energy inputs and the space we have available to us in relation to where we tend to spend most of our time. For example, there's not a lot of point in planting a bed of 'Cut and Come Again' mixed salad leaves on your allotment a mile away from your house if you only visit it once every couple of weeks. When you are knocking up a salad for tea, human nature and the law of minimum effort dictates that you will pop round to the corner shop and buy a salad bag whilst your crop sits running to seed. In other words, your wonderfully succulent and deliciously flavoured lettuces, rocket, mizuna and mustard are simply planted in the wrong place.

Zoning is therefore an important permaculture analysis and design tool that helps us to think about our energy inputs and decide where things best belong. Traditionally, zones are numbered from 0 to 5, and can be thought of as a series of concentric rings moving out from a centre point, where human activity and need for attention is most concentrated, to where there is no need for intervention at all.

- Zone 0 is the house or home centre. In terms of food production this might be about using energy efficient cooking and storage methods, or designing an ergonomic kitchen layout.
- Zone 1 is immediately next to your back door, the place nearest the house where the gardener's shadow, 'the best fertiliser of all', according to an ancient Chinese proverb), most often falls. This is where to put crops that require frequent attention and harvesting, those 'Cut and Come Again' salads mentioned above that need to be plucked regularly, fresh herbs that are added to daily meals, strawberry plants, those seedlings in trays that need watering a couple of times a day until they are established, the worm compost bin that needs to be added to little and often and cold frames for tender plants that need to be opened in the morning and closed at night.
- Zone 2 extends out from Zone 1, and in the larger garden might be where we grow more crops for household use that do not require quite as much attention – maybe a variety of vegetables in beds that require watering and weeding every couple of days, or possibly a small forest garden area with a few dwarfing fruit trees, currant bushes and perennial herbs and vegetables.
- Zone 3 is main crop production – perhaps that once a week cycling distance allotment where we might plant larger amounts of staples; these can be onions, beans or potatoes that take up quite a bit of space but don't require that much attention beyond occasional weeding and watering – maybe once a week or even less once established, especially if utilising techniques such as mulching that conserve soil moisture and suppress weed growth. It is also where we might think about sourcing the bulk of the cereal grains and other staples that are grown on a more extensive farm scale.
- Zone 4 is semi-wild, for example coppice managed woodland used for timber, woodland products like charcoal, poles, fencing, etc. Attention here might be necessary only once a year or less, especially if managed on a rotational basis.
- Zone 5 is wild nature, where we don't design. Instead we observe. Apart from some foraged wild foods, the main 'yield' here is the opportunity to look at and learn from natural ecosystems and cycles.

If zones are about understanding our own patterns of energy use, then 'Sector Analysis' helps us to consider natural energy flows such as sun, wind or wildlife and how these might affect our microclimate. For example knowing where and when the sun rises and sets at different times of the year in relation to our garden can help us decide where to position our sun loving or shade tolerant plants, and knowing the prevailing wind direction can determine the best potential location for a protective shelter-belt hedge or wind turbine. It's also useful to think about slope and the implications this might have on your land in terms of its limitations, potential and management strategies such as water flow, preventing erosion and so on.

The tool of zoning can be utilised in many ways other than thinking about how land is used. Try, for example, applying it to determine scales of community organisation and how relevant these are to you. Where might your energies best be employed in effecting change, and when do different strategies become appropriate? Zone 0 could be the people you share a home with, i.e. your partner, family or room-mates; Zone 1 your friends, immediate neighbours or work colleagues; Zone 2 the streets around you, or within your district or parish boundaries, and so on outwards, with Zone 5 perhaps representing national government and its intractable jungle of bureaucracies. What are your 'circles of influence' or strategic leverage points if you truly want to make a difference? Do you approach your partner about their habit of always leaving the towel on the bathroom floor in the same way that you address a community meeting about road safety outside your kid's school, or the way that you engage in a national scale Anti-War protest event? Probably your strategies are different in each case, just as you wouldn't use a hand fork and trowel as your main tools to landscape a 1,000 hectare farm or hire a JCB to tend your window box...

Zones and Sectors

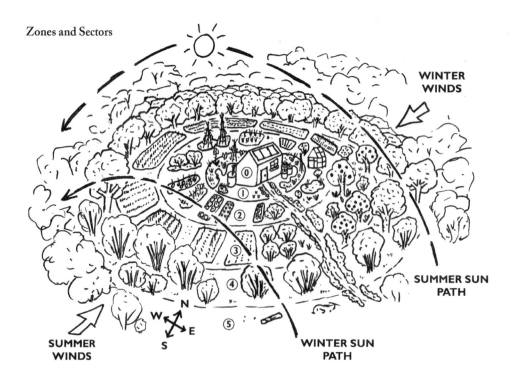

How This Book Is Organised

For the remainder of this book I've loosely used the concept of Zoning as a theme to explore our own relationships to land, food and community. Each chapter focuses on an aspect of creating greater self reliance in our day-to-day lives, as well as looking at a wider picture of building more resilient and regenerative futures for ourselves, our children and our world.

- Zone 0 looks at the energy flows within the house, along with the food producing potential of the average kitchen, such as sprouting, growing windowsill greens, fermentation and small-scale mushroom production.
- Zone 1 focuses on the application of a permaculture design process to the small back garden of a typical urban household, as well as some ideas for using the salad crops that even those of us with very limited space could grow.
- Zone 2 provides an overview of vegan organic methods of growing fruit and vegetable crops in a larger back garden, as well as plenty of recipe ideas for how these might be used.
- Zone 3 looks at sourcing the main crops and staples of our dietary requirements on a scale beyond what most of us would be able to grow ourselves, including some ways in which we might develop more regenerative local food links. It also includes plenty of recipe ideas for cooking with staples such as grains and pulses.
- Zone 4 focuses on the potential of tree crops to feed people kind and meet other needs in a more compassionate and sustainable future, as well as exploring the concept of forest gardening and using the amazing diversity of crops these can yield. This section also includes ideas for using fruits, nuts and leaf protein as alternative staples.
- Zone 5 looks at our relationship with the wilderness and the harvests it can offer us both in terms of wisdom and the useful wild plants that we can forage.
- So far I haven't mentioned a seventh important zone in permaculture design, that which is sometimes referred to as Zone 00. This means the person or persons at the very heart of any human-based system. Perhaps this is the most important part of the design of all. Thus it is where the journey through this book both begins and ends, respectively focusing on how we as individuals can become more effective in changing ourselves and the world around us, and finally looking at the amazing power of community when World Changers come together.

CHAPTER 2

Personal Health
and Effectiveness

"You start with your nose, then your hands,
your back door, your doorstep.
You get all that right, then everything is right.
If all that's wrong, nothing can ever be right."

Bill Mollison

Zone 00

The interconnected permaculture ethics of earthcare and peoplecare imply that wholeness and earth repair is not just about the wider 'out there' of our gardens, farms, forests and oceans, but is just as importantly to do with the 'ecology of the self'. Paying attention to our own physical, emotional and spiritual needs and development is fundamental to good Zone 00 design. Just as peace is not simply the absence of war, so too health is not just about being free from disease. Therefore self-care – setting up holistic mind and body systems in order to avoid sickness, depression, stress and burnout – is a vital part of enhancing well-being and developing personal effectiveness.

Healthy Body

Luckily many activities that lessen our negative impacts upon the planet tend to at the same time have positive effects on our own personal health and well-being. Cycling or walking instead of using the car not only reduces road congestion, pollution and fossil fuel usage, it provides vigorous aerobic exercise that increases stamina, strengthens the muscles and has cardio-vascular benefits (not to mention saving us money!). Eating good quality, locally grown organic fruit and vegetables doesn't just support local producers, cut 'food miles' and reduce unnecessary packaging and pesticide usage, it provides our bodies with the best possible building blocks in terms of quality, balance and nutrition. Growing at least some of your own food is even better. Gardening, once described by Bill Mollison as 'a gentle form of Tai Chi', offers a multitude of mental and physical health benefits.

From swimming to 5-a-side football to massage, there are all manner of exercises and forms of physical stimulation that we can design into our lives, depending on what is appealing. The physical aspects of yoga, for example, combine awareness of the body – how one stands, how one sits, how one breathes – with focus on the mind and the inner self. The 'Sun Salutation' sequence (illustrated) stretches all of the main muscle groups, yet can be performed in just a few minutes each day. Dance too can have wonderful physical benefits, whether it's grooving at the salsa bar, getting down to the latest trance cuts or moshing at a punk gig. Gabrielle Roth's 'Endless Wave' CDs provide a great percussion based soundtrack to an energising and cathartic full body workout, progressing over 40 minutes or so through the five rhythmic archetypes of 'flowing', 'staccato', 'chaos', 'lyrical' and 'stillness'. I've found these particularly useful when using music and movement therapy with groups of adults with learning disabilities, and more personally, they are a good way of connecting spiritual and physical practice.

Salute to the sun

As important as eating well and having plenty of physical exercise is the need for adequate rest and relaxation. Obvious maybe, but in our busy, busy culture it's surprising how often we forget to just chill out and take a bit of time for ourselves. *The Idler*,[7] a publication whose very ethos is a riposte to the idea of the 'work ethic', has a healthy attitude that we all might do well to emulate from time to time:

"The idler's work looks suspiciously like play. Victims of the Protestant work ethic would like all work to be unpleasant. They feel that work is a curse, that we must suffer on this earth to earn our place in the next... The idler on the other hand sees no reason not to use his brain to organise a life for himself where his play is his work, and so attempt to create his own little paradise in the here and now."

Or as another wise person once said, "Don't just do something – sit there!"

Healthy Mind

Despite the dualistic ways of thinking, separating mind and body, that have dominated the last few hundred years, there cannot be many nowadays who would deny that physical and mental well-being are complementary. Yet rather than exercising and nourishing the brain, a far more common pattern is to allow it to atrophy, stunted by the cathode rays of indiscriminate televisual passivity.

Education should be about lifelong learning, but for many of us it's something we forget about after leaving school or college. Maybe this is because our past experiences within the formal education system have been negative or bring up painful memories. Traditional educational thinking has tended to emphasise more formal talk 'n' chalk style learning, based on the imposed order of classrooms, lectures and written note taking. However, more recent research has shown that we all have our own individual ways of effectively assimilating information, knowledge and experience, broadly falling within one or more of seven 'intelligences' – which of these learning styles fits you best?

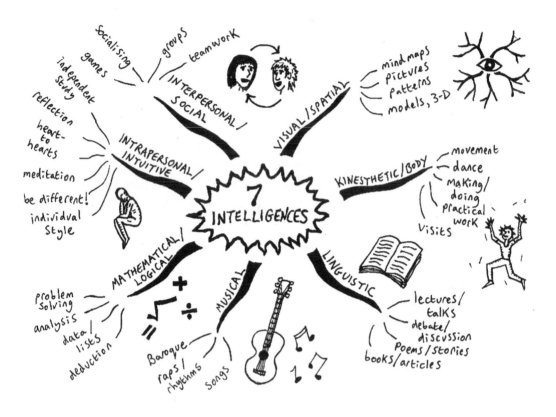

Seven 'Intelligences' – which of these best fit your learning and thinking styles?

'Consciousness Raising' is a term that was coined by the feminist movement during the 1970s. These pioneers understood that coming to terms with the internalised nature of oppression was a vital first step towards fulfilling personal potential. As we enter the new millennium we too can develop our awareness of the 'destructoculture' forces at work around us, and of where and how we fit into the picture. Be discriminating when informing yourself, and think about just who controls the media. Publications such as *Schnews*,[8] the weekly Brighton based alternative newssheet, local community and neighbourhood bulletin sheets, as well as independent web-based resources such as *Indymedia*,[9] *Corporate Watch*[10] and *Wikileaks*[11] often make available information and analysis that the vested interests who benefit from destructoculture might prefer us not to access. Knowledge is power, and being well informed exponentially increases our ability to make positive change happen!

Positive Thinking – Positive Action!

Permaculture is about world change, moving away from the present dominance of 'destructoculture' and towards creating resilient abundance in harmony with nature. Yet perhaps the greatest barriers to positive change come from within us, the result of often lifelong attitudes that can severely limit our effectiveness. Deeply embedded tendencies such as procrastination, impatience or criticism of self and others are reinforced by the fatalistic messages we repeat to ourselves; "It's not fair", "I'll never be able to do that", "What's the point?" Our past histories and social conditioning can instil and constantly replay these paralysing internal 'meta-negative' scripts. Yet it is within us all to find the power to consciously 'switch' our thinking to a 'meta-positive' mode, and realise that in becoming compassionate, creative and empowered beings we CAN make a difference.

We are all familiar with the saying 'think globally, act locally'. Despite this, we often still tend to be REactive rather than PROactive. This is something that our society and media encourages. Think of the mainstream press and TV 'soap operas' or 'reality shows'. They thrive on despair, gossip and confrontation. 'If it bleeds it leads', as the old Fleet Street saying goes. A constant stream of bad news and 'car crash' entertainment taps into our negative fixations and has a cumulatively dis-empowering effect on us. We learn that blaming and complaining, like living on a diet of junk food, offers short term pay-offs that might fill the empty gaps in our lives for a while but in the long run don't actually make us feel satisfied in a good way. In the meantime, we have avoided taking responsibility for our own part in making real change happen. Things aren't too different in the world of politics. The main parties often seem more interested in rivalries, posturing and short-term vote grabbing than in focusing on real solutions to social conflicts and environmental threats. The Native American Navaho people taught that when planning for the future, we should always think at least seven generations ahead. Yet I'm hard pressed to recall a recent politician who looks much more than seven days past their own tabloid-friendly sound bites and spin.

Pass Me Another Issue

For my own part, I became involved in campaigning activities around the time I left school during the late 1970s. Politicised by the lyrics of punk bands like The Clash, Crass and The Ruts, my eyes were opened to the injustices of the real world beyond the school gates by organisations like Rock Against Racism and the Anti Nazi League. Shortly afterwards I became involved with animal rights groups such as the Hunt Saboteurs and various Anti Vivisection organisations. Throughout the 80s and up until the mid-90s I was a regular at meetings, pickets, protests, demonstrations and direct actions: Ban the Bomb, Anti-Apartheid, Smash the Poll Tax, Boycott Shell, Oppose the Criminal Justice Act, No to GM crops, Stop the Road Building Program and so on. Notice the pattern yet? Like so many radically motivated and socially concerned people, my focus was almost exclusively on 'Stopping' rather than 'Starting'. Don't get me wrong, protest and resistance movements are of course vital in raising awareness as well as advancing and protecting our rights and freedoms, and their importance and value should never be underplayed or dismissed. Often they are what Buddhist earth-activist Joanna Macy terms 'holding actions':

> "(These) slow the destruction caused by the industrial growth society. This economic system is doomed because it measures its success by how fast it uses up the living body of Earth – extracting resources beyond Earth's capacity to renew, and spewing out wastes faster than Earth's capacity to absorb. It is now in runaway mode, devouring itself at an accelerating rate. Holding actions are important because they buy time. They are like a first line of defence; they can save a few species, a few ecosystems, and some of the gene pool for future generations."[12]

But for me personally, I had begun to feel that I was defining myself more in negative terms of what I was Against rather than what I was positively For. I was also beginning to feel the symptoms of 'activist burnout'. I was despondent, cynical, convinced that nothing could get better and not wanting to know when it actually did. The problem was that whether 'We' won or lost on any particular issue, 'They' always had the next struggle lined up for us. The next social injustice, the next environmental threat, the next war. And always in 'Their' terms, in the arena that 'They' defined...

About this time I was reminded of a little Sufi story I'd read some years earlier:

Late one evening an innkeeper walked into the main guestroom now lit by several oil lamps. One of the guests was peering under tables and into corners obviously looking for something.

"What have you lost?" asked the innkeeper.

"My purse", replies the guest, pushing a bench aside to look underneath.

"Do you know roughly where you lost it?"

"Yes, in the garden."

"Then why on earth are you looking for it in here?"

The guest grunts, heaving at a heavy piece of furniture. "This is where the light is," and continues the search.

For me personally, maybe it was time to get back to the garden.

Stella's Window Box

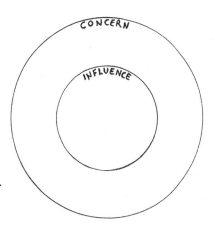

Permaculture asks us to think in terms of solutions rather than problems, and perhaps paradoxically it seems that the more we focus our positive energies and time on the things in our lives that we can affect directly, the greater and wider our 'circles of influence' actually become, expanding outwards and creating opportunities to make ever bigger changes.

During the mid 1990s my friend Stella lived on a housing estate in southeast London. Like so much of the inner city, this area was blighted by poverty, crime, poor transport links, lack of green spaces and vandalism. However Stella had a belief in the abilities of ordinary people to make a difference, and started at the 'end of her nose'. She planted up a small wooden box of flowers on the window ledge of her flat to add a splash of colour to the street. Some of her neighbours informed her that she was wasting her time, and sure enough, by the next day the box was smashed up and the flowers and soil were strewn and trampled across the pavement. So she replaced it with another window box. And exactly the same thing happened again. So she replaced it with another. And exactly the same thing happened again. So she replaced it with another. And this time something interesting happened. A box of bright marigolds, petunias and geraniums appeared on the ledge of the house across the street. Then another a little further down the road. Soon window boxes, tubs and containers of flowers and herbs began to pop up all over the estate. People began to talk to each other, and from the confidence gained from these small beginnings grew Green Adventure, a multicultural urban regeneration project that encompassed a vegetable box delivery scheme, food growing initiatives, a Local Exchange Trading System (LETS), a bicycle trailer building and repair workshop, play schemes, educational and employment projects and forest gardens and community orchards. Stella decided to be a model rather than a critic, and never let anybody tell her that an individual can't make change happen.

Where Do YOU Want to Go?

Becoming effective in this way means finding your ethical core, and setting aims and goals that accord with this rather than more short term motivations like financial gain, status, etc. Of course, any attempt at defining a personal moral system is highly subjective as we all have our own views about what is 'right' or not. However, I believe that the three permaculture ethics of Earthcare, Peoplecare and Fair Shares provide a sound basis for anybody who is interested in working for positive change at whatever level.

Creative Visualisation techniques have long been used as tools for self-empowerment. It's well known that world-class athletes usually have a very clear mental picture of themselves being first across the finishing line. In the same way we can develop our own 'visions' of where we want to get. For example, maybe your long-term goal is to leave the city and set up some kind of woodland eco-community. Spend some time creating an image of yourself, say, five years into the future, living as a part of this community. In a relaxed and comfortable position where you won't be disturbed, try to empty your thoughts of distractions and slowly build up a clear vision in your mind's eye. Imagine as much detail as possible using all of your senses. See the higgledly-piggledy assortment of benders, timber huts and other low impact dwellings dotted in the clearings amongst the tall oaks and coppiced hazel and chestnut stands. Taste the fresh woodland fruits, nuts and leaves from the smoothly carved bowl as their juices permeate your mouth. Smell the wood smoke from the communal fire circle on your clothes and listen to the birdsong and the breeze playing through the branches of the canopy above. Feel the rough finish of the home-made rustic wooden chair you are relaxing in, as well as that tired sense of physical well-being that comes at the end of a long day of working hard outdoors. Begin with your end in mind and use your creative, visual 'right brain' to define your own personal 'life compass'.

The Tao reminds us that 'every journey of 1,000 miles starts with a single step'. Realising our goals is a pathway of change, and like any journey needs to be undertaken in manageable stages. What are your next achievable steps? What practical things can you do today? Enrol on that green woodworking course you have seen advertised? Get your rusty old bike that you haven't ridden for years out of the shed? Join your neighbourhood LETS scheme? In much the same way as the signposts that you pass will change as you journey from London to Glasgow, so the next phases of your personal journey (your future 'next achievable steps') will become apparent as their relevance arises.

Keep Yourself Healthy: UK Home Grown, Plant Based Sources of Nutrients

One personal 'next step' might be to adopt a healthier diet that contains less animal products. Much of the available information about vegan dietary requirements and nutrition can be complex and sometimes contradictory. Therefore it's not the purpose of this book to give comprehensive nutritional advice, and neither am I qualified to do so. These general guidelines, however, are adapted from information provided by the late Kathleen Jannaway in a number of Movement for Compassionate Living publications, and from Liz Cook's beautiful self-published laminated vegan nutrition wall-charts. For a much more in-depth overview of the subject I'd recommend *Becoming Vegan: Comprehensive Edition: The Complete Reference on Plant-based Nutrition* or *Becoming Vegan: Express Edition: The Everyday Guide to Plant-based Nutrition*, both by Brenda Davis and Vesanto Melina.

Protein for Body Building

Recommended daily amount (RDA): 1-3 years 14.5g, 4-6 years 19.7g, 7-10 years 28.3g, average adult 45-50g (approx 2oz).

Whole cereals – wheat, oats, barley, rye. Also quinoa, a grain alternative from South America that can be grown in gardens here (see page 177).

Pulses – peas and beans: haricot, czar, field – ripe and dried (see page 180).

Nuts and seeds – almonds, hazels, walnuts, acorns (see page 233), beech and pine, sunflower, marrow, pumpkin.

Potatoes – small percentage, but high value.

Leaf curd (see page 236)

Cereals and pulses taken together yield increased value.

Sugars, Starches and Fats for Energy (Carbohydrates)

(Shouldn't be a problem in a balanced diet, oils should be cold pressed however)

All of the above – they will be used by the body for energy if enough cheaper energy foods are not provided.

All fruits – raw, dried, cooked.

Pasta

Vegetables – all kinds.

Wholemeal bread

Oil for cooking can be obtained from sunflower and rapeseeds, and beechnuts. It may be possible to grow olives in some southerly parts of the UK, but at present it is unlikely that yields will be high enough to provide a sustainable source of olive oil.

Vitamins for Healthy Functioning

A (retinol) – carrots, greens (especially dark green), broccoli, spinach, parsley, endive, apricots, peppers, tomatoes.

B12 – essential for health, and especially important for women of child-bearing age. Vegans should note that B12 is not present in plant tissue. It is, however, widely present in the environment, including the soil, and may possibly be found on some plants, e.g. on leaves, if not washed too thoroughly. B12 is always synthesised by microorganisms. It is obtainable from bacteria grown in laboratories and added to processed foods, especially yeast extracts (check label for RDA).

Other B vitamins (B1 (Thiamin), B2 (Riboflavin), B3 (Niacin), B6 (Pyridoxin), Folic acid, Pantothenic acid) – yeast extracts, green leafy vegetables, nuts, pulses

(peas and beans), bean sprouts, mushrooms, currants, other seeds, whole cereals.
C (ascorbic acid) (RDA: 0-1 year 25mg, 1-10 years 30mg, average adult 40mg.
N.B. easily destroyed by light and heat) – fresh raw fruits and vegetables,
especially blackcurrants, rose hips, parsley, peppers, leafy greens, broccoli and
alfalfa sprouts.
D (calciferol) – sunlight. D2 produced by sunlight on yeast is added to vegan
margarines.
E (tocopherol) (shouldn't be a problem in a balanced diet) – wheatgerm, nuts
and seeds, pulses and vegetable oils.
K (phytomenadione) (shouldn't be a problem in a balanced diet) – dark greens,
cauliflower, tomatoes, seaweeds.
Cooking can destroy many vitamins, hence the need for raw fruits and salads
daily. Vitamin pills should only be taken on professional advice: they are usually
unnecessary and excess can cause toxicity.

Minerals

Calcium (RDA: 0-1 year 525mg, 7-10 years 550mg, 11-18 years 900mg, average
adult 700mg) – dark green vegetables – especially kale, spinach, broccoli – also
haricots, almonds, oatmeal, hazels. Vitamin D is essential for the utilisation
of calcium. Brittle bones in elderly women are probably caused by hormone
changes and lack of vitamin D.
Iodine (RDA: 1-3 years 70mcg, 4-10 years 100mcg, average adult 140mcg) –
green leafy vegetables, seaweeds, kelp.
Iron (RDA: 0-3 months 1.7mg, 7-12 months 7.8mg, 7-10 years 8.7mg, average
male adult 8.7mg, average female adult 14.8mg) – dark greens, beans and pulses,
almonds, oatmeal, wheatgerm, parsley, figs, raisins, apricots, pumpkin seeds,
millet. Absorption of iron is aided by vitamin C.
Magnesium (shouldn't be a problem in a balanced diet) – green leafy vegetables,
almonds, broccoli, wholegrains, wheatgerm, prunes.
Phosphorous, sulphur, potassium (shouldn't be a problem in a balanced diet) –
wholegrains, wheatgerm, pinto beans, chickpeas, pumpkin seeds, potatoes, yeast
extract, many fruits and vegetables, nuts.
Zinc (RDA: 0-3 years 4-5mg, 7-10 years 7mg, average male adult 9.5mg, average
female adult 7mg) – wholegrains, pumpkin seeds, almonds, wheatgerm, oats.
Others: e.g. **fluorine, copper, cobalt, chromium, manganese, etc.** (shouldn't be
a problem in a balanced diet) – brewer's yeast, green leafy vegetables, potatoes,
wholegrains, almonds, beans and pulses, seaweeds.

Fibre

(Not usually a problem with a plant based diet.)
Beans and pulses
Lots of **fresh fruit and vegetables**
Nuts
Oats
Wheatgerm
Wholegrains

Please note that the above information is for guidance only. Amounts required for health vary greatly: a good rule is to eat to appetite and watch your weight. If it settles at the recommended level and you feel well, you are eating enough. If in doubt or you have specific health concerns, seek qualified advice. Eating with the rhythms of the seasons is also a sensible pattern as this reconnects us with the cycles of the year.

Eating with the Seasons

Seasonal food is fresher and so tends to be tastier and more nutritious, supports local farmers and growers and has a number of environmental benefits, such as reducing the energy (and associated CO_2 emissions) needed to grow and transport the food we eat. The suggested menu ideas below can be adapted to other foods that are available throughout the year.

Spring

Muesli, bean sprouts, seasonal greens, salads, chickweed, spring onion and alfalfa sprouts, nuts, sunflower and pumpkin seeds, green juices, sprout and spring leaves detox salad, steamed vegetables, fresh beetroots, leek and broccoli croustade, pasta and tomato sauce, spinach soup, broad bean patties, raw energy nut loaf, barley risotto, sea beet soup, vegetable curry, dried and stored fruit.

Summer

Muesli, bean sprouts, seasonal greens, new potatoes, salads, nuts, sunflower and pumpkin seeds, green juices, tomato soup, green bean medley, raw spicy leek and broccoli soup, ratatouille, gazpacho, pasta and tomato sauce, roasted summer vegetables, raw nut balls, raw energy nut loaf, spinach and chickpea curry, buckwheat casserole, stuffed peppers, English curry, stir fry with sweet and sour sauce, seasonal fruit salad.

Autumn

Muesli, bean sprouts, seasonal greens, salads, nuts, sunflower and pumpkin seeds, green juices, steamed seasonal vegetables, new potatoes, Bircher potatoes, courgette and tomato bake, marrow and butternut squash tagine, bean and vegetable casserole, raw carrot savoury, nut roast, mushroom flan, barley risotto, acorn roast, quinoa pudding, sea beet and tomato soup, apple casserole, apple and blackberry cobbler, fresh seasonal fruit.

Winter

Porridge oats, bean sprouts, seasonal greens, winter salads, nuts, sunflower and pumpkin seeds, green juices, steamed seasonal vegetables, shepherd(ess) pie, lentil pie, colcannon, roasted winter vegetables, leek and potato soup, chestnut roast, cream of celeriac soup, parsnip, kale and lentil soup, vegetable wellington, stewed fruit, puddings, fruit cake, fruit from storage.

Eat More Raw

Note that this isn't a raw food recipe book. Nevertheless, including a greater percentage of uncooked produce to our diets can only be a positive step in terms of adopting a healthier and more ecologically harmonious life style. Humankind is the only species on earth that cooks its food – a process that in many ways reduces much of its nutritive value. Unprocessed, organically grown fruit, green leaves, seeds, nuts, vegetables and cold pressed oils such as flax and hemp can provide us with all the vitamins, minerals and even proteins that we need to promote vibrant health in highly accessible forms. Other possible benefits are said to include increased energy, heightened awareness and improved mood, less tendency to be overweight, less need for sleep and clearer skin. Some followers of raw diets also claim to have a deepened connection to nature and other people. Raw food can take less time to prepare, consumes much less fossil fuel or nuclear based energy and could lead to the planting of increased numbers of fruit and nut trees, thereby also having a number of environmental benefits.

That said there are also some good reasons for cooking our food. Hot food in cold weather is psychologically comforting for many of us, and also decreases its bulk, therefore making a higher intake possible. This is important for young children whose stomachs may not be able to deal with sufficient bulk of uncooked food. It is said that cooking renders certain nutrients more available for use in the body, e.g. pro-vitamin A in carrots and niacin in cereals. Cooking also makes grains and other starchy foods more digestible by causing cell walls to burst open and release their contents. In addition much of the diet of many of the raw food eaters I have met relies on foods that are not always easily grown in our cool temperate maritime climate. This includes exotic fruits such as mangos, bananas and avocados that rely on long hours of sunshine to ripen successfully. Whilst I'm not advocating completely excluding such imports from more seasonal and locally sourced menus, perhaps such items should be considered more as 'luxuries' rather than the bulk of a sustainable UK diet (see page 27). Substituting these with home grown fruits and vegetables can be challenging, although isn't impossible, especially if adopting polycultural growing practices like forest gardening. Raw advocate and permaculture teacher, Steve Charter, therefore suggests adopting a '50:50' raw diet as a good personal goal, and not to try and do everything at once if it doesn't feel right to you, nor to be hard on yourself if you don't 'get it right'!

CHAPTER 3

The Permaculture Home and Kitchen

"A house is not a home unless it contains food and fire for the mind as well as the body."

Benjamin Franklin

Zone 0

In permaculture design terms, the house or home is often referred to as 'Zone 0', the very heart of all our activities. Here we tend to think about issues such as efficient use of energy, recycling and waste reduction, or else creating a comfortable and stress free environment in which to live and relax. However, our 'Home-Zone' can also have a direct role to play in increasing our levels of food self reliance.

Reducing Your Ecological Footprint

'Ecological footprints' are a rough measure of the impacts that our present ways of living are having on the earth. These are derived by calculating the land and resources a region, city or even a single household needs to sustain itself, based on its usage of energy, food, water, building materials and other consumer goods. London, for example, is said to have an ecological footprint of almost 20 million hectares, that is about 125 times its size, or taking up 95% of the productive land in the UK. Calculating the footprint of your own household is a valuable exercise, although can be complicated if maths isn't your forte. However, there are a number of computer-based ecological footprint calculators that are either downloadable or can be used online. These range from highly complex spreadsheets based on keeping long-term detailed records of your personal consumption patterns, to far simpler, user-friendly programs such as those provided by WWF[13] and Best Foot Forward[14] that give instant but much more approximated estimates. Such tools are very useful (and often sobering) in terms of the awareness they can raise, but they don't always offer a lot of practical advice about how to actually lessen our impacts.

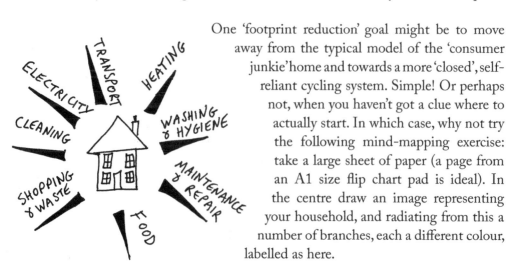

One 'footprint reduction' goal might be to move away from the typical model of the 'consumer junkie' home and towards a more 'closed', self-reliant cycling system. Simple! Or perhaps not, when you haven't got a clue where to actually start. In which case, why not try the following mind-mapping exercise: take a large sheet of paper (a page from an A1 size flip chart pad is ideal). In the centre draw an image representing your household, and radiating from this a number of branches, each a different colour, labelled as here.

Now, with the people you live with (or by yourself if you live alone), spend some time thinking about and discussing the inputs, outputs and implications of each of these activities within your household, adding the key points to each relevant branch. Do this over a period of time, maybe revisiting your mind map after a few days or even weeks. Redraw it if necessary. Importantly, this exercise shouldn't be about inducing guilt or causing arguments, and nor should it be some onerous task. Hone your listening skills, and keep things light-hearted and fun – children in particularly will enjoy getting involved if it's seen as a family game. In time you will have created a 'base-line' showing where you are at now that will help you make changes that everybody in the home can live with.

Don't get too hung up on the idea of 'perfection'. We all live in a world we didn't make, and are all caught up in destructoculture, the very foundations of which are built upon an unsustainable oil based economy. It would be extremely difficult, if not impossible, for most of us to completely extricate ourselves from such systems overnight. Instead adopt what Centre for Alternative Technology co-founder Peter Harper calls the 'Quit While You're Ahead' principle: a footprint reduction of between 10 to 20% can be achieved with little effort or cost just by adopting sensible habits and management. A 50% reduction takes some investment but is worthwhile. Beyond this it might be better to re-focus on quick and easy solutions in other areas before going round again. Use the 'circles of influence and concern' tool (see page 25) to help you to 'roll out' your own change pathways, deciding what can be achieved straight away or with comparatively little effort, and what might be longer-term goals. Some ideas might include:

- Heating: Draught proof your home efficiently, e.g. draught strips at the bottom of doors (but don't forget air must be able to still circulate). Fit double or secondary glazing. Ensure pipes and hot water tanks are lagged, and that lofts are properly insulated. Think about cavity wall insulation; although the materials used can be toxic find safe alternatives! Site radiators and heaters away from windows, and ensure thermostats/timers are working. Use wood burners in preference to electric/gas fires. Wear extra layers of clothes in preference to turning the heater on. In winter try to base most of your activities around one room, preferably south facing. Ensure curtains are open during the day to allow in maximum sunlight and close them as soon as it gets dark. Use heavy lined curtains. Darker furnishings will absorb sunlight, whilst lighter ones reflect light and heat. Wall hangings provide insulation. Utilise thermal inertia of building materials; brick floors will retain heat. Hug more!

- Transport: Is your journey really necessary? Why not walk or cycle? Use public transport and campaign for its improvement, as well as for safer streets and more cycle networks. If you must drive, why not hire a car only when you need it or start a car share scheme. Keep your car well tuned and running as efficiently and cleanly as possible.

- Household maintenance and repair: Teach yourself DIY and self-repair skills, buy a good set of tools and look after them. Don't get timber or building materials from 'DIY Superstores'. Contact your local demolition contractors. Loads of wood is also dumped in skips or left lying around, and what isn't good enough for use can always go in the wood burner! Don't use (new) tropical hardwoods. Start with building shelves and work up to a solar conservatory!

- Electricity and appliances: Turn off unnecessary lights, use low energy, LED long life bulbs, and low wattage bulbs in hallways, etc. Reduce unnecessary appliances, e.g. dishwashers, microwaves, and gadgets, handwash instead of using a machine, or wash full loads only on short, cooler cycles. Use a washing line or clothes-horse in preference to a tumble dryer. Don't wash your clothes so often, give up ironing, or do it in bulk. Keep your freezer full, or don't have one and learn how to dry and preserve instead. Watch less TV (it stunts your mind anyway). Hoover less. Use hand tools rather than power tools. Choose a power supplier that is committed to the development of renewable and sustainable energy.

- Washing and hygiene: Don't leave taps running, or wash in running water. Have showers instead of baths, and not as often; better still, shower with a friend! Don't flush every time you pee. Put a 'hippo' or a plastic bottle full of water in your cistern to reduce volume. Re-route 'grey' water from washbasin to the cistern. Install a compost toilet. Recycle bath/shower/washing up water to use in the garden, or clean up through a reed bed system.

- Cleaning and household chemicals: Reduce toxic elements that affect your home and the wider environment, most of which will have been tested on animals. Avoid potentially dangerous products on the supermarket shelves and use basic items for household cleaning tasks. Bicarbonate of soda will scour sinks, baths and fridges, table salt is a disinfectant and distilled vinegar will remove stains and descale kettles. Use 'simple' soaps and shampoos. Choose water rather than solvent-based paints and natural varnishes when decorating. Other pollutants in the home can include: formaldehyde from wood treatments, MDF furniture and synthetic fabrics; CFCs from refrigerators; low level electromagnetic radiation from TVs, computers, microwaves, etc. Houseplants e.g. spider plant, weeping fig, are said to absorb many pollutants – grow them everywhere!

- Shopping and waste: question your consumption habits: do you have to have the latest state of the art computer when an older model (or even a typewriter!) will meet your needs? What's in your rubbish bin each week? How can you reduce it? What can be reused? What don't you need? What can you recycle? Support local shops and small ethical businesses. Buy second hand, and pass on stuff you no longer use/need.

- Food: Avoid additives and processed foods. Reduce consumption of animal products and consider 'Food Miles' issues (that is, the distance produce has travelled, often thousands of miles, before it reaches your plate, and the energy/fuel costs this implies). Use a wholefood co-op or box scheme rather than supermarkets. If you do use imported goods, try to ensure they are fairly traded. Eat more raw food, sprout beans and mustard etc. on the windowsill. Use a haybox cooker, or a pressure cooker for beans and pulses. Simmer on a low heat rather than boiling. Recycle all kitchen scraps through the compost bin.

A Garden in Your Kitchen

The kitchen can be a 'garden' in its own right, using the minimum amount of space to produce intensively grown, nutrient rich crops all year round, especially during the winter months when other fresh vegetables can be hard to find. They can make an important contribution to any healthy diet, being high in enzymes – that assist digestion, help cell repair and boost immunity – and chlorophyll – 'liquid sunshine' that acts as a blood cleanser and helps to remove toxins from the body.

Seeds or beans such as mung beans, alfalfa, chickpeas and fenugreek can be sprouted on any spare window ledge or shelf, and are easily available from health food stores and many grocers. The main requirements for successful sprouting are moisture and warmth, and providing a few guidelines are followed, it's easy to obtain good results that require very little time or effort. Run a small handful of seeds under a tap and place them in the sprouting vessel. This can range from a simple upside down jam jar with a piece of net curtain secured over its rim by an elastic band, to specially designed multi-level self-draining sprouters. There are several makes on the market, but we've had great success with our 'Biosnacky' three-tiered mini-greenhouse germinator that allows us to keep a constant succession on the go. What is important is that the vessel is maintained at room temperature (approx. between 13-21°C (55-70°F)) and is free draining, for waterlogged sprouts will quickly rot. The seeds will germinate within a day or two, and should then be rinsed at least twice a day, possibly even three or four times in hot weather. When around 2.5-7.5cm (1-3in) in length – that is, after 3-4 days – they will be ready for use. If left much longer they will begin to develop leaves and can become bitter tasting, although the growth process can be halted by placing them in a cool place until needed.

Mung beans are a particularly popular indoor crop, and can be sprouted either in light or dark conditions, for example, an airing cupboard. Those sprouted in the dark will be whiter and crisper in texture, but have less nutritional content. Growing in full sunlight, however, should be avoided as this may cause the beans to overheat or dry out. Subjecting the sprouts to pressure, e.g. by placing a weight on top of them in their sprouting container, will result in larger, crunchier sprouts similar to those sold in Chinese grocery stores. They are a valuable source of vitamins A, B, C and E, calcium, iron, magnesium, potassium, amino acids and consist of 20% protein. However, they are fast growing and quickly pass their nutritional peak. It's also worth experimenting with combinations of seeds and sprouts. Among our favourite mixtures are mung, alfalfa, fenugreek and broccoli, and alfalfa, radish and green lentils.

It should however be noted that all raw legumes contain varying levels of toxins. These are reduced by soaking, sprouting and cooking (e.g. stir frying), although some have advised that to be on the safe side one shouldn't eat more than about 550g (20oz) of raw legume sprouts a day. In reality the risks are probably minimal in most cases, although kidney beans are one legume that should NEVER be eaten uncooked.

Wheatgrass and Other Windowsill Herbs and Greens

Herbs such as chives, parsley, basil, thyme, sage, etc. can also be grown indoors on a sunny windowsill. These can of course be raised from seed, but if you have trouble getting them started off they are often sold grown-on in supermarkets, health food shops and garden centres for 'fresh picking'. Divide them up from the pots they are sold in and re-plant in small containers of potting compost and they will last indefinitely! Most of us are probably familiar with the mustard and cress we grew at school, but other leafy vegetables such as wheatgrass, buckwheat and sunflower greens can also be cultivated indoors. Soak the seeds overnight then drain thoroughly. Germination should begin after about 24-48 hours, when they should be planted in 5cm (2in) deep seed trays half filled with soil or organic potting compost. The sprouting seeds should be gently spread on the soil surface and covered with newspaper (not soil) to exclude the light, then positioned in a warm place. When the growing shoots push off their coverings (usually after about four days) place them in full daylight and water regularly. The leaves will turn green and be ready for harvesting after about a week. This can be done by cutting with kitchen scissors as close to the soil as possible, leaving a mat of soil held together by a root mass that can then be composted. Harvest with scissors when between 15-25cm (6-9in) in length.

As well as having high mineral, vitamin and enzyme content, wheatgrass is a great dietary source of chlorophyll. However the human stomach is not able to effectively digest wheatgrass properly due to its high levels of cellulose. The best way to use wheatgrass is by extracting its juice, either with a hand or electric juicer. A masticating juicer such as a Green Star is best (although they are expensive). Cut the grass into 5cm (2in) lengths to prevent it clogging up the equipment. Juice the wheatgrass a small amount at a time, alternating with a small amount of water if needed.

You can drink wheatgrass juice on its own, or it can be added to other fruits or vegetables such as carrots, apples, celery or green leaves such as kale (not too much as this can be very bitter), spinach, broccoli, etc. Alternating wheatgrass with carrots through the juicer will help to prevent it foaming up.

'Cut 'n' Come again' salad plants like red and green 'salad bowl' lettuce, rocket, chicories and oriental 'saladini' mixtures can be cultivated in large seed trays in the same way, but will re-grow after harvesting, providing a succession of edible leaves rather than just a single crop.

Some Ideas for Using Sprouts and Windowsill Greens

Sprouts and windowsill greens can be used in a whole variety of ways, either juiced, eaten raw in salads or added to dishes such as soups, stews, curries, stir fries or bread. Some ideas include:

- Try sprinkling a handful of sprouted alfalfa seeds over pasta sauce dishes in the same way you might use Parmesan cheese.
- Blend with vegetable juices or smoothies, especially wheat grass (see page 39).
- Stir into soups, curries or stews when serving up.
- Eat them fresh and uncooked in a sprout salad.
- Add to vegetarian sushi (particularly hot/spicy flavoured sprouts such as radish, mustard or fenugreek).
- Sauté lightly with onions.
- Steam and serve dressed with olive or hemp oil.
- Use in sandwiches, or blend together to make a sandwich spread.

EVE'S GOOD HEALTHY SPROUT SALAD RECIPE

Mixed sprouted seeds
(alfalfa, lentil, mung, radish, sunflower, etc.)

Ginger, grated

Fresh herbs from the garden - lots, chopped (not basil though)

Sunflower seeds, roasted

Carrot, grated (optional)

Dressing (lots) - mix cider, wine, vinegar, Dijon mustard, tahini, a little hot pepper sauce (if you want)

1tsp miso, mix with a little hot water until creamy

Pour dressing over salad mix.

Unbelievable flavours and you can feel it doing you good!

With thanks to Eve Libertine

WINTER SPROUT SALAD

Gently toss all ingredients.

Serve with dressing (see page 73).

1 cup of each:
Alfalfa sprouts
Fenugreek sprouts
Mung bean sprouts

½ cup of each:
Broccoli sprouts
Buckwheat sprouts
Sunflower seed sprouts
1 carrot, grated
1 celery stalk, chopped
1 red pepper, chopped

SPROUT SALAD (2)

Place bean sprouts, broccoli sprouts, red pepper and spring onions in a large bowl.

Add dressing (see page 73) and sesame seeds, and toss gently.

Chill for one hour before serving.

1 cup alfalfa sprouts
1 cup broccoli sprouts
2 cups mung bean sprouts
Spring onions
1 small red pepper
Sesame seeds, roasted

BEAN SPROUTS WITH SCALLIONS

2 cups mung bean sprouts

5-6 scallions (spring onions)

Dash olive or other oil

A handful of parsley, chopped

1tbsp soy sauce

Sauté scallions for a few minutes, stir in sprouts and cook for a few more minutes. Stir in soy sauce. Sprinkle with parsley and serve.

SPROUT BREAD

Add 3 or 4 cups of mixed sprouted beans or seeds (e.g. alfalfa, broccoli, chickpea, fenugreek, mung) as well as a handful of dry sunflower and/or pumpkin seeds to the basic bread recipe (see page 158) before baking.

The finished bread has a beautifully moist texture throughout, whilst the crust has an aroma that is slightly reminiscent of freshly ground coffee.

STIR-FRIED SPROUTS AND VEGETABLES

Heat olive oil in a heavy pan (or wok) until very hot. Chop onions and other vegetables into small pieces, and drop into the pan, taking care to keep them constantly on the move, add bean sprouts to pan, and continue to stir.

After a few minutes splash wine, vinegar and soy sauce into the pan, continue to let the veggies and sprouts cook in this sauce for a few more minutes until veg is crunchy but not over-cooked.

Serve with couscous or noodles topped with sweet and sour sauce (see page 141).

N.B. You could add a splash of chilli sauce if you want to give this dish a bit of a kick, although be warned that when the chilli sauce hits the hot pan it can give off quite eye-watering fumes!

2 cups fresh sprouts (alfalfa, lentil, mung, radish, sunflower, etc.)

1 medium onion

Any other vegetables you fancy, e.g. broccoli, carrots, chard, courgette, mange tout, mushrooms, green or red peppers, sweetcorn, etc.

A dash of cider vinegar

A dash of fairly traded olive oil

A dash of red wine

A dash of soy sauce

OYSTER MUSHROOMS FROM YOUR KITCHEN

Did you know that you can grow mushrooms in your kitchen even if you haven't got much room? Coffee shops and cafés are a source of plentiful used coffee grounds that can be used as substrate for growing oyster mushrooms on a home scale. Most will be more than happy for you to take away as much as you like provided that you ask nicely, in fact you will be doing them a favour as otherwise they will need to pay to get rid of what is for them a waste product. Growing fresh mushrooms on coffee grounds should provide you with a crop in about five weeks.

Oyster mushroom spawn (obtainable online from suppliers such as Anne Miller Mushrooms)[15]

Fresh, used coffee grounds (no more than 1 day old)

Large mixing bowl

A clean plastic container, e.g. large freezer bag, small plastic bucket of some sort

Plastic gloves

Spray bottle

Tetrapack fruit juice or soya milk carton (for use as growing container)

Place fresh coffee grounds and oyster spawn together in mixing bowl in a 3:1 ratio. Mix the oyster spawn into the grounds with your hands, making sure to break up any large pieces and distribute evenly. It's a good idea to wear latex gloves in order to prevent any contamination from unwanted moulds that might be on your skin.

Sterilise your growing container (e.g. fruit juice carton) by cutting it open at the top, rinsing out thoroughly then filling with boiling water.

Put the mixture in your growing container so that it is around three quarters full and place in a warm, dark place such as an airing cupboard, under a bed, etc.

After about three weeks, the mixture should be completely colonised with white oyster mushroom mycelium, and ready to fruit. Make a 5cm (2in) diameter hole in your container and place in an airy spot with indirect light. A humid location is good.

Spray with water regularly – it's important that it doesn't dry out. Mushrooms should appear within a few days and will be large enough to harvest a few days after that.

The grounds will continue to crop until all the nutrients are spent – you can also keep some of the mixture in order to inoculate the next batch.

REJUVELAC

Rejuvelac is a fermented drink made from wheat or other grains such as oats, millet, barley, etc. that is said to improve digestion and be a source of B vitamins, amino acids and simple sugars.

Soak wheat for 12 hours in water. Rinse and drain.

½ cup wheat berries
Water

Sprout wheat for three days in a sprouting jar or other vessel, then three-quarter fill jar with fresh water.

Leave at room temperature for 24 hours. Rejuvelac is now ready to drink – it should have a pleasant smell with a slight flavour of lemonade. Drink soon after it is made, or store in a refrigerator for up to four days.

Fermentation

Fermentation is a series of techniques that use certain yeasts or bacteria to convert the carbohydrates in foodstuffs into alcohols and carbon dioxide or organic acids. It has many benefits: it preserves food and nutrients; it breaks nutrients down into forms that are easier to digest; it creates new nutrients (although claims that it can make vitamin B12, an important vitamin that can be lacking in a vegan diet, are debatable); it removes toxins and may create antioxidants in some foods. Live fermented foods such as sauerkraut and kefir include 'good' bacteria that live in our guts and promote healthy immune systems. However many shop bought fermented foods have been heat treated or pasteurised, which will kill these beneficial organisms, therefore it is useful to get into the habit of producing our own fermented foods in the kitchen. For more information on the fascinating subject of fermentation, I'd strongly recommend Sandor Katz's books *Wild Fermentation*[16] and *The Art of Fermentation*.[17]

SAUERKRAUT

1 large cabbage head
2-3tbsp coarse or sea salt
1tsp caraway seeds
(optional)
Water as needed

Cut cabbage finely and pack into large sealable storage jars (e.g. 'Kilner' jars) with a sprinkling of salt and caraway seeds between each layer. Pack the cabbage down as tightly as possible. Add water to overflowing. Close jar and seal.

Keep an eye on the jars over the next few days and add water if necessary to keep jar full and ensure cabbage is covered (exposed cabbage may develop moulds; this should be removed although the rest should be OK). The sauerkraut will be ready in about a week, and should keep indefinitely.

KIMCHI

Kimchi is a traditional Korean dish made of vegetables that have undergone lactic fermentation. The most commonly used ingredients are Chinese cabbage, carrots and radishes, although practically any other vegetables can be used.

Cut the cabbage in half lengthwise, then crosswise into 5cm (2in) pieces, discarding the root end. Place in a large ceramic bowl with salt and add enough water to cover. Weigh the cabbage down with a plate to ensure it remains submerged. Leave for between 12-24 hours or so, then drain and rinse.

Shred the carrots and radish and finely chop the spring onions and garlic, then combine all ingredients together, ensuring that all are evenly coated with the chilli, garlic and paprika mixture.

Pack into large fermenting jars. The mixture should begin bubbling after a few hours.

Leave for a week or so, opening the jars occasionally to let the gasses escape. Kimchi should keep indefinitely, but needs to be refrigerated once a jar is opened.

1 large Chinese napa cabbage

4 medium carrots

1 medium daikon radish

6-8 garlic cloves (one bulb)

¼ cup fresh ginger, minced

¼ cup paprika

¼ cup red chilli pepper powder

½ cup sea salt

A handful of spring onions

Water

YOGHURT

Dairy free alternatives to milk based yoghurts can be successfully produced in a number of ways.

Soya milk

Live soya yoghurt starter

Heat soya milk to boiling, simmer for a few minutes and allow to cool to body temperature.

Stir in two or three tablespoons of soya yoghurt starter (several brands are available). Keep covered in a warm (not hot) place for 8-12 hours.

When it is ready it should have set, and will have a distinctive acid smell and taste. Keeps for about a week – store in a cold part of the fridge – do not freeze or cook as this will kill the beneficial bacteria.

Future batches can be made in the same way using this home-made yoghurt as a starter, although it is advisable to make a new batch using fresh starter culture every now and then in order to prevent the build up of undesirable bacteria.

OATMEAL YOGHURT

Stir water into the oatmeal in a bowl until it has a smooth creamy consistency, cover and leave in a warm place for 12 hours or so until fermentation begins.

It will become increasingly acidic over the next few hours; when desired flavour is achieved, store in the fridge. Discard if any unpleasant smells are detected as this indicates the presence of undesirable bacteria.

This yoghurt substitute can be flavoured with lemon juice, fresh fruit, chopped nuts, etc.

1-2 cups oatmeal
Filtered or spring water

SUNFLOWER SEED YOGHURT

Soak seeds for around 12 hours. Drain and leave covered to sprout for a further 12 hours.

Finely chop sprouts in a blender or liquidiser, combined with 1tbsp of starter culture with a little filtered or spring water (you could use the seed soak water), until it has a smooth creamy consistency. It may be necessary to add a little more water during processing.

Keep covered in a warm place for a few hours – it will acquire a pleasant acid taste. Keep refrigerated and use within 2-3 days.

Note that this yoghurt cannot be used as a starter culture.

1-2 cups raw sunflower seeds, hulled
Live soya yoghurt starter

KOMBUCHA

Kombucha is a fermented drink with a distinctive slightly sour taste said to have probiotic properties particularly beneficial to the digestive system. It is made by adding a Symbiotic Culture of Bacteria and Yeast (SCOBY) 'mother' to a brew of sweetened tea. The process is extremely easy, although it can be difficult to source a SCOBY mother to begin. The best (and traditional) way is to find a friend who is already making kombucha who can pass some onto you – mine was given to me by permaculture teacher Aranya – although it can also be obtained through sellers online.

1 SCOBY mother

4 black or green tea bags

¾ cup sugar

2 litres (3½ pints) water, filtered

Boil the water and stir in the sugar. Add the teabags and leave to steep for 20 minutes or so.

Strain the tea into a sterilised, wide necked glass or ceramic vessel (note that kombucha needs a wide surface area, and works best if the diameter of the container is greater than the depth of the liquid).

When liquid has cooled to lukewarm temperature add the mother culture with the firm, opaque side facing upwards.

Leave in a warm spot to ferment for a few days until a skin has formed on the surface. The longer it is left the more acidic it will become.

Once it has reached your preferred degree of acidity start a new batch, storing the mature kombucha in the fridge. You now have two mothers, one that you can use for your next batch, and one to pass on to a friend! It can also be added to the compost if you don't have anybody to share with.

Preserving Your Abundance

Apart from fermentation, there are several other preservation methods that can be used to store and prolong the life of any surplus garden produce.

Bottling Fruit

Particularly useful for preserving fruit that only has a short season. Only the very best clean, fresh and undamaged fruit should be used for bottling, and requires proper vacuum sealing jars and bottles that are scrupulously clean. The fruit is packed into sterilised bottles with sugar or syrup, which helps to maintain the flavour. Water may be used instead of syrup, but the fruit will need to be sweetened and reheated before use. The jars are then closed tight and unscrewed a quarter turn, submerged in water and heated to the required temperature.

Apples, blackberries, gooseberries, loganberries, raspberries, rhubarb and strawberries need a temperature of 75°C (165°F) for 10 minutes. Apricots, cherries, currants, damson, citrus fruits, peaches and plums require 80°C (180°F) for 15 minutes.

Drying

Apples, beans, grapes, mushrooms, peas, pears, plums and all manner of herbs can be successfully dried without using any special equipment provided that a constant correct temperature can be maintained and that there is adequate ventilation to enable a good air flow to carry away any moisture. An airing cupboard above a hot water tank or rack over a solid wood stove would be suitable, or else produce can be dried overnight in an oven on a very low setting with the door left open.

Apples and pears – slice into rings 0.5cm (0.25in) thick, then submerge in salt water for five minutes or so to preserve their colour, then spread on an oven tray or thread through twine to prevent them touching each other.

Grapes – dry when fresh and fully ripe – seedless varieties are best. Fruit should be kept whole and spread on trays in a single layer, or can be hung in bunches. The drying process is complete when no juice appears if the fruit is squeezed.

Mushrooms and onions – string up (cut onions into rings first). When dry, store in airtight boxes in a cool, dark, dry place.

Peas and beans – shell and tie in a muslin bag. Place in boiling water and leave for five minutes, then plunge into cold water. Dry gradually in a thin layer.

Jams and Syrups

The only equipment needed is a large stainless steel or enamel pan (avoid aluminium as this can leach toxins). For a basic jam recipe, wash, core and clean fruit, removing any stones or pips. Weigh fruit and add equal weight of sugar. Place in a pan adding a little water if fruit is dry. Boil rapidly then reduce heat a little (be careful or it will boil over), skimming off any rising scum. To test that the jam has set, drop a little onto a cold plate until jam gels. Remove from heat and when cooled a little, ladle into jars sterilised by boiling water then dried in an oven, then seal.

Syrups can be made by cooking fruit very slowly, then drawing off the juice through muslin. The juice is put in bottles that are then simmered in water for 20 minutes and sealed.

Chutneys

Chutneys are mainly based on spiced vinegars and sugar as the preservative. Finely chop all fruit and vegetables such as onions, garlic, marrows, apples, green tomatoes, ginger, courgettes, etc. and add all the ingredients into a large pan. For every 4kg (9lb) of fruit/vegetables add about 20g (1oz) salt, 400g (14oz) sugar and 0.5-1 litre (1-2 pints) vinegar. Bring to the boil and simmer uncovered for 30 minutes to 3 hours depending on the ingredients until the mixture is glossy, thick, rich in colour and well reduced. Leave to cool slightly and pot into sterilised jars.

CHAPTER 4

Designing the Permaculture Garden

"If you have a garden and a library,
you have everything you need."

Marcus Tullius Cicero

Zone 1

For many, the small back garden, or Zone 1, is the logical place to begin implementing permaculture. It's where we can begin to have some control over the production of crops such as fruit, vegetables and herbs.

The difference between the permaculture garden and its more 'conventional' counterpart is basically to do with design or at least an approach towards design. Of course, 'design' is very much addressed by the TV gardening programmes and multitude of glossy 'lifestyle' books and magazines around at the moment. However these tend to be focused primarily in terms of aesthetics – what colours and shapes go well together, where to place your decking or water features for best visual effect, etc. Permaculture design on the other hand isn't so much about what looks attractive on a cosmetic level. Rather it's to do with creating an integrated landscape that produces food, medicines, seeds (for propagation or distribution), craft and building materials, fibres, dyes, and much more. The permaculture designer recognises that nature is abundant and will emulate her patterns and principles in creating sustainable human habitats.

This isn't to say that productive landscapes should be about visually dull utilitarianism. Form follows function, and all the permaculture gardens I've ever seen are places of great beauty. But this kind of beauty flows from the relationships to be found in a polycultural ecosystem, at once elegant in its simplicity, yet at the same time diverse in its complexity. A pond is not just a place to store water, grow water mint and attract pest predators such as frogs, toads and dragonflies. It also has its own sense of mystery and calm where it is easy to spend half an hour simply gazing into its depths, meditating upon the myriad interactions between its many remarkable denizens. A keyhole bed is not only a technique for increasing productive growing edges, its flows and curves are also pleasing to the eye, emulating natural forms rather than the imposed straight lines of the traditional square or rectangular vegetable bed. And a forest garden not only utilises every productive niche of space and time, it also has qualities that seem to touch something within the inner 'spiritual' being. Furthermore, a well-designed permaculture garden has many other 'uses' beyond simply 'growing stuff': play area (for children and 'grown ups'), chill out zone, spiritual retreat, open air art gallery, wildlife sanctuary, nattering with the neighbours, yoga space, biodiversity storehouse, tree nursery or somewhere to dry your washing.

Above all, the permaculture garden should be somewhere for relaxation and enjoyment, not yet another place to get hung up about whether or not you are 'doing it right' or meeting others' expectations. For me, there's nothing like our small urban garden on a summer's afternoon. The bushes and trees are literally dripping with cherries, apples, loganberries, blackcurrants and raspberries, whilst burnet, sorrel, rocket, lemon balm, mints, Welsh and tree onions, chives, lovage, lettuces, day lilies, marigolds, poppies and other edible leaves and flowers fill the salad beds. Buddleia and evening primroses scent the warm air and frogs and newts plop into the pond. Blue tits search the trees for bugs whilst starlings polish off the cherries that are out of human reach. Cuban or dub grooves drift from the open kitchen window and I'm under the shade of the quince tree in a deck chair with a few bottles of fine local ale and the latest edition of *Permaculture* magazine or maybe *The Idler* – truly the embodiment of Bill Mollison's concept of 'the designer as a recliner'.

'SADIM' - Survey, Assess, Design, Implement, Maintain

SADIM is a handy little acronym used to describe a systematic process of permaculture design and development. It's a tool that enables good task management, helping us to do things in logical stages and make intelligent placement decisions. It can be relevant to any situation, from land development, creating communities, setting up a small business enterprise, building a house, to preparing a meal. For now I'm going to apply the steps to the design of a small permaculture garden, roughly based around my Zone 1 plot here in the very urban setting of Westcliff on Sea in Essex.

Survey Stage

The first step in any design process is to observe and collect information about your site, for example:

- Create a base map indicating any existing physical features, for instance, boundaries, fences and walls, greenhouses, ponds, paths, trees and bushes, as well as orientation (e.g. south or north facing, sun paths at different times of the year, shady spots, frost pockets, etc.). Take photographs or make sketches – you can also download quite high-resolution aerial photos of most of the British Isles – including your back garden – from various internet sites such as Google maps.

- Gather data about your soil type and condition. A simple hand test will determine if it is sandy, clay or silty, and pH (alkalinity or acidity) can be measured using an inexpensive kit bought from any garden centre. Discover what you can about the history and previous usage of the garden – if cultivated, were chemicals used? Any long-term soil contamination? Any evidence of compaction?
- Investigate local weather patterns; prevailing wind direction, annual rainfall figures and dates of first and last frosts. Much information can be gleaned from public sources such as the library, internet or meteorological office, but buildings, trees, walls and fences can have significant effects on the micro-climate of your garden, and should also be taken into account.
- Slopes and contours. These can be measured accurately enough with simple home made tools such as an 'A' frame or bunyip.
- How does water influence your garden? Is your site dry or boggy? Any springs or ponds (natural or left by the previous occupant)? Any watercourses passing through? The presence of moisture-loving trees such as willow or alder might well indicate water underground. What is the water quality? Discolouration could indicate mineral or chemical deposition. Any sources or potential contamination pollution nearby, e.g. industrial sites upstream?
- Do a flora and fauna audit; look at the animals and plants that share your land. Many wild plants are indicators of soil type, condition and pH – look at plant communities rather than individual specimens that may not be typical. What else lives with you? Foxes, frogs, newts, birds, fish, snakes, bees, wasps, worms, slugs, centipedes. What do they tell you about your garden?
- Some other issues to think about: access (existing paths, steps, entrance gates, etc. and their condition); electricity and mains water supplies; security and susceptibility to 'human predation' (e.g. vandalism, burglars and other uninvited visitors); 'cultural' history of your site (activities of previous inhabitants, attitudes of neighbours, planning or legal issues, tenancy agreements, etc.).

At this stage it's important to try to be as 'value free' as possible as at the moment we are concerned only with collecting data, not with making decisions. Many permaculture designers recommend that the observation period should last at least 12 months in order to view all of the seasonal changes. In reality this isn't always practical, as we usually need to obtain some kind of a yield before this, especially if our livelihood or sustenance depends on it! However the 'leave it a year' rule is certainly good advice to follow before making any changes that may be difficult to reverse, such as any major landscaping, pond creation, tree or hedge planting, building permanent structures (for example, sheds, greenhouses), etc.

As well as gathering information about your plot on a physical level, it's also important to ask questions of the people who are going to be using the site, and finding out as much as possible about their needs and wants. Note that this might mean you and your family, or any client that you may be designing for, thus it can be very useful to develop your listening

skills, and refrain from imposing your own ideas too much. What are their dietary requirements or preferences; are they vegan, vegetarian or omnivorous? How much time, money or inclination are they likely to devote to their garden? Any children (actual or planned)? Any special needs? We all have our own understanding of what 'special needs' might mean and we all have them to one extent or another, but examples might include allergies, physical disabilities, visual impairments, therapeutic needs (especially if the garden is to be a retreat from stress and anxiety) and so on.

Ours is a four bedroomed Victorian terraced house situated about a mile inland from the mouth of the Thames Estuary. When we moved here in 1994 the sheltered north facing 5.2m x 8.2m (17ft x 27ft) garden was fairly typical for an urban situation. It consisted of an overgrown lawn with a straight concrete path running its length. This was edged by a rectangular bed with four rather scraggy looking rose bushes in it whilst the lawn itself was dominated by a self-sown elder bush and a large pile of assorted debris and rubbish. The pH neutral soil, based on underlying London Clay bedrock with Ice Age gravel deposits on top, was of good quality, with a reasonable degree of organic matter present. However, we suspect that the previous occupants had periodically applied herbicides to control the 'weeds' (They offered to give the garden a 'quick dose' to 'smarten it up' before vacating the property. Needless to say we politely declined this magnanimous gesture.), but their attitude apart from this seemed to be general disinterest.

As for the new occupants, we were an 'alternative green' inclined vegan family of five at that time, two adults and three children aged eight, three and one year old. We didn't have much money to spend on the garden (still don't!), although I had a fair degree of 'conventional' organic gardening experience, and a predilection for urban skip scavenging. I was employed full time at a local care home, mainly shift work, including weekends and some nights, but often with free time on weekdays. My partner Debby was a full time mum, also doing some child minding from home, but didn't have much interest in gardening at that time. My 'wants' from the garden included a place to grow fruits, herbs and veggies to supplement our allotment's production, as well as try out all the wonderful and inspiring ideas I was discovering in the permaculture books I'd just started to read. Debby and the kids' main interest garden-wise were to have somewhere to relax and play respectively. We also wanted a garden that was aesthetically pleasing and attractive to wildlife. A break-in shortly after moving in also made us realise that the lack of a proper fence onto the back alley was leaving us vulnerable to the 'energy' of 'human predation'!

Assessment and Analysis Stage

The 'assessment' phase of the design process is about analysing and evaluating the data gathered during the 'survey' stage, such as looking at your 'boundaries' (what are your limiting factors?) and 'resources' (what can you make use of?), and how to fit these together. Think about needs and outputs – which of these can be met by the existing system and what changes might need to be made?

For us, 'boundaries' were not only the physical parameters of the garden (i.e. the property lines delineated by our neighbours' fences), but also included time and money. However, these could all be seen as 'resources' as well, especially once we started to use our imagination and think creatively.

Having listed our 'wants' from the garden, we divided it into distinct 'conceptual' areas in order to meet those needs. The productive part of the garden would principally be for fruit and vegetable growing, favouring perennial plants. Our allotment already produced most of our 'staples' such as onions, beans, potatoes, brassicas and root crops, besides which space was very limited, hence the focus here would be more on leafy salads and herbs, as well as small trees and bushes. We were also keen to get away from the existing, very linear (i.e. boring) layout of the garden, and develop a far more organic, flowing feel.

Making Design Decisions

We are now ready to start thinking in more detail about placement decisions in order to maximise beneficial connections. It's useful to spend as much time as possible working on the design of your project. That way hopefully most of your mistakes will have been made on paper rather than on the land itself!

There are a number of books that go into permaculture design in great depth, including Patrick Whitefield's *The Earth Care Manual*[18] and Aranya's *Permaculture*

Design: A Step-by-Step Guide,[19] and money spent on these will be an investment that will repay you many times. However, one very useful tip is to make a number of photocopies of your original base map on to which you can try out all of your design ideas. These might range from the pragmatic and sensible right through to the completely wild and impractical and everything in between. Get them all down and learn to temporarily ignore your 'inner critic', that little voice in the back of your head that always seeks to censor your creativity and imagination. Let your artistic 'right-brain' have free range. Use bold colours, maybe crayons or felt tips or even different coloured pieces of card or small models to represent the shapes of beds, structures, trees or ponds that can be moved around. In effect this is a 'brainstorming' process, where, in the initial stages at least, it is far more important to get down the flow of ideas rather than appraise what will or won't work. To me, a major part of permaculture design is about unlocking creative potential and overcoming the barriers of restrictive thinking. Besides which, even the craziest idea might actually lead to you to some very good practical insights you might not otherwise have thought of.

Some design 'overlay themes' in our garden included:

Beds

In order to maximise the potential growing area of the garden as well as give it a more natural, flowing character, we decided to create no-dig beds around a spiral pattern formed by a central 'key-hole' shape. The 'key-hole' bed is a common feature of Zone 1 permaculture garden design that provides a variety of aspects, maximises 'edge' and the available growing area as well as providing easy access to all plants without the need to walk on and compact the soil. They also encourage 'mix and match' cottage-style planting rather than putting in straight lines of one thing, a good way of creating mutually beneficial companion 'guilds' of fruits, vegetables, herbs and flowers.

Trees, Shrubs and Climbers

Even a small garden such as ours can include room for a few productive fruit trees and bushes. We decided to choose compact yet productive new strains of blackcurrant such as Ben Sarek, which has large, tasty fruits that are tolerant to a degree of shade. We were also able to fit in a surprising number of fruit trees by choosing varieties grown on 'dwarfing' rootstocks (see page 107). We chose varieties that would be compatible in terms of their flowering (and thus pollination) periods, and that would do well in our part of the country. Vertical space such as fences would be utilised for climbers such as grapes, tayberries and honeysuckle, extending their height with trellises.

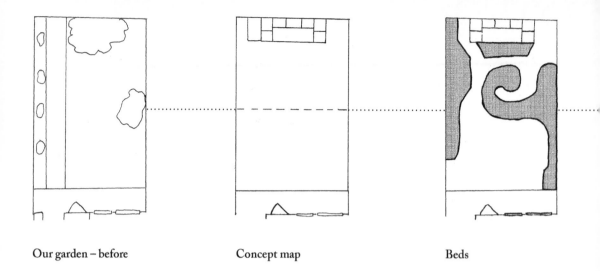

Our garden – before   Concept map   Beds

Water

Our main reason for wanting a pond in the garden was to provide a wildlife habitat. The importance of creating such an oasis in the urban environment cannot be overstated, and even a tiny pond with a diameter of just a few feet will have innumerable benefits for frogs, toads, newts and dragonflies, as well as a source of drinking water for birds. And hopefully our visitors will repay our hospitality by consuming slugs, snails, aphids and other 'pests'. The pond and its margins also act as a growing medium for edible and useful plants such as watercress and water mint.

Another aspect of water in the garden is harvesting, every opportunity for which should be maximised. As well as placing butts below gutter run-off points, this can be achieved by adding lots of organic matter to the soil in the form of compost. This will greatly improve its moisture retaining capacity. According to permaculture designer Toby Hemenway, "soil with as little as 2% organic matter can reduce the irrigation needed by 75% when compared to poor soils with less than 1% organic matter".[20]

Water in the garden also has safety implications if young children are likely to be around. Therefore it was important to ensure that our pond would be adequately fenced off. Eventually we decided to create a trellis barrier separating the 'leisure' and 'productive' zones, secured with a gate that would be kept bolted shut whenever the children couldn't be fully supervised.

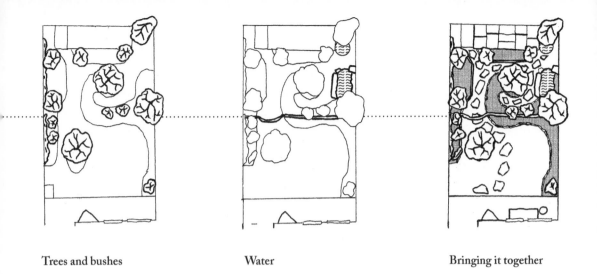

| Trees and bushes | Water | Bringing it together |

Pulling it Together and Adding Features

Bill Mollison once described slotting together all of the elements of a permaculture design as being 'more fun than chess', giving careful thought and consideration to what will fit where to the best advantage. As well as making decisions about greenhouse location, bed shaping, permanent plantings, fencing and pond placement, other features to be integrated into our garden design included compost bins, stepping stone pathways, seats, pots and containers and so on.

Implementation Stage

My own golden rules for the implementation phase – that is, turning the design into reality – are basically these:

- Don't overdo it. Keep within your physical and financial limitations. It's better to thoroughly develop a small area – probably not more than a few square feet for a beginner – than take on too much and simply exhaust yourself and your enthusiasm.
- Take it easy. Learn to fit in with the rhythms of the seasons, and take time to listen to the experience and advice of others. But don't let a lack of confidence or experience intimidate you into indefinite procrastination. You won't always get things right first time, but that's fine. Remember that the person who never made a mistake never learned anything either!
- Enjoy yourself. If creating a sustainable garden feels more like a chore than a pleasure, it's probably not worth doing in the first place!

Here in our Westcliff garden we got stuck in by breaking up the straight concrete path we had inherited, the fragments of which we saved to make 'stepping stones' and a rockery by the pond. Scavenged and scrounged timber, bricks, roof tiles, wine bottles and split chestnut logs were used to create bed edging, and soil excavated from the pond creation was used to build up the height of the beds. A 'child-friendly' trellis fence that protects the pond and veggie beds was made from the stems and branches of the grubbed out elder bush. Seeds, plants and fruit trees and bushes were donated, propagated from cuttings or purchased either locally or from reputable specialist suppliers.

I had lots of help from friends with manual labour tasks, in particular building the greenhouse. This project mainly utilised scrap timber from a neighbour who was carrying out a major house renovation project, cedar frames rescued from an abandoned commercial greenhouse, plus any bits of scrounged glass cut to fit this. Construction skills were not my forte, and I wanted to find ways of repaying all those who had given me invaluable assistance. This led me to find out about and join my Local Exchange Trading System (LETS). LETS became a great way of putting back into my community what I had withdrawn, even if the skills I had to offer weren't reciprocated in a direct way.

Maintenance and Management

A living system such as a permaculture garden is never finished. Elements evolve, our needs and commitments change, climatic conditions alter. Sometimes even the best and most considered plans don't work out; nature has a habit of not following the blueprint! Permaculture design maintenance is therefore about creating 'feedback loops'; a constant process of observing, reassessing, redesigning and implementing tweaks and changes.

During the decade or so that we have been developing our garden, annual vegetable crops such as carrots, quinoa and tomatoes have slowly given way to leafy spring perennials and top fruits as the trees' canopies have spread. A grey water harvesting system that we installed was abandoned when it became clear that the smell of stored static bathwater is intolerable in the summer, especially as it was right next to the dining room window. It has since been modified to collect roof run-off rainwater only, and even with 5 x 200 litre (44 gallon) water butts to collect it, still yields more rainwater than we can ever capture or for that matter make use of on our garden!

Possibly my biggest design mistake was planting what appeared to be a quite innocuous looking cherry plum seedling given to us as a house warming present in a spare spot that looked like it needed filling up. Within four or five years this 20cm (8in) whip had shot up 6m (20ft) and was shading out the entire garden, making it a dank, unproductive and depressing place. Showing no signs of slowing down, it became clear that it would have to go. But on the plus side, I now know far more about tree surgery and cherry plum growth habits than I did before, and was also able to use the wood to make a rustic table and stool set! What's more, I coppiced it rather than digging it out, so the stems can regrow, meaning that some years it still bears a crop of succulent bright yellow cherry plums. On others, when it again outgrows its welcome, I coppice it back again to produce more stems for rustic furniture making, firewood or other projects.

....

A Top 10 of Perennial Vegetables Suitable for the Small Garden

Common Name	Latin Name
Dandelion	*Taraxacum officinale*
Fennel	*Foeniculum vulgare*
Lemon Balm	*Melissa officinalis*
Lovage	*Levisticum officinale*
Ramsons (Wild Garlic)	*Allium ursinum*
Sorrel	*Rumex acetosa*
Sweet Cicely	*Myrrhis odorata*
Three Cornered Leek	*Allium triquetrum*
Tree Onions	*Allium × proliferum*
Wild Rocket	*Eruca sativa*

Salad Days

Most people will have space for at least a few leaves and herbs that can be added to salads, even if you only have a window box or a few pots by the back door. Luckily the days are now long gone when a 'salad' meant a bit of limp lettuce, a watery tomato, a few bits of cucumber and a spring onion or two to add a hint of the exotic. Nowadays they can be healthy, satisfying meals in their own right, or perfect accompaniments to main dishes whatever the time of year.

Don't forget the aesthetic dimension when creating a salad; aim for a pleasing mix of colours, smells, textures and flavours. It's good to have larger amounts of relatively 'mild' tasting ingredients such as lettuce leaves, chickweed, etc. to provide 'bulk' (or 'background') to the salad, and smaller amounts of strongly flavoured leaves such as dandelion, lemon balm, lovage, radicchio, wild rocket, etc. as 'foreground' tastes that would otherwise be overpowering. Edible flowers (see list below) used as a garnish can add an attractive visual touch and make your salad a marvellous centrepiece to the table.

Salads can quickly lose nutrients through oxidisation, so when cutting up ingredients, the smaller the area of cut or peeled surface exposed to the air the better. Adding a dressing will help prevent the loss of vitamins, and can also enhance the flavours. A salad should be prepared as close as possible to eating time, so if being used as a side dish, the salad should be made up last, preferably just a few minutes before serving.

EVERYTHING SALAD

Combine ingredients in a large bowl and serve as a meal in itself, or with, say, a nut roast, baked potatoes and cooked beetroot.

Serve with a dressing or with plenty of chutney on the side.

More 'minimalist' salads can be made by combining just a few of the ingredients above, e.g. chopped apple, chicory, onion and red cabbage, sliced, or kidney beans, butter beans, sliced runner beans and chopped red onions. As ever, use your own preferences and imagination.

1 apple, chopped – A 'cooking' variety such as Bramley is best

1 cup cooked beans, e.g. broad beans, butter beans, flageolet beans, etc.

1 small beetroot, grated

½ small red cabbage, shredded

1-2 carrots, chopped or grated

1 handful of cauliflower or broccoli florets

2 sticks celery (including leaves), chopped

½ cucumber, diced

1 lettuce (red or green lettuce, Salad Bowl or Little Gem is particularly nice in a mixed salad)

1-2 handfuls of chopped nuts, e.g. almonds, walnuts, hazels, etc.

1 onion, chopped into rings. Red onions are especially suitable

1-2 cups cooked pasta shells

1 red or green pepper, sliced

3-4 radishes, sliced or topped and tailed

1 cup sweetcorn – use tinned if you can't get it fresh

2-3 tomatoes, firm and sliced – in addition to the usual red tomatoes try yellow or stripey varieties such as Golden Sunrise or Tigrella

Herbs, such as chives and parsley, chopped

1 handful of sunflower seeds

The list goes on as long as you like: add bean sprouts, chard, chicory, courgettes, cress, endives, French beans, chopped leeks, raisins, rocket, spring onions, spinach. Need I go on?

AN EASTER SUNDAY SALAD

PICKED FROM OUR GARDEN

Blackcurrant leaves

Chives

Dandelion leaves

Hop shoots

Lemon balm

Ramsons (wild garlic)

Raspberry leaves

Sorrel leaves

Sweet cicely

Three cornered leek
(stems and first flowers)

SUMMER SOLSTICE SALAD

PICKED FROM OUR GARDEN, WINDOW BOXES AND GREENHOUSE

Basil

Blackcurrant leaves

Dandelion

Day lily flowers

Garden cress

'Little Gem' lettuce

Marigold flowers

Oregano

Parsley

Salad burnet

Sorrel

Tsi leaves

Turkish rocket

Tarragon

Watercress (from pond)

Water mint (from pond)

Welsh onion

Wild rocket

CLASSIC GREEN SALAD (1)

*A simple green salad is the perfect accompaniment to a main meal
such as roasts, pasta dishes or anything else in fact!*

Tear up the lettuce and combine with the remaining
ingredients in a large bowl.

Dress with a splash of fairly traded olive oil and cider or
white vinegar.

¼ cucumber, diced

1 small lettuce, Little Gem

3-4 spring onions, finely
chopped

1 green pepper, cut into
small strips

2 good handfuls of fresh
small spinach
or chard leaves

Cider vinegar

Olive oil

GREEN SALAD (2)

Combine all the fresh ingredients in a large bowl.

Dress with a splash of fairly traded olive oil and cider or
white vinegar.

1 head chicory, outer leaves
removed

Cos lettuce

½ cucumber, peeled and
sliced thinly

1 small onion, chopped

1 handful of rocket leaves

1 handful of three cornered
leeks or wild garlic,
chopped

1 handful of watercress

SPROUT AND SPRING LEAVES DETOX SALAD

*A nutrient and mineral rich refresher to revitalise and detoxify the body
as the nights draw out and the dark days of winter start to fade.*

A couple of handfuls of mixed bean and seed sprouts,
e.g. alfalfa, broccoli, fenugreek, mung, radish,
red clover, etc.

A combination of annual or perennial green leaves
available from the garden or from under glass in
late winter/early spring, e.g. broccoli, chard, kale,
purslane, sorrel, winter lettuce, etc. as well as wild
plants such as chickweed. Some of these will just
be starting to appear as fresh shoots, so only take a
small amount to ensure abundant crops later on in
the year.

A smaller amount of strongly flavoured garden and wild
spring leaves and shoots, e.g. dandelion, red dead
nettle, green garlic shoots, hairy bitter cress, lovage,
yarrow, etc.

Welsh or other perennial onions (these will just be
starting to grow, so use sparingly) or annual onions
from store.

Tear up or roughly chop 'bulk' leaves.

Chop much smaller amounts of the
strongly flavoured leaves and shoots.

Dice up the onions.

Mix all ingredients together with the
sprouts.

BROAD BEAN, BASIL AND TOMATO SALAD

Cut tomatoes into quarters, tear up basil and combine with broad beans in a salad bowl.

Lightly dress with olive oil.

2 cups fresh young broad beans, or mature beans, cooked for 10 minutes or so

Fresh basil leaves

4-5 fresh tomatoes

Olive oil

SUMMER PASTA SALAD

Cook pasta in a large saucepan of boiling, salted water until tender. Drain and allow to cool.

Toss in oil then combine with other ingredients and serve.

Dry pasta shells or spirals

½ cup fresh basil leaves, shredded

1 cup black or green olives

1 handful of baby spinach leaves

Cherry tomatoes, quartered

2tbsp olive oil

¼ cup pine nuts, toasted

AUTUMN APPLE, BEETROOT AND SPROUTS

1 apple, chopped

2 cups mixed bean and
  seed sprouts, e.g. alfalfa,
  chickpea, fenugreek,
  mung, etc.

1 medium beetroot, grated

3-4 rainbow chard leaves,
  torn into small pieces

6-7 cherry tomatoes,
  halved

½ cup chopped hazel nuts
  and almonds

4-5 chopped Welsh or
  spring onions

Combine ingredients and serve with a light dressing of
olive oil and cider vinegar.

PANZANELLA

This traditional Tuscan salad is a great way of using up old bread.

Stale loaf of wholegrain or
  crusty bread

A good handful of basil
  leaves

1 small cucumber

½ cup red onion, sliced

2 large fresh tomatoes

½ cup extra-virgin olive oil

A good splash of red-wine
  vinegar

Tear the bread into small chunks and place in a large
bowl. Splash generously with the olive oil and the red
wine vinegar and leave to soak these up for 20 minutes
or so.

Roughly chop the tomatoes, cucumber and basil and
combine together. Leave to stand for a little while
longer to allow the juices to soak up some more
before serving.

MOROCCAN STYLE BUTTERNUT SQUASH SALAD

Baste pumpkin cubes in olive oil with the ground spices in a pan and roast in oven at 200°C (390°F) for 20 minutes or so until tender.

Allow to cool, then combine with chopped coriander, chickpeas, figs and onion in a large bowl.

Dress with lemon juice and olive oil.

1 small butternut squash, peeled, deseeded and cut into cubes

1tsp ground coriander

1tsp ground cumin

¼ cup olive oil

1 handful of coriander leaves, roughly chopped

2 cups chickpeas, cooked (or use tinned)

1 small red onion, sliced

1 cup dried figs, finely chopped

1 large lemon, juice of

Edible Flowers

Kitchen gardeners often favour vegetable and fruit crops over ornamentals. Yet flowers not only enhance the aesthetic dimension of any garden, but many are also invaluable in terms of attracting pollinators and pest predators. In addition many are delicious to eat, especially in salads, and have medicinal as well as nutritional value.

Borage (*Borago officinalis*): Delicate blue flowers with a cucumber like flavour.
Chicory (*Cichorium intybus*): The blue or pink flowers have a slight taste of coffee.
Chives (*Allium schoenoprasum*): The purple flowers have a distinctive mild onion flavour similar to the leaves.
Cowslip (*Primula veris*): Treat as primroses. Cowslips are also increasingly rare in the wild.
Daisy (*Bellis perennis*): Whole flowers can be used as a salad garnish. Pick just before they are to be used.
Dandelion (*Taraxacum officinale*): All parts of this common so-called 'weed' are edible. The roots can be roasted as a coffee substitute, the leaves used in salads, also the bright yellow flowers as an attractive garnish.
Day lily (*Hemerocallis spp.*): Petals are crisp and juicy with a mild sweet flavour. The nectar at the base of the flower is particularly sweet.
Elderflower (*Sambucus nigra*): A lovely delicate flavour, the flowers can be eaten whole or sprinkled over a salad. Also used for elderflower champagne (see page 253).
Geraniums (*Pelargonium spp.*): The scented leaves of some varieties can be used in salads.
Iron cross plant (*Oxalis deppei*): Has a delicious lemony flavour. However they do contain oxalic acid so should not be eaten in large quantities.
Lavender (*Lavandula spp.*): Use sparingly, finely chopped, in salads.
Mallow (*Malva sylvestris*): Has a slightly glutinous texture.
Nasturtium (*Tropaeolum majus*): The peppery flavoured leaves and seeds can be eaten in salads along with the flowers. Seeds can also be pickled as a substitute for capers.
Pansy (*Viola wittrockiana*): This colourful flower brightens up any salad.
Pot marigold (*Calendula officinalis*): This self seeding annual cheers up any garden all year round with its yellow to orange flowers. Has a delicate saffron like flavour.

Rose (*Rosa spp.*): Petals can also be crystallised or used to make rose petal jam.

Squash flower (*Cucurbita pepo*): These can also be stuffed; try a filling of gently sautéed onion and mushrooms mixed with a little couscous.

Three-cornered leek (*Allium triquetrum*): An abundantly growing allium with a milder garlic flavour, the white flowers can also be added to the salad bowl.

Violet (*Viola odorata*): Sweet violet in particular has an attractive flavour, often flowering in late winter to early spring, and often the only edible flower available at this time of the year.

Dressings

It's easy to create a basic salad dressing by combining equal parts of oil (olive oil is more expensive but makes a worthwhile difference, although an ordinary sunflower oil will do – you could also try using alternatives such as hemp, walnut, sesame or wheatgerm oils which have their own distinctive flavours) with vinegar (a cider or wine vinegar is preferable, although I have improvised with malt vinegar with passable results), two or three cloves of garlic, lemon juice and herbs such as basil, sage, tarragon, etc. and a teaspoon of mustard powder or a couple of tablespoons of French mustard. Combine all ingredients in a jar with a tight lid and shake vigorously. Pour liberally, according to taste, over your favourite salad.

Although the above is a good base to work from, once again the sky is the limit with dressings when you start to use your imagination. Sara Davies, former grower at Growing Communities in north London, has kindly allowed me to reproduce some of the winning entries from the project's regular 'Dressing of the month' competition submitted by apprentices and volunteers.

RU'S ORIENTAL DRESSING

This one flavours the salad leaves

100ml/3.5fl. oz malt vinegar
100ml/3.5fl. oz sesame oil
25ml/1fl. oz soya sauce
Sprinkling of ground pepper

Thanks to Ru Litherland

ANNIE'S MINTY MIX DRESSING

While this one complements them

½ lemon, juiced
1 handful of mint
1tsp mustard - Dijon
Balsamic vinegar - a bit
(These ingredients make up about a third of the jar)
Olive oil - a bit more
(The oil makes up two thirds of the dressing)

ANNIE'S SWEET DRESSING

For strongly flavoured leaves

1 part balsamic vinegar to 1 part olive oil (use Palestinian for best result)
1tsp blackcurrant and sloe jelly ("or any old jam, to be honest," says Annie)
2tsp Dijon mustard

Thanks to Annie Stables

JANET'S CAESAR-STYLE DRESSING

½ cup apple cider vinegar
½ cup olive oil
½ cup white wine vinegar
½ tsp dried basil
1tbsp maple syrup
1tsp dried tarragon
250ml/8.5fl. oz soya yoghurt
Salt and pepper to taste

Thanks to Janet Davies

SARA'S SUNFLOWER SEED DRESSING

*Described as 'simple, not too many flavours' by one judge
and as 'unusual and complex' by someone else!*

1 handful of sunflower seeds, roasted*
and then smashed

1 lemon, juiced

2.5cm/1in of ginger and 1 garlic clove, both finely chopped

A generous splash of soya sauce

A few grinds of a pepper mill

A couple of glugs of good olive oil

* If you haven't done this before, it's easiest to toast the seeds in a dry pan on the top
of the stove, lessening the chance of your forgetting them in the oven or letting them burn.

Thanks to Sara Davies

CHAPTER 5

The Vegan Organic Vegetable Garden - The Basics

If everybody had a garden, wouldn't it be great?

We could sit and eat our dinner, and know that we'd grown everything that we ate!

Without you sailing cross the oceans, without you driving down the roads

Without you going to the garages, without your World Bank loans

Tragic Roundabout, 'The Garden Song'

Growing your own vegetables, herbs and fruit in your back garden is like learning to cook. Start with the basics and your skills will soon increase along with your confidence. In permaculture design terms, Zone 2 provides us with opportunities to extend our food growing activities further beyond Zone 1. In the larger garden for instance, more space is available for producing a wider range of crops, particularly if we consider giving up our attachment to the weed-free and manicured 'green deserts' that are suburban lawns.

Top of the Crops

There are many reasons why making your garden more productive is a good idea for you, your family and for the wider environment. For a start you'll be cutting down your 'food miles' and helping to save the Earth's precious resources by reducing your carbon footprint. Home-grown produce is as fresh and locally produced as it's possible to get, and unlike what is sold in the supermarkets, you will know exactly what has gone into producing it! If you have children, involving them in growing their own will help them to understand where our food really comes from, giving them a real sense of achievement and self esteem, and will equip them with vital life-skills. Gardening also provides plenty of gentle outdoor exercise that will keep you fit, and is an excellent way of relieving the stresses of modern living. Growing your own is also good for your pocket – not only will you will be making considerable savings on your weekly food shopping bill, you'll be driving to the supermarket less. Plus who needs an expensive health club membership when you've got your own 'green gym' in your back garden? Gardening can also be a great social activity. For example, why not share surplus produce with your neighbours – who knows what you might get in return?

Start with the Soil

The soil in your garden is mainly composed of non-living components produced by weathering of surface rocks, together with soluble nutrients, gasses and water and organic matter (humus). In a balanced soil, plants grow in an active and vibrant environment. The mineral content of the soil and its physical structure are important for their well-being, but it is the life in the earth, and the interactions between these organisms, that powers the soil's cycles and provides its fertility. The soil biota includes:

- Megafauna: size range 20mm upwards, e.g. moles, rabbits, rodents, etc.
- Macrofauna: size range 2-20mm, e.g. woodlice, spiders, earthworms, beetles, centipedes, slugs, snails, ants, harvestmen, etc.
- Mesofauna: size range 100 millimicrons-2mm, e.g. mites, springtails.
- Microfauna and Microflora: size range 1-100 millimicrons, e.g. yeasts, bacteria, fungi, nematodes, protozoa, rotifers, etc.

Depending on soil particle size, it is broadly divided into one of three categories, clay, sand or loam. It's possible to find out which you have, by performing the simple hand test shown below.

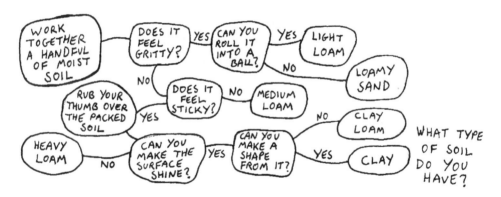

Your soil type will affect what will grow well in your garden – brassicas (the cabbage tribe) and potatoes will do well on heavy clays, whilst carrots, parsnips, peas and early outdoor crops may not. The reverse is the case with sandy soils, whilst beetroots and onions prefer clay loam soils.

Your soil type will also determine the best way of managing your garden. Clay and clay-loam soils should be cultivated only when just moist – not too wet or too dry.

Avoid walking on clay soils, especially when wet, as this may cause it to become compacted. Due to the tiny size of clay particles, these soils tend to be rich in nutrients, but many of these are locked up and unavailable to your plants as they are tightly bound to the particles due to a small electrical charge.

The addition of plenty of organic matter in the form of humus will improve the soil's overall structure as well as nutrient availability. A sandy soil is very free draining and thus does not hold nutrients well. Adding organic matter will improve its structure and water holding capacity. Mulching (adding a protective layer of material on top of the soil such as compost or straw, cardboard, etc.) will help prevent moisture loss as well as keeping down weed growth. All soils will benefit greatly from adding as much compost and organic matter as you can spare.

Digging out a soil profile (that is, a smooth sided square hole 45cm (18in) or so wide and deep) should reveal a number of distinct layers to your soil:

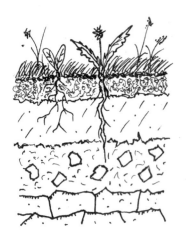

a) Humus: organic matter in relatively un-decomposed form. This layer tends to be dark and rich in smell and texture. Raw, semi-decomposed organic matter may be recognisable amongst its components, e.g. leaf mould, twiggy material, etc.
b) Topsoil: well-decomposed organic matter, mixed with a smaller amount of minerals
c) Layer of mixed, decomposed organic matter and mineral content
d) Subsoil or mineral layers, the content of which varies according to the nature of the soil and its parent material
e) Bedrock or parent material, which breaks down at the upper surface due to the effects of weathering and decay

The acidity or alkalinity of your soil (its pH) is important, as this will affect its overall fertility. It can be measured using a simple testing kit that you can buy in any garden centre, or by observing the predominant flora. Calcifuge plants (those that prefer an acid soil) include: azaleas, birch, *Digitalis* (foxgloves), Ericas, gorses and Scots pine. Calcicole (lime loving) plants include: ash, beech, buddleia, dogwoods, hazel and honeysuckle. Most soil life, including earthworms, as well as the majority of the fruit and vegetables that we want to grow prefer a neutral soil, although brassicas prefer slightly alkaline conditions whilst potatoes and strawberries like a soil that is slightly acidic.

Over-acidity can be corrected by applying lime as a short term measure (ground limestone, sold in garden centres, is available, but be aware that this will be depleting resources elsewhere) whilst adding plenty of organic matter will help to move both alkaline and acid soils towards a neutral pH as a longer term solution.

To Dig or Not to Dig

The primary reasons for digging our plots are to remove weeds, to loosen and aerate the soil and to incorporate organic matter such as compost or manure. However, too much digging can harm the soil's health and actually cause more weed problems than it solves. Whilst digging is an effective way of removing perennial weed roots, it can also cause dormant seeds to come to the surface and germinate.

Mulching your garden is fun and easy.

①

FLATTEN ANY GRASSES, WEEDS ETC. ON YOUR SITE. DON'T BOTHER TO CUT THEM DOWN OR REMOVE. SOAK GROUND WELL IF DRY, AND MAYBE ADD AN ACTIVATOR SUCH AS SEAWEED MEAL

②

COVER WITH A THICK LAYER OF LIGHT EXCLUDING, ORGANIC MATERIAL, EG, CARDBOARD OR NEWSPAPER (NOT COLOURED PRINT). ENSURE PLENTY OF OVERLAP TO PREVENT WEEDS GROWING THROUGH GAPS.

③

COVER WITH A THICK LAYER (3-6") OF WELL-ROTTED COMPOST, TOPPED WITH A FINAL LAYER OF STRAW, HAY (ENSURE FREE OF WEED SEEDS) GRASS MOWINGS, ETC TO PREVENT SURFACE DRYING OUT.

④

LARGE SEEDS & TUBERS (EG, BEANS, POTATOS) OR STRONGLY ROOTED AND PERENNIAL PLANTS CAN BE PLANTED DIRECTLY INTO OR THROUGH THE MULCH. WAIT A YEAR OR SO UNTIL BROKEN DOWN BEFORE SUITABLE FOR SMALLER SEEDS.

Digging will always damage soil structure to some extent, and will disturb the soil life balance, and, by exposure to the air, tends to burn up nutrients that then need to be replenished. It can also cause long term problems like compaction. No dig methods rely on nature to carry out cultivation operations. Organic matter such as well rotted compost, etc. is added directly to the soil surface as a mulch layer at least 5cm (2in) deep, which is then incorporated by the actions of worms pulling it downwards. No dig systems are said to be freer of pests and diseases, and moisture is also better retained under mulch.

Converting to a no dig system can be a long term process, and requires plentiful organic matter to provide mulch material. No dig techniques are not appropriate in all situations, but any gardener would do well to at least develop an awareness of when it is really necessary to dig, as well as considering minimising any soil disturbing practices.

Adding Fertility

'Feed the soil, not the plant' is the age-old organic gardener's mantra, and with good reason. Compost is at the heart of any fertile plot. This is the main source of humus, the very stuff of life itself, providing both nutrients and structure when it is added to the land. It is advisable to have at least two compost bins (these can be built out of old scrap wood – palettes are ideal – and ought to have a lid to keep the rain off), so that one heap can mature whilst the other is being built. Aim for a good balance of 'brown' (i.e. high in carbon materials such as tough, woody plant stems, straw, twigs, etc.) and 'green' (i.e. high in nitrogen materials such as grass mowings, fresh weeds, raw fruit and vegetable wastes, kitchen peelings, etc.) ingredients. In a few hours this should be too hot for you to comfortably insert your hand into its centre – this means it is active! Turn it over regularly, don't allow it to either become too wet or dry out too much, and the books say it will be good, friable compost in as little as six weeks in summer, although my experience is that at least six months is a far more realistic timescale!

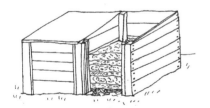

Autumn leaves should not be added to compost piles as they decompose very slowly. Instead these should be piled up separately and allowed to break down over a year or so into leaf mould, an excellent free-of-charge soil conditioner.

Smaller gardens may not have space for a double compost bin, in which case you might be better off with a smaller plastic 'cone' composter such as those often sold in garden centres or by Local Authorities that are trying to encourage recycling.

Another option to consider is 'worm composting'. These are also suitable for dealing with cooked kitchen scraps that might otherwise either putrefy or attract rats, and involves feeding such scraps to brandling worms in a special plastic bin. These small red 'wriggler' worms will quickly break them down into a high nutrient worm compost that is too rich for use as a seed compost, but is useful as a top dressing or as an addition to potting composts. You can buy worm composting kits from garden centres or by mail order, but it's very easy to make your own using an old plastic rubbish bin.

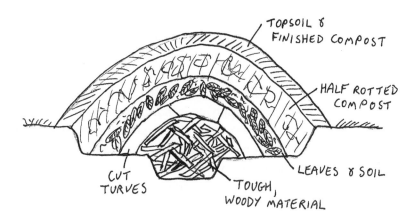

Hugelkultur, also known as magic mound composting, is a good way of dealing with excess amounts of woody garden materials such as twigs and tree prunings, hedge clippings, tough brassica stems, brashwood, etc. Dig a circular trench about 0.5m (1.5ft) deep and 1.4m (5ft) wide, into the centre of which the rough material is piled. Turves are then stacked face down onto this pile, then layers of compost and well-rotted leaves, etc. are added. The layers gradually break down, slowly releasing nutrients and creating rich humus over four or five years, ideal for growing hungry crops such as courgettes or strawberries.

'Green manuring' is another method of building long-term fertility. Most commonly this is achieved by sewing a temporary or semi-permanent cover crop such as alfalfa, buckwheat, grazing rye or mustard, that provides a protective cover for bare soil over winter that helps to prevent erosion and the leaching of nutrients, as well as breaking up the soil and accumulating minerals from deep in the subsoil with their root systems. The plant foliage is then chopped down either in spring or before flowering, and either lightly hoed into the soil or left on the surface as a rough mulch, whilst the roots are left in the soil to break down and improve its structure. This practice can cause temporary depletion of available nitrogen in the soil, but this can be reduced by using leguminous green manure crops such as field beans, lupins, red clover, trefoil or winter tares, that are able to fix their own nitrogen supply in root nodules that is released as the plants decay. Proponents of this system argue that green manuring and sheet composting causes fewer nutrients to be lost through leaching than heap methods; also that fresh organic matter provides a slower release of minerals when applied than when decayed. It is also said that in the long term, sheet composting leads to higher nitrogen levels in the soil, as much is lost by vaporisation when a traditional heap heats up.

Whatever composting system you prefer, one thing is certain – you can never make enough of it! Therefore the wise gardener will plan the usage of this valuable commodity with care. Rather than applying it indiscriminately around the garden, priority should be given to those plants that require a rich soil, for example, blackcurrants, brassicas, celery, onions, peas, potatoes, raspberries, runner beans and strawberries. Next are those that will produce a reasonable crop on a less good soil, e.g. beetroot, broad beans, leeks, lettuce, spinach, turnip. Fresh compost should definitely not be applied where carrots and parsnips are to be grown immediately afterwards, as this will lead to distorted growth and forking roots.

When applying compost to permanent crops such as trees or fruit bushes, it can be forked very gently into the top few inches of soil so as not to cause any root disturbance, or applied to the surface as a 'spot' mulch, especially if it still contains recognisable elements of the original plant material. Such material should not be dug in as the bacterial activity required to complete its breakdown may cause temporary nitrogen robbery. Worms will ensure that it is eventually fully incorporated into the soil. Well-matured compost can also be added to the planting hole when establishing new fruit trees and bushes to ensure plenty of available fertility and a healthy root structure.

Fenugreek
(Trigonella foenum-graecum)

Green Manures

Common Name	Latin Name	Nitrogen Fixer?	Comments
Alfalfa	*Medicago sativa*	Yes	A deep rooting hardy perennial legume. Sow April-July. Can be dug in after a few months or left for a year or two, in which case it can be cut for mulch or compost material.
Bitter Blue Lupin	*Lupinus augustifolius*	Yes	A deep rooting annual legume. Sow from March to June to stand for 2-3 months. Dig in before flowers open. One of the best for light, slightly acid soils.
Buckwheat	*Fagopyrum esculentum*	No	An attractive half hardy annual sown from April to August for 2-3 months' cover. Dig in when flowering or before. Hoverflies love its tiny pink flowers.
Crimson clover	*Trifolium incarnatum*	Yes	An annual legume with crimson flowers that are attractive to bees. Sow March-August, to give 2-3 months' soil cover. Later sowings can be left to overwinter. Dig in when flowering, or before.
Essex red clover	*Trifolium pratense*	Yes	A deep rooting perennial legume. Sow March to August to stand for a few months, overwinter or for a whole season or two. Dig in any time up until flowering, or cut back after flowering to encourage fresh growth.
Fenugreek	*Trigonella foenum graecum*	Yes	A fast growing, slightly hardy annual. Although it is a legume it is unlikely to fix much nitrogen in the UK. Sow in spring and summer, to stand for 2-3 months. Dig in before it gets tough.

Common Name	Latin Name	Nitrogen Fixer?	Comments
Grazing rye	*Secale cereale*	No	An annual rye grass with an extensive root system which makes it an excellent soil improver. Sow August to November to stand overwinter. Dig in as soon as flowering stems are seen, or before.
Mustard	*Sinapis alba*	No	A very fast growing annual green manure. Sow from March to September, to give up to 8 weeks cover. Dig in before flowering. Note that mustard is susceptible to club root.
Phacelia	*Phacelia tanticetifolia*	No	A flowering annual with fern like foliage and bright blue flowers that are very attractive to bees. Sow April to August to stand for up to 2 months. Later sowings may overwinter in some areas. Dig in when flowering, or before.
Trefoil	*Medicago lupulina*	Yes	An easy to grow annual/biennial legume. Sow from March to August to stand for several months, overwinter or for a full season. Dig in when flowering or before. Will tolerate some shade so suitable for undersowing with other crops, e.g., sweetcorn. Will grow on light soils but does not like acid conditions.
Winter field beans	*Vica faba*	Yes	A hardy annual legume related to broad beans. Sow September to November to overwinter. Dig in any time before flowering.
Winter tares	*Vicia sativa*	Yes	A fast growing annual legume. Sow March to May for summer/autumn cover, or July to September to overwinter. Prefers heavier soils. Dig in when flowering, or before.

Comfrey the Wonder Plant

Comfrey (*Symphytum officinale*) is a perennial herb that has long been recognised by both organic gardeners and herbalists as having great usefulness and versatility. Its only drawback is that it can seed prolifically and spread through the garden as a weed. The 'Bocking 14' cultivar of Russian comfrey however is sterile and will not spread to where it is not wanted, thus is a particularly valuable source of fertility in the vegan-organic garden. It has very deep roots, and acts as a 'dynamic accumulator', mining a host of nutrients from the soil by tapping into reserves that would not normally be available to plants. These are concentrated in the leaves of the plants, which can be cut three or four times a year, and can be utilised in a number of ways:

- Freshly cut comfrey is wilted for a day or two, then laid in potato trenches about two inches deep. The leaves will rapidly break down and supply potassium rich fertiliser for the developing potato plants. Avoid using flowering stems as these can root.
- 5-7.5cm (2-3in) deep layers of comfrey leaves in the compost heap will encourage bacterial activity and help to heat the heap. However, comfrey should not be added in great quantity, as it will quickly break down into a dark sludgey liquid that needs to be balanced with more fibrous, carbon rich material.
- Comfrey liquid feed can be produced by either rotting leaves down in rainwater to produce a ready to use but very smelly 'tea', or else by stacking dry leaves under a weight in a container with a hole in the base. When the leaves decompose a thick black comfrey concentrate is collected. This should be diluted at 15:1 before use.
- A 5cm (2in) layer of comfrey leaves placed around a crop as a mulch will slowly break down and release plant nutrients. It is especially useful for crops that need extra potassium, such as tomatoes, and also fruit bushes like currants and gooseberries.
- A potting mixture can be made in a black plastic sack, alternating three to four inch layers of well decayed leaf mould and chopped comfrey leaves. Add a little dolomitic limestone to slightly raise pH. Leave for between two to five months depending on the season, checking that it does not dry out or become too wet. The mixture is ready when the comfrey leaves have rotted and are no longer visible. Use as a general potting compost, although it is too strong for seedlings.

Crop Rotation, Polycultures and Beneficial Guilds

Rotation is the traditional gardening practice of moving crops around your plot from year to year so that they don't grow in the same place all the time. There are a number of reasons why this is a good idea, including:

- In order to prevent diseases like clubroot, eelworm, etc. building up in the soil
- Control of weeds is easier to achieve by regularly changing their growing conditions
- To prevent the soil becoming exhausted
- To make best use of soil nutrients as different plant families have different requirements

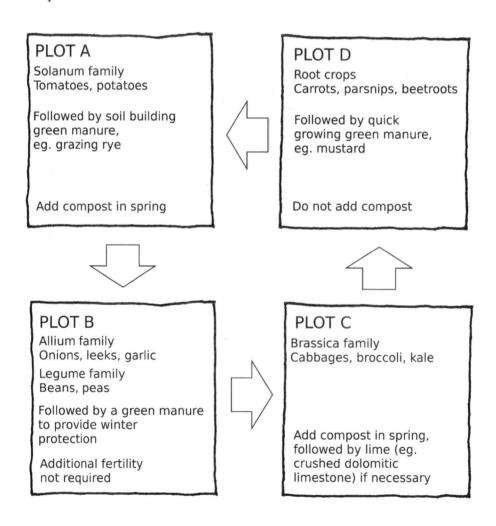

PLOT A
Solanum family
Tomatoes, potatoes

Followed by soil building
green manure,
eg. grazing rye

Add compost in spring

PLOT D
Root crops
Carrots, parsnips, beetroots

Followed by quick
growing green manure,
eg. mustard

Do not add compost

PLOT B
Allium family
Onions, leeks, garlic
Legume family
Beans, peas

Followed by a green manure
to provide winter
protection

Additional fertility
not required

PLOT C
Brassica family
Cabbages, broccoli, kale

Add compost in spring,
followed by lime (eg.
crushed dolomitic
limestone) if necessary

On the previous page is a suggested four year crop rotation scheme that can be adapted to your situation. This may be impractical in a smaller garden, but it's still a good strategy to move your crops around from year to year.

More complex and multifunctional 'polycultural' edible landscapes can be achieved by practising 'companion planting', that is growing vegetables in complementary plantings or communities. Although often discounted by the linear thinking 'conventional' scientific establishment, co-operation and symbiosis can be the most powerful patterns to be found at work within natural systems. By carefully observing such interactions, we can replicate them to our advantage by creating mutually beneficial 'guilds' of plants and animals. The 'stacked' structure of a well-planned forest garden (see pages 195-202) is one example, another is the traditional Native American 'Three Sisters' partnering of corn, beans and squashes. The beans are leguminous – that is, their root nodules support bacteria that are able to convert nitrogen from the air into the soil nitrates that plants need to grow well. In this way they provide nutrients for not only themselves but also the corn and squashes. Meanwhile the tall corn stems offer a vertical support structure for the climbing beans, and the broad leaves of the squash plant provide ground cover, shading out weeds and keeping the soil moist and cool so that all three plants can thrive.

Companion planting is about encouraging biodiversity. Tall growing, sun-loving plants may share space with lower growing, shade tolerant species. Tomatoes, French marigolds and basil are another beneficial guild. Marigold roots exude a chemical that deters harmful nematodes from attacking tomatoes, and their pungent smell can also help to confuse other insect pests, whilst growing tomatoes and basil together is said to increase the vigour and flavour of both crops. Carrots and onions are said to exude strong odours that help to mask each crop from the others' respective pests such as carrot fly and onion fly.

Companion Planting Guide

Please note that this list is not exhaustive, also that many of the relationships are based on anecdotal observation and are not scientifically proven. The interactions between various combinations of plants in a living garden are incredibly complex and difficult to quantify, therefore this list should be used as a basis for your own experimentation rather than considered as definitive. Many thanks to Alan and Elaine Garrett of the Vegan Self Sufficiency Network.

Common name	Latin name	Beneficial effects	Antagonistic effects
Basil	*Ocimum basilicum*	Repels flies and mosquitoes. Companion to asparagus and tomatoes (said to improve growth and flavour).	Do not plant near rue or tansy.
Garlic	*Allium sativum*	Deters aphids and many other bugs. Companion to raspberries, strawberries. Lettuce, tomatoes, beets, roses. Said to generally improve growth and health of neighbouring plants.	Said to inhibit growth of peas and beans.
Marigolds	*Tagetes* and *Calendula* species	Deter eelworms, wireworms, whitefly and other 'pests'. Companion to potatoes, beans, cucumbers, marrows and roses.	None noted.
Mint	*Mentha spicata* and others	Repels moths, ants, flea beetles and caterpillars of cabbage butterflies. Companion to cabbages, tomatoes and potatoes.	Should not be planted with comfrey.
Horseradish	*Cochlearia armoracia*	Said to discourage bugs from potato plants and to improve the disease resistance of the crop.	Do not plant with peas or beans.

Common name	Latin name	Beneficial effects	Antagonistic effects
Nasturtium	*Tropaeolum majus*	Deters aphids and whitefly. Companion to fruit trees, tomatoes, radishes, cucumbers and marrows.	Should not be grown near broad beans.
Rosemary	*Rosemarimus officinallis*	Repels carrot fly and weevils. Companion to carrots, cabbages, beans, and sage.	Do not plant with cucumbers or marrows.
Rue	*Ruta graveolens*	Repels flies. Companion to raspberries and roses.	Do not plant it next to basil.
Sage	*Salvia officinalis*	Deters carrot fly and cabbage butterflies. Companion to carrots, cabbages and rosemary.	Do not plant with cucumbers or marrows.
Southernwood	*Artemesia arbrotanum*	Repels moths and cabbage butterflies. Grow near cabbages and fruit trees.	None noted.
Summer savoury	*Satureia hortensis*	Deters bean weevils and blackfly. Companion to beans and onions.	Do not plant with radishes or turnips.
Tansy	*Tanacetum vulgare*	Deters flying insects, fleas, ants, cutworms and many other bugs. Companion to raspberries, roses, marrows, cucumbers, cabbages and fruit trees.	Do not plant it next to basil.
Thyme	*Thymus vulgaris*	Deters cabbage root fly and cabbage butterflies. It is a companion to cabbages, broad beans and roses.	Should not be grown with cucumbers, marrows or rue.
Wormwood	*Artemesia absinthium*	Repellent to flea beetles, moths, weevils, fleas, aphids and the caterpillars of cabbage butterflies. Companion to cabbages.	Inhibits the growth of tender vegetables, basil, fennel, sage and caraway.

Mycorrhiza - Nature's Internet!

Important guilds have also co-evolved between members of the plant and fungi kingdoms. Mycorrhiza are fungi that form symbiotic associations with most living plants, including most trees and edible crops (apart from brassicas (the cabbage family)), creating a relationship that is beneficial to both. Plant root hairs are invaded and colonised by the mycelia of the mycorrhiza, which may either cover the length of the root hair as a sheath or be concentrated around its tip. Fungi lack the cells that produce chlorophyll and are thus unable to manufacture their own carbohydrates through the process of photosynthesising sunlight. The mycorrhiza therefore obtain these from the plant, and in return provide the plant with an extended secondary root system that can take up increased moisture and nutrients such as nitrogen, phosphorous and potassium from the soil. In a healthy forest, mycorrhiza will act as 'nature's internet', creating a fine underground mesh that extends well beyond the limits of the tree's roots, greatly increasing their collective feeding range, and actually causing neighbouring trees to become physically interconnected. Soils that have been excessively cultivated or have had artificial fertilisers applied to them tend to be low in mycorrhizal fungi, although the vegan organic gardener can stimulate their presence by adding plenty of well composted organic matter to the soil as well as mycorrhizal root powders that are sold by some commercial growers. Soils that have mycorrhizal fungi present tend to give significantly higher yields of fruit and vegetable crops than those that do not.

Who's Who in Your Garden?

The healthy garden is a living ecosystem, and you will inevitably be sharing it with a variety of other birds, amphibians, insects, molluscs and arthropods, not to mention the other billion or so bacteria or fungi microorganisms to be found in every teaspoon of healthy soil. It's worth knowing which of these are welcome and which less so. Bear in mind that even those that are sometimes labelled as 'pests' have their part to play (such as providing a source of food for beneficial insects), so aim to manage their populations rather than trying to get rid of them completely.

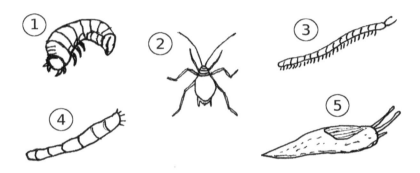

1. Chafer grubs, 2. Aphids, 3. Millipedes, 4. Leatherjackets, 5. Slugs
Discourage those visitors that can become crop damaging pests in the vegan organic garden.

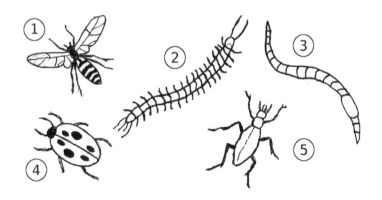

1. Hoverflies, 2. Centipedes, 3. Earthworms, 4. Ladybirds, 5. Predatory beetles
Other garden visitors help to control pests or have other beneficial roles to play such as acting as pollinators or building fertile soil.

Maintain your growing plot so that pests and diseases are dealt with by natural methods that do not threaten your allies, or in the long run increase your problems by producing resistant strains – in other words, avoid chemicals and pesticides. An important part of the ecological gardening approach is to become familiar with the various life forms that inhabit the garden, predators as well as pests, and also their life cycles, patterns of feeding and the habitats that they prefer. Planting flowers such as marigolds, nasturtiums, poached egg plant (*Limnanthes*) or herbs such as chives, garlic or thyme amongst your vegetables, helps to create a balanced ecosystem where the former attract insects or birds that eat pests such as aphids, caterpillars and slugs, whilst the smells of the herbs mask those of your cabbages, tomatoes and so on. Frogs and toads will consume any number of slugs and snails so encourage their presence by providing a small pond. An old bowl or wash basin sunk into the soil will do, but ensure that your amphibian visitors are able to get in and out, and also that any ponds are made safe if small children are about. Spreading something abrasive like ash, lime or sand will further discourage slugs, at least until it rains! Fruit or young seedlings can be protected from an otherwise beneficial bird population with netting or other physical barriers.

Finally, the most effective way of defeating pests and diseases in your garden is by growing strong healthy plants using good quality seeds, and by keeping the soil itself healthy and well fed with plenty of organic matter.

A Weeder's Digest

Weeds are often described as 'any plant growing in the wrong place'. Indeed, given half a chance many will compete with our food crops and quickly return cultivated land to wilderness. However, consider tolerating those that are growing away from productive areas to some degree, for they can actually be very useful. They can tell us much about the condition of our land (for example, nettles indicate fertile soil, whilst horsetail suggests compaction and drainage problems) or be a source of nutrients for the compost heap or encourage beneficial wildlife. Many are edible or have medicinal properties. Weeds are generally either annual or perennial in habit.

Annuals grow from seed each year and die at the end of the season. They are usually fairly easily controlled by light hoeing.

Perennials live for several years. These tend to be deeper rooted and harder to permanently remove, needing to be either deeply dug, or else mulched out with a light excluding soil cover for at least a season.

Annual weeds: 1. Goosegrass, 2. Chickweed, 3. Fat Hen, 4. Groundsel

Perennial weeds: 1. Coltsfoot, 2. Dock, 3. Plantain, 4. Horsetail, 5. Yarrow, 6. Couch Grass

Growing from Seed

Whilst many vegetables can be directly sown where you wish them to grow, others will do much better if started indoors or given some protection from the elements at least until established. Relevant information on each is given below, or will be found on seed packets, but the following are a few basic guidelines:

When starting seeds indoors, always use seed compost. This is different from the garden compost discussed above, having a finer texture, lower nutrient content and is better able to retain moisture in order for seedlings to become established. Note that many commercially available seed composts are peat based. These are unsuitable for the ecologically conscious gardener due to the unsustainable extraction of peat from bogs and uplands, a practice that both endangers non-renewable resources and diminishes natural habitat. A range of peat-free alternatives are available that are suitable for the vegan organic gardener, such as coir, a waste product of the coconut fibre industry. This holds more air and water than peat, but its importation also raises questions regarding environmental sustainability. Other options include composted brewing industry by-products, and 'Moorland Gold', a brand that is not peat-free, but consists of peat that is collected as a by-product of the water industry in the Pennines. The water pouring off the mountainside naturally picks up particles of peat that are then collected in filters before the water enters the reservoirs, thus has not been 'mined' and is not ecologically destructive in its production.

Better still would be to make your own seed compost using two parts sieved garden compost, one part leaf mould, one part loam and one part sharp sand.

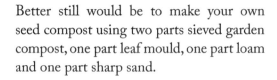

Fill a clean seed tray with moist seed compost and gently press the surface down so that it is firm and flat, but not compacted. Note that a half size tray is usually more than adequate if growing on a garden scale and will take up less space, plus use less compost. Sprinkle seeds sparingly on the surface of the compost. Most seed packets contain far more seeds than you will actually need, so just use a couple of pinches and save the rest for future years or to exchange with friends.

Gently water taking care not to disturb the compost too much (a child's watering can is ideal for this task).

Cover the seeds with a thin layer of compost and then a tight cover of polythene or piece of glass. Place in a warm sunny position, preferably a south-facing window until seeds germinate (usually a week to 10 days), then remove polythene.

When large enough, use a household fork to gently remove ('prick out') the best seedlings from the soil and pot these on using a potting compost consisting of one part garden compost, one part loam, one part leaf mould, one part worm compost and one part sharp sand or grit. Handle only by the leaves, and take care to minimise any damage to the roots. Yoghurt pots or fruit juice cartons, cut in half (make a drainage hole in the bottom of each with a sharp knife) are perfect, but whatever you use, ensure they are scrupulously clean in order to avoid diseases or pests.

Grow on in pots, watering and feeding with a liquid fertiliser regularly until large enough to plant out into their final growing positions. During the last couple of weeks of this stage seedlings should be 'hardened off' by putting them outside for a few hours each day so that they become accustomed to the changeable, harsher conditions they will be facing outdoors.

Seed Saving

For generations growers have saved their own seeds from year to year, and with good reason. Apart from saving money, the practice ensures a supply of guaranteed organic seed and preserves many of the older and less commercially popular vegetable varieties that are disappearing from the seed catalogues due to EU regulations that ban their sale. With care and practice the quality of crops can also be improved, adapting them to local conditions through selective breeding.

Always collect seed from the very best plants, i.e. those that show optimum health and resistance to pests and diseases, have yielded well and have the flavour, texture and other qualities that you prefer.

Harvest seeds from fully mature pods or fruits on a dry, sunny day so that they are not damp. Spread out on newspaper in a dry airy place and store in labelled envelopes in clean, dry jars in a cool place – the fridge is ideal. The viability of seeds varies. Parsnips will keep for one year, peas and beans for two, tomatoes for three years, beets, spinach and brassicas for five, and cucumbers, courgettes and squashes for six.

Plants with self-pollinating flowers will produce seeds that will grow true to type, but those that cross-pollinate with other plants will produce different characteristics according to both parents. Hybrid 'F1' and 'F2' varieties often sold by commercial seed merchants will not grow true to type and are often sterile thus should not be used as plant breeding stock.

Lettuce and tomatoes are self-pollinating and peas and beans usually so. Beets, carrots, celery, courgettes, cucumber and swedes are cross-pollinating. Most brassicas (i.e. broccoli, cabbages, cauliflowers, kales, and kohl rabi) do not breed true, thus if seed is to be saved no two types should be allowed to flower within 60m (200ft) of each other.

Crop by Crop

The following is a selection of some of the most commonly grown vegetable crops. If you are new to gardening it might be best to start with these in order to gain confidence and experience before moving on to some of the less usual veggies. Some recommended varieties are listed, but these suggestions are very subjective and will vary according to your own region and specific climate and growing conditions. Use these as a starting point for your own research and experimentation.

Beetroot, Chard and Perpetual Spinach

Sow thinly from April to July for successional crops. Each 'seed' is in fact a cluster of several beetroot seeds, so they will need thinning as soon as they are large enough. Final spacing should be about 12cm (5in) apart in rows 2.5cm (1in) apart. However if you intend to harvest beetroot when it is about golf-ball sized, and its flavour is at its best, this spacing can be reduced. Although spinach-like in appearance and taste, chard is in fact closely related to beetroot and can be grown in the same way and is much less fiddly in its requirements than true spinach. The leaves of beetroot can also be used in salads or as a spinach substitute. Boltardy and Cylindra are reliable beetroot standbys. A range of multi-coloured rainbow and Swiss chards provide visual interest on the plot, whilst sowings of perpetual spinach will mean that green leafy vegetables suitable for cooking or using in salads are available nearly all year round.

Cabbages and Other Brassicas

Different varieties of cabbage can be sown from February to August to provide plants for eating virtually all year round. Seed should be started indoors, thinly sown in trays. Seedlings should then be planted out about 45cm (18in) apart when they have five or six leaves. They prefer a firm rich soil with a little lime added if it tends to be acidic. Feed occasionally with comfrey or seaweed liquid fertiliser, keep weeded and water regularly. Watch out for pests such as slugs or cabbage white butterfly caterpillars that will eat the leaves, and avoid problems like club root by practising crop rotation. Follow the same general rules for other brassicas such as broccoli, cauliflower and Brussels sprouts. The latter however prefer a VERY firm soil, and it can be quite difficult for beginners to obtain successful results. Members of the brassica tribe do not breed true, thus if seed is to be saved no two types should be allowed to flower within 60m (200ft) of each other.

Purple sprouting broccoli is a must for any productive garden, whilst Nine Star Perennial is a perennial variety that will last several years provided all the flowering heads are picked, and is especially suitable for the permaculture garden. Romanesque cauliflower produces an amazing head consisting of hundreds of tightly packed spirals arranged as fractal patterns.

Seed saving of brassicas on a garden scale is not usually a practical option for most home growers.

Carrots

Sow very thinly in rows a foot or so apart directly into the soil between March and July. Fortnightly sowings will give successional crops. Carrots don't really like heavy soils, but appreciate a soil that has been composted for a previous crop – fresh compost can cause the roots to fork. Carrot fly can be discouraged by watering with comfrey and nettles rotted down in rainwater, by mixing with onions that disguise their smell or by providing physical protection such as surrounding the bed with a 1m (3ft) high Perspex barrier or covering with commercially available agricultural fleece.

To save seed select about six of the best quality roots, not too large, and with care, trim off the leaves about an inch from the root. Store in sand in a cool, frost-free place for the winter. In spring replant the roots and they will send up flowering stalks with seed heads that ripen in autumn. Cut these off and hang up to dry, putting boxes lined with paper underneath to catch the seeds. Treat parsnips and beets in the same way.

Courgettes, Squashes and Cucumbers

Members of the cucurbit family can be started indoors in pots, or alternatively, dig a hole in a sunny, sheltered spot about 15cm (6in) wide and deep and fill with well rotted compost. In mid May to early June plant two or three seeds under a cloche made with something like a large clear plastic bottle cut in half. When they germinate, thin out all but the sturdiest seedlings and allow to grow on. Courgette and squash plants can be very large and trailing, so give them plenty of space, positioning them up to three foot apart, whilst climbing outdoor cucumbers will need to be supported with canes. They are heavy feeders and require plenty of watering.

To save seed leave selected fruit until fully ripe and yellow, cut in half and scoop out the seeds and place in a bowl of water. Viable seeds will sink to the bottom. Dry and store.

Leeks

Sow seed sparingly in trays around March/April. Transplant into final growing positions with about 15cm (6in) between plants from June onwards when they are about 15cm (6in) long. Make a hole about 12.5cm (5in) deep with a dibber (or use the end of a rake handle) and drop in a seedling, water well but no need to backfill the hole with soil. Apart from an odd watering in very dry weather they will require little attention provided they are in fertile soil. Leeks can be left in the ground over the winter months until required, but will start to set seed and become tough and unpalatable by late spring.

If you wish to save your own leek seed, reject any plants that have bolted in their first year. Allow the best bulbs to overwinter in situ, or else lift and store over winter and replant the following spring. The flower stem may need support when it emerges. Cut the seed heads as soon as the tiny black seeds are visible and dry for a few weeks before collecting by shaking them out onto newspaper and storing.

Lettuce

With careful planning and by choosing appropriate varieties, lettuces from the garden are available pretty much all year round. Lettuces do best on a light, friable moisture retentive sandy loam, but can be grown in most gardens. They benefit from plenty of well-rotted organic matter, and must be kept moist throughout hot, dry weather or they are inclined to bolt and run to seed. Sow seed indoors or under glass in a tray, and pot on the best specimens ready for planting out in their final positions, or else 'saladini' mixes can be broadcast sown and treated as 'cut and come again'. Little Gem is a reliable compact Cos lettuce. Red and Green Salad Bowl, also known as oak leaf lettuce, produce large loose heads of serrated leaves suitable for 'cut and come again' growing. Lolla Rosa is a reliable variety with beautiful red leaves, adding a splash of colour to your plot.

Save seed from the plants that are slowest to go to seed. When the flowers have changed into downy white seed heads they can be removed and dried for a week or so before storing.

Onions

Can be grown from seed but I've had more success growing from 'sets' (sold as bags of tiny onions in garden centres). Rake a flat bed to a fine tilth between March and April. Plant sets in rows about 15cm (6in) apart, pushing them into the ground so that only the tips show above the surface. Keep well watered and weed regularly until established, after which they need minimal care apart from occasional weeding. Birds tend to pull newly planted sets from the ground, discourage them with scarers made from old CDs on sticks. Pulled out sets can be pushed back into the soil. Lift mature onions between July and September when foliage has died off. Leave in the sun to dry before hanging up in 'ropes' to store. Japanese onions can be planted in the autumn to overwinter, ready for harvesting in late May or early June.

See Leeks (page 101) for seed saving advice.

Peas and Beans

Plant peas about 5cm (2in) deep in rows about 45cm (18in) apart, with 5-8cm (2-3in) between seeds. They prefer a rich soil, so add plenty of compost the previous autumn, or dig a pea trench. This is a shallow trench that is lined with fresh kitchen wastes, e.g. vegetable peelings, etc. Peas are leguminous, which means they fix their own nitrogen from the air, so as the wastes decay they will not cause 'nitrogen robbery' to the peas that would be a problem for other plants. Sow in succession between March and June, choosing appropriate varieties (seed packets will tell you this information). Support with canes or twigs when they begin to climb. Most beans have similar requirements to peas. Broad beans however can be sown in the autumn. Growing them over winter then gives them a head start against blackfly. Runner beans require poles up to 2.5m (8ft) in length to supply them with adequate support.

Saving seed: French, runner beans and peas – select best specimens. Leave pods on the plant to dry. Pick, shell and dry. Broad beans – autumn sown varieties are best for seed saving. Leave the pods on selected plants until they are dry and start to split. Cut the plants and spread them in a dry airy place until pods split right open. Pick out the seeds, selecting the best to dry for keeping.

Potatoes

Buy certified virus-free Scottish or Irish seed potatoes in late winter and leave to stand in a cool place in seed trays until healthy sprouts appear. Plant in rows about 15cm (6in) deep and 30-45cm (12-18in) apart with the sprouts facing upwards. Give them plenty of compost; they really do benefit. As the shoots (or haulms) grow, earth them up (or cover with layers of mulch) to increase yield and suppress weed growth. Water heavily during dry periods, although mulches will help to retain soil moisture. A selection of first early, second early and main crop varieties will give you harvests from June to October. Clean, dry and undamaged potatoes can be stored over winter in large brown paper sacks. In the smaller garden, potatoes can be grown in compost

using old tyres as containers. Simply stack on more tyres and add more compost as they grow up.

Potatoes are very susceptible to viruses, therefore seed from the previous year's crop should not be saved for replanting.

Radish

Radishes are probably one of the easiest crops to grow, so are perfect for beginners or to grow with children – early success builds confidence and a 'can do' attitude! Sow thinly straight into the ground from March to September in rows about a foot apart and they will quickly germinate, although avoid letting them dry out as this may cause them to bolt or split. Fast maturing, they should be ready for harvesting after as little as a month in summer. Pick young and eat straight away or let them grow on to produce tasty seed pods that add a little heat to your salads. 'French Breakfast', 'Sparkler' and 'Scarlet Globe' are small red varieties suitable for fast growing and using in salads. 'Munchen Bier' is the best variety for producing edible seed pods. Larger white daikon varieties include 'Japanese Mooli', which produces long white fleshy roots suitable for stir fries, for cooking as a root vegetable or for fermentation.

Radish is a member of the brassica tribe, which do not breed true, thus if seed is to be saved no two types should be allowed to flower within 60m (200ft) of each other. Seed saving on a garden scale is not usually a practical option for most home growers.

Sweetcorn

Although sweetcorn takes up a lot of space and can sometimes be difficult to grow successfully, the taste of fresh cobs picked straight from the plant before the sugars have had a chance to turn into starch, makes the effort worthwhile. Sow seeds indoors in individual pots in May and plant out in blocks rather than rows to ensure good pollination with about 45cm (18in) between plants. Sweetcorn needs full sun and a well drained fertile soil, and should be kept well watered during dry periods. Harvest when fully ripe between early August to late September.

Seed saving of sweetcorn on a garden scale is not usually a practical option for most home growers.

Tomatoes

Sow seed indoors in a tray in a sunny spot in March or April. Transplant the best seedlings into individual pots as soon as they are large enough to handle. Keep well watered, and plant out when the last danger of frost has passed, e.g. mid June onwards. As they grow, pick off side shoots, and when they have four trusses (groups of flowers at one level), break the tops off the plants so that all the plant's energy will be diverted into fruit growth. Tomatoes have a trailing habit so will need support with canes. They can be thirsty plants, and may require a potassium rich feed (e.g. comfrey liquid (see page 87)) for the best crops. Marigolds are said to be a beneficial companion plant for tomatoes. There is a huge range of tomato varieties of virtually every colour and size imaginable, with a choice in the better seed catalogues that can be overwhelming! Some personal favourites of mine include Black Crim, a large fleshy and succulent variety originating in Russia, Tigrella that has beautiful orange, red and yellow stripes, San Marzano, a plum variety suitable for cooking, and Golden Sunrise, a tasty golden variety.

To save your own tomato seed select the best fruits from the third and fourth trusses when slightly over ripe. Squeeze out the pulp and seeds and wash thoroughly. Spread the cleaned seeds on blotting paper and leave to dry at room temperature for one week.

Herbs

In terms of maximum flavour for minimum space requirements, home grown herbs are hands down winners, so it's always worth making space for them in the vegan organic garden. Rosemary, tarragon, sage and thyme are fairly easy to grow from cuttings. Mint and lemon balm can be propagated from sections of root, but can spread and become weeds amongst your other crops if not contained. Try growing them in an old bottomless bucket sunk into the ground.

Creeping thyme and pennyroyal provide good ground cover. Borage and chives are particularly valuable for attracting bees, which aid the pollination of your other crops.

Basil, garlic (also medicinally valuable), parsley, sage and savoury (very high in vitamins A, C and calcium) are other essential culinary herbs, but you could also try growing less common specimens such as alecost, bergamot, chamomile, Good King Henry, hyssop, lovage, salad burnet, sorrel (has a wonderfully sharp lemony flavour), skirret, sweet cicely, tansy or wild rocket. Many of these herbs are becoming rarities as they are no longer fashionable. Growing them in our gardens provides them with a sanctuary that ensures their survival for future generations.

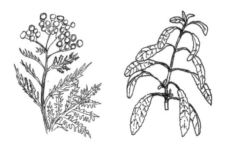

Fruit in the Garden

Consider giving over part of your growing area to fresh fruit production. Modern compact varieties of bush fruit such as blackcurrants, gooseberries or Worcesterberries take up little space, whilst climbers like blackberries (thornless varieties are available) or loganberries can be used to cover ugly walls and fences as well as provide a crop. Even apple trees can be grown in a small garden by utilising M27 'dwarfing' and M106 'semi-dwarfing' rootstocks.

By using grafted 'family' trees you can grow two or three different types of apple on one tree.

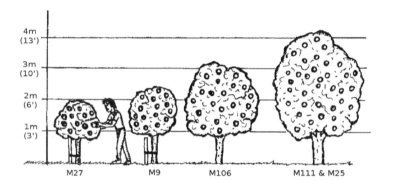

Apples can be grafted onto various different rootstocks that will determine their size and other characteristics.

Bare rooted trees and bushes can be planted between November and March when they are dormant, whilst container grown specimens can be planted all the year round. As they are a permanent feature of the garden it is advisable to make sure they are going to be in the best position (e.g. avoid spots which tend to be frosty) and to prepare the soil well before planting. Ensure all perennial weeds have been removed and dig in plenty of organic compost. Most importantly, ensure that drainage is adequate, especially if your soil is heavy clay. Water well for the first year until established, and prune according to nursery instructions in order to optimise health and fruit production.

Forest gardening is a way of growing edible and useful crops modelled on the ecology of the woodland, allowing us to combine fruit trees and bushes in a small area to create a healthy low maintenance system that creates its own fertility. Despite the name, the methods are very suitable for use in small urban gardens where both time and money are in limited supply. (See page 195 for more information.)

Ways with Vegetables

Greens

Green leafy vegetables should be a daily part of the vegan diet. As well as being grown in the garden, many of these can also be foraged (see chapter 8). They can be eaten raw or added to salads, although some are strongly flavoured so might be better used in moderation with blander tasting leaves such as lettuce to counteract them. Alternatively they can be steamed or lightly boiled. Avoid over cooking or they will lose colour, flavour and their nutritional value. They can also be juiced to make vibrant and invigorating drinks. Leafy greens can include:

Beetroot tops
Broccoli (tops and leaves)
Brussels sprouts (sprouts, leaves and tops)
Cabbage greens (spring greens)
Celery leaves
Chard
Dandelion (have quite a bitter flavour that
    can easily dominate if over used!)
Kale
Leeks (including green leaves)
Lovage
Oriental greens (e.g. pak choi, Chinese
    cabbage, mizuna, etc.)
Parsley
Rocket (wild and salad)
Savoy cabbage
Spinach
Swede tops
Turnip greens
Watercress

PEACE'S ALKALISING MORNING GREEN JUICE

You will need a good quality juicer such as a twin gear Greenstar for this, or a blender and a nut milk or jelly bag to strain off the liquid. If using a blender, add 2 cups of water to the ingredients, blend and then squeeze all the liquids through your bag to create a juice. The left over fibre can be added to soups, stews or roast recipes, or composted.

Pass all the ingredients through the juicer.

Serve immediately and 'chew' each mouthful to activate the digestive juices in the mouth and stomach.

By juicing in the morning you gain maximum benefit from all the goodness in the foods, taken on an empty stomach, allowing your body to flush any toxins through without being hampered by digestion.

Thanks to Peace Raven

2 apples
1 head of celery
1 cucumber
3 cups spinach or kale

GREEN GODDESS SMOOTHIE

*You will need a good blender for this, either a hand blender or jug blender,
but with a hand blender you may need a bit more liquid.*

2 apples

2 very ripe fairly traded
bananas

12 leaves (approx) kale

2 pears

1 Romaine lettuce

1tbsp sweetener of your
choice, e.g. agave or
maple syrup

1 cup filtered water

Optional extra - 1tsp
spirulina powder for
extra protein and energy

Gently chop the leaves and fruit into chunks that your
blender will be able to cope with. Add the fruit first,
then the leaves and water.

Blend until nice and smooth. If you want it cold, add a
handful of ice cubes if your blender will cope with that
or pop it into the fridge for an hour before drinking.

This drink can form the basis for many green smoothies
and you can alter the ingredients to suit your tastes,
garden produce and time of year, making sure that
greens make up the largest quantity of ingredients
each time!

By using ripe bananas you will have a nice creamy
smoothie every time as they add that lovely texture and
prevent the more watery ingredients from separating in
the smoothie.

Thanks to Peace Raven

EVE'S DELICIOUS 'EALTHY AND SIMPLE VEG

Steam broccoli, carrot, garlic, ginger and onion (or anything – watercress was nice with it tonight).

When done, put in a dish, pour over some olive oil and some tamari. Sprinkle lots of groundnuts on top. Put in oven.

Boil some spaghetti or buckwheat noodles or both. When done add a big spoon of miso and tahini and mix until it's melted and covered.

Serve with vegetables.

Thanks to Eve Libertine

Steamed Vegetables

A dedicated metal steamer pot that will fit on top of a large cooking pan is one of the most useful pieces of equipment in the vegan permaculturist's kitchen. Steaming vegetables rather than simply boiling them in water is less likely to overcook them, and will preserve their flavours and nutritional value. Softer vegetables such as broccoli florets or greens will only take a few minutes to cook over a pan of boiling water, although hard vegetables such as carrots or parsnips will take a while longer, so if you wish to cook both together the latter should be chopped into small pieces and added seven or eight minutes beforehand. The cooking water left in the pan underneath afterwards can be saved as a vegetable stock and added to soups, etc.

FRIED GREENS WITH NUTS

1 handful of greens
   (e.g. broccoli, cabbage,
   chard, spinach, etc.)

1 small onion

Nuts, e.g. hazels, walnuts,
   etc. chopped

1tsp dark soy sauce

Vegetable oil

Heat oil in a pan that can be closely covered with a lid.

Slice onions and shred greens. Place in the pan with chopped nuts and cook gently for 10-15 minutes. Steam is released from the vegetables so that they are part steamed and part fried.

Season with soy sauce and serve as a side dish.

AGEDASHI TOFU WITH BLACK KALE

1 pack of tofu

2 large garlic cloves

1 large onion

A good handful (around 12
   leaves) black Tuscan kale

Organic tomato paste

Olive oil

Black pepper

Tamari

Cut onions into half moons and chop garlic. Slice tofu into long thin strips.

Chop kale and steam for a few minutes.

Lightly sauté onion and garlic in olive oil then add tofu strips. Be careful not to overcook. Add steamed kale to pan, then add tomato paste and olive oil, quickly mix together.

Serve with noodles.

Thanks to Eve Libertine

SWEET AND SOUR CABBAGE

Shred cabbage, grate onions and chop apples into small pieces. Blend all ingredients in a saucepan.

Cover and simmer gently for 10 minutes and serve.

4 tart apples

1 large cabbage

3 small onions

3tbsp apple juice concentrate

1tbsp caraway seeds

¼ cup cider

2 lemons, juiced

2tbsp olive oil

½ cup raisins

Pinch of mixed spice

ROASTED WINTER VEGETABLES

Cut root vegetables and onion into largish chunks or cubes. Line them on the base of a good quality baking tray with the rosemary and drizzle with olive oil.

Break garlic into cloves and place amongst the veg. Don't worry about peeling the cloves; the insides will soften as they cook and the garlic skins can be discarded afterwards. Roast in a moderately hot oven at 200°C (400°F) for an hour or so until the vegetables are beginning to soften.

Remove from oven and top with the sliced mushrooms, pepper and tomatoes and place back in the oven for another 30 minutes or so.

2 large beetroots

4 medium carrots

1 garlic bulb

1 large red onion

2 medium parsnips

5-6 medium potatoes

1 large sweet potato

2 sprigs of fresh rosemary

Fairly traded olive oil

Topping:

4-5 large mushrooms, sliced

1 large red pepper, sliced

4-5 large tomatoes, sliced

MARROW AND BUTTERNUT SQUASH TAGINE

A handful of dried apricots, chopped

1 medium butternut squash, cubed

1 tin of chickpeas

2 garlic cloves

1 medium marrow, cubed

1 medium onion, chopped

2tbsp sultanas

1 tin of tomatoes

150ml/¼ pint vegetable stock

1tsp chilli powder

2tsp cumin

1tsp powdered ginger

Fresh mint, chopped

Gently fry onion until soft. Add garlic, marrow, squash, and all your spices, fry and coat in spices until browned. Add apricots and sultanas, then your chickpeas.

Stir for 2 minutes then add tomatoes and hot stock, season to taste. Gently simmer for 20 minutes or so.

Top with fresh mint and serve with couscous and some pitta bread.

BIRCHER POTATOES

Scrub and thickly slice potatoes. Place in a well-oiled shallow tin, sprinkle with caraway seeds and a little sea salt. Bake for 30 minutes in a hot oven 200°C (400°F). The potatoes should be brown and crispy.

POTATO PATTIES

Mash all ingredients together in a bowl and form into flat burger shapes, lightly dust with wholemeal flour and fry until golden brown.

4-5 medium potatoes, mashed

2 large carrots, grated

4-5 mushrooms

1 small onion, chopped

½ tin of sweetcorn

3-4 fresh tomatoes, chopped

Any other left over vegetables

Mixed herbs

A dash of soy sauce

½ cup rolled oats for binding

COLCANNON

Adapted from a traditional Irish dish. This could also be adapted to make Bubble and Squeak, simply add any 'leftovers' such as cooked Brussels sprouts, peas, carrots, parsnips, etc.

Cook potatoes and mash with the yeast extract.

Shred the kale or cabbage and stir into the mixture.

Heat oil in a sturdy pan. Press in the potato mixture and cook over a low heat until brown underneath. Cut in half and turn, then cook the other side until brown.

Serve with tomatoes and parsley.

A good handful of dark kale leaves, or ½ medium cabbage (savoy is good)

4-5 medium potatoes

1tsp yeast extract

Oil

SAUTÉED MARROW AND TOMATO

1 marrow

5-6 ripe tomatoes

Cover the bottom of a heavy pan with 2 tbsp oil. Add marrow flesh cut into cubes and sliced soft ripe tomatoes.

Cover with lid and simmer for 25 minutes, turning occasionally so that all sides of the marrow are browned.

LEEK HASH

1 cooking apple

2 large leeks

2 large potatoes

A handful of sultanas

2 tbsp vegetable oil

A splash of tamari

2 tbsp water

Spread oil in a heavy bottomed pan and heat.

Slice leeks and potatoes and chop apples. Add potatoes to pan, then leeks, sultanas and apples. Cover with lid and cook over a gentle heat until potatoes are crisp.

Add a splash of tamari (or yeast extract dissolved in water). Stir well.

LEEK AND BROCCOLI CROUSTADE

Pre-heat oven to around 180°C (350°F).

Combine breadcrumbs, ground almonds, nuts or seeds and mix with vegetable oil until the mixture has a crumbly texture. Spread the mixture over the base of an oiled baking tin. Bake for about 10 minutes, until the top starts to brown.

Clean and chop the leeks and broccoli, and gently fry in olive oil until tender. Spread the leeks over the baked base.

Next make a white sauce. Heat the oil in a pan, stir in the flour, then gradually add in the soya milk, stirring constantly until the sauce thickens. Pour the sauce over the leeks and return the dish to the oven for about half an hour, or until the top is golden brown.

Serve with potatoes or a green salad.

Variations – instead of leeks try broad beans, courgettes, mushrooms, sweetcorn or anything else you fancy.

1 head of purple sprouting broccoli

2 large leeks

½ cup ground almonds

1 cup breadcrumbs

¼ cup of nuts and/or seeds, e.g. sunflower or pumpkin, finely chopped

Vegetable oil

For the white sauce:

1 tbsp cornflour

2 tbsp oil

1¼ cups sugar free soya milk

FRIED ROOTS AND GREENS

Greens, such as chard, kale, spinach, or wild garlic

Root vegetables, such as beetroot, carrot, celeriac or parsnip

¼ cup apple cider vinegar

1tsp fennel seeds

¼ cup olive oil

Cut vegetables into medium-sized chunks. Boil in salted water until cooked and drain, reserving cooking water as vegetable stock to make soup.

Allow to dry, then shallow fry in olive oil until browned on both sides. Add fennel seeds and cook for another minute, then add chopped greens.

Add more greens if needed to absorb remaining oil, season, sprinkle with a little apple cider vinegar and serve.

Thanks to Growing Communities[21]

AUTUMN VEGGIE BOX BAKE

*Everything in this dish apart from the soy sauce and olive oil
came from our veg box delivery one week.*

Parboil potatoes and drain, saving the cooking water for
gravy.

While they are cooking chop the carrots, onions,
parsnip, pepper and shred the kale and sauté them in
a large heavy pan. When the veggies are beginning to
soften, add the potatoes and continue to sauté for a
while longer.

Chop up the apple and add to the veggies, before
transferring all to a baking tray. Top with the sliced
mushrooms and tomatoes drizzled with a good splash of
olive oil. Add soy sauce. Bake in a moderately hot oven
at 200°C (400°F) for an hour or so.

1 apple

2-3 carrots

A handful (about 6 leaves)
of kale

1 small onion

1 parsnip

½ green pepper

6-8 mushrooms, sliced

2-3 potatoes

3-4 tomatoes, sliced thin

A dash of soy sauce

Fairly traded olive oil

SPICY ROAST VEGETABLES

1 aubergine

1 tin of chickpeas

A handful of coriander
    leaves

2 courgettes

3-4 garlic cloves

2 onions

1 red pepper

1 large sweet potato

1 tin of tomatoes, chopped

A dash of curry powder to
    taste

Vegetable oil or fairly
    traded olive oil

Cut aubergine, courgettes, pepper, sweet potato and one onion into approx. 3cm (1in) sized chunks. Place in an earthenware casserole dish, brush with olive oil and roast the vegetables in a moderately hot oven at 400°C (200°F) for 20 minutes or so.

In the meantime, chop and gently fry the other onion in olive oil until soft. Add curry powder, garlic and coriander and continue to cook for 1-2 minutes, then stir in the chopped tomatoes followed by the chickpeas. Simmer on a gentle heat for 5 minutes or so to create a spicy sauce.

Remove roasting vegetables from the oven, and pour the sauce over these. Return to oven and continue to cook for about 30 minutes until the vegetables are tender.

SUMMER VEGETABLES IN OLIVE OIL

Slice or chop the beans, carrots, courgette, onion, pepper and spinach and combine in a heavy ovenproof pan, placing the garlic cloves amongst them. Don't worry about peeling the garlic beforehand; the insides will soften as they cook and the garlic skins can be discarded afterwards.

Slice the tomatoes (or use whole if small) and place as a layer on top of the other veg, then thinly slice the mushrooms and add as a topping. Add a generous splash of white wine, and then pour over some olive oil.

Cover and place in a hot oven at 220°C (425°F) for 45 minutes to an hour until vegetables are soft and simmering in their juices. Remove cover and cook in oven for a further 20 minutes or so until the mushrooms on top are roasted.

Serve with couscous and a green salad.

1 cup fresh broad beans or runner beans, sliced

2 medium carrots

1 large courgette

5-6 garlic cloves

10-12 mushrooms

1 medium onion

1 large red pepper

A good handful (12 or so leaves) of fresh spinach

6-10 fresh tomatoes (cherry tomatoes are good)

Fairly traded olive oil

A generous splash of white wine

RAW CARROT SAVOURY

2 large carrots

1 onion

A good handful of nuts
(hazels, walnuts, beech
nuts, almonds, etc.)

1 cup porridge oats

A splash of shoyu soy sauce

A little oil

Herbs to taste

Grate carrot and finely chop onion. Finely chop nuts in coffee grinder or food processor.

Combine all ingredients with enough oats to make a firm mixture. Put in dish with a weight on top.

Serve with a salad and baked potato.

PUMPKIN SAVOURY

1 small onion

1 medium red pepper

1 small squash

A handful of sunflower
seeds

Herbs to taste

Vegetable oil

Peel squash and slice into chunks, and soften in a little water.

Finely chop onion and pepper and sauté with sunflower seeds in oil for a few minutes. Add herbs to taste.

Pour over drained squash and serve with vegetables.

Thanks to the late Kathleen Jannaway

COURGETTE AND TOMATO BAKE

Grease an ovenproof dish. Wash and slice courgettes and steam for a few minutes.

Chop the onion and garlic. Heat the oil and fry gently for a few minutes. Chop up the mushrooms and add these, frying for another couple of minutes.

Add the very ripe tomatoes (or tinned, or paste diluted in water), chopped basil and ground sunflower seeds and mix well to give a firm but moist texture. Add soy sauce.

Put a layer of sliced courgettes in the baking dish followed by a layer of sliced tomatoes then a layer of the fried mixture. Repeat until all ingredients are used, finishing with a layer of the fried mixture. Bake in moderately hot oven at 400°C (200°F) for 35-45 minutes.

2 medium courgettes

6-8 mushrooms

1 large onion

2 large, firm fresh tomatoes

1 tin of tomatoes (or ½ tube of tomato paste diluted with half a cup of water)

A handful of sunflower seeds

2tbsp oil

A handful of fresh basil leaves

1 garlic clove

1tsp yeast extract or a good splash of soy sauce

RUNNER BEAN PROVENÇAL

1 large onion

450g (1lb) fresh runner
   beans

1 tin of tomatoes (or ½ tube
   of tomato paste diluted
   with half a cup of water)

A few chopped fresh basil
   leaves

2 garlic cloves

2tbsp fairly traded olive oil

Slice and lightly boil runner beans for a few minutes.

At the same time gently fry the onion and garlic in olive oil. Remove beans from heat and strain, and then add to cooking onion. Add tomatoes and simmer for a while, then add chopped basil.

Simmer for another few minutes until runner beans are just tender.

Serve with new potatoes and a green salad.

GREEN BEAN MEDLEY

1½ cup broad beans

2 cups fresh peas (shelled)

450g (1lb) runner beans
   (make sure they are not
   too large or stringy)

Grated rind of 1 lemon

Freshly ground black
   pepper

Place broad beans, sliced runner beans and peas in a pan of boiling water. Cook for 2-3 minutes then drain well.

Tip all the vegetables into a large bowl, add grated lemon rind and black pepper.

RATATOUILLE

Chop courgettes, garlic and onion. Lightly sauté in a large heavy-bottomed pan. When soft add the tinned tomatoes and tomato paste, adding a little water if it is too thick.

Slice up the aubergine and quickly add to the sauce before it starts to oxidise and go brown.

Slice up the other ingredients and add, along with plenty of paprika. Let the veggies simmer in their own juices on a low heat for 20-30 minutes or so.

Serve with baked potatoes or on a bed of pasta. Garnish with 2 or 3 sprigs of parsley.

1 aubergine

2-3 large courgettes

A few garlic cloves

10-12 mushrooms

1 large onion

1 large green pepper

2 tins of tomatoes

1 tube of tomato purée

Paprika to taste

Parsley, 2 or 3 sprigs

Soup Ideas

Any old vegetables will go into a soup. They are a good way of using up any vegetables that have sat around for a while. The smaller you cut the ingredients the quicker the soup will cook but larger chunks can make for a more interesting texture. 'Stock' is an important ingredient of any soup to give it 'body'. You can make a stock by boiling down vegetable wastes you can't otherwise use – e.g. skins and peel, roots, outer cabbage leaves and stems, etc. Make sure they are scrubbed well, and use your common sense – anything that is too far gone belongs on the compost heap! Alternatively you can buy vegetable stock cubes, or else use about one tablespoon of yeast extract to a pint of boiling water.

BORSCHT

A beetroot based soup originating from Eastern Europe.

1-2 large beetroots

½ white cabbage

2 garlic cloves

1 large onion

1-2 large potatoes

1 tin of tomatoes

1.5 litres (3 pints) vegetable stock

A generous dash of red wine vinegar

Mixed herbs, e.g. oregano, rosemary, sage, thyme

2tbsp vegetable oil

Cooked green beans

Chop onion and garlic and sauté in the vegetable oil until tender.

Cut potatoes into chunks and grate the beetroots and cabbage. Add to pan with the tomatoes, red wine vinegar, stock and herbs. Bring to the boil then simmer on a low heat for 30-40 minutes.

Add cooked beans to the soup before serving and garnish with parsley if you want to.

TOMATO SOUP

*A good way to use up a glut of tomatoes, or keep your eye out for seasonal bargains
– the other day (late July) I got a huge box of tomatoes from Southend market
for a quid before my own allotment crop had begun to ripen...*

Finely chop onion and fry in a large, heavy pan until golden brown. Add flour and garlic and fry for a little longer.

Liquidise or finely chop the tomatoes – as many as you want – add to the pan, then add stock using your judgement, so the soup is pretty thick, but not too dry or 'stodgy' – add more liquid if necessary. Simmer for 25-35 minutes or so. Flavour with herbs.

If you've made loads, freeze it or share it out! Great with garlic bread and a glass of red wine (see page 217).

1 large onion

As many tomatoes as you want - the more and the riper the better!

2 garlic cloves, crushed

1-2tbsp wholemeal flour

1 litre (2 pints) stock - use proportionally with the tomatoes

Herbs, e.g. basil, tarragon, sage, etc.

CREAM OF CELERIAC SOUP

1 large apple

1 medium carrot

1 medium celeriac, use root and leaves (scrub well to remove any soil)

1 large onion

1 large potato

2tbsp almond flour

A dash of cumin

1tbsp dried mixed herbs

1 litre (2 pints) stock

Chop and fry onion with herbs.

Dice potato, carrot and celeriac into small pieces and add to pan. Add stock, bring to boil for a few minutes.

Peel, core and chop apple and add to pan along with the cumin. Simmer for 25-30 minutes.

Liquidise through a blender, mix almond flour to a paste and stir in, then gently reheat before serving.

LEEK AND POTATO SOUP

Perfect to warm you up in winter, but can be rather bland tasting –
this, however, is a perfect base for a vegetable soup. Bung in whatever is around
– beans, shredded cabbage, carrots, courgettes, lentils, parsnips, pasta, peas,
turnips... Don't worry if it gets too thick – then it's a vegetable stew!

1-2 large leeks

2-3 potatoes

1 litre (2 pints) stock

Herbs, e.g. oregano, sage, thyme, etc.

Olive oil

Chop up leeks, including the leaves (make sure you have cleaned out any of the dirt that can get trapped between the layers as it grows), and fry gently in the oil for a few minutes.

Add potatoes, herbs and stock and bring to the boil for 10 minutes or so. Simmer for 20-30 minutes until the potatoes are soft.

PARSNIP, KALE AND LENTIL SOUP

Put lentils on to boil. In the meantime, chop the onion and garlic into a large solid saucepan and gently sauté on a low heat.

Roughly chop the parsnips and carrot into cubes, and add to the pan. Continue to sauté for a few minutes then add a 500ml (1 pint) or so of boiling water. Stir in the stock, then add the lentils, which should by now be soft.

Roughly chop the greens and add to the pan. Simmer for half an hour so until ready.

Serve with a good crusty loaf for some winter cheer!

1 large carrot

A good handful (10-12 leaves) Black Tuscan kale, or any other fresh green leaves you can find

1-2 garlic cloves

1 large onion

2 parsnips

1 cup fairly traded puy lentils

1 litre (2 pints) vegetable stock

SPINACH SOUP

Chop up potato and onion and lightly sauté for a few minutes.

Finely chop spinach and add to pan, continue to sauté for a little longer then add stock. Simmer for 15-20 minutes or until potato is tender.

Liquidise, then add nutmeg, salt, pepper and lemon juice. Stir in soya milk to give it a more creamy texture.

1 onion

1 medium potato

A good lot of fresh spinach leaves ('perpetual' spinach is easier to grow than true spinach) or Swiss chard, well washed

1 litre (2 pints) stock

Lemon juice

A little grated nutmeg

Salt and pepper

1 cup unsweetened soya milk (optional)

GAZPACHO
(COLD SUMMER SOUP)

Perfect to cool you on those long hot summer days

1 medium courgette

½ large cucumber

2 garlic cloves

1 large onion

1 green pepper

7-8 large, very ripe fresh tomatoes

1 bunch of watercress

2 large lemons, juice of

Olive oil

A generous dash of red wine vinegar

Herbs and seasoning, e.g. black pepper, oregano, etc.

Blend all ingredients in a liquidiser.

Chill for half an hour or so and serve with crusty white bread.

HOT AND SPICY RAW
BROCCOLI AND LEEK SOUP

A raw recipe that only takes 5 minutes to prepare!

1 head broccoli florets

1 courgette

1 garlic clove

½ leek

1tsp miso

1tsp fresh mustard

2tbsp nutritional yeast (optional)

½ tsp Cayenne pepper and turmeric

3tbsp olive oil

Mineral salt and hot water

Blend ingredients together and serve straight away.

Thanks to Peace Ravenwood

DIY CURRY POWDER

For a curry powder that is generally more satisfying than the little plastic pots sold in the supermarket or wherever, try mixing the following spices which can be bought in any Asian grocery shops (try to ensure fair trade if possible): equal parts of coriander, cumin, fenugreek, ground ginger, poppy seeds and turmeric to a smaller proportion (a quarter or less) of chilli pepper. There are loads of other spices you could experiment with: cardamom, cinnamon, cloves, mustard seeds or nutmeg. They will keep indefinitely if stored in airtight jars, and their flavours will improve over time.

Catherine and Dean Yates suggest this 'English Curry Powder' that uses only ingredients that can be grown in the UK:

1 bay leaf

½ tsp caraway seed

¼ tsp dried chilli

2-3tsp coriander seed

1½ tsp cumin seed

½ tsp dill seed

1tsp fennel seed

1tsp powdered horseradish

2tsp lovage root

2tsp mustard seed

A few nasturtium seeds

1tsp poppy seed

1tsp rosemary

Ideas for Curries (and accompaniments)

Another perfect way of using up leftovers or bits of veg that have been sitting around for a while. Get your imagination and sense of experimentation going! Two points to bear in mind however: it's easy to 'overdo' it with the curry powder. The spices should enhance the flavours of the other ingredients, not overpower them! Also tastes differ from person to person, and if you are not keen on super-hot curries remember to go easy on the chilli. Gradually increase the amount used until you discover what suits you. This is particularly important to bear in mind if you are cooking for others!

'ENGLISH CURRY'

2tbsp buckwheat

½ white cabbage, chopped

1 large carrot

1 celery stick

1 onion

3 garlic cloves

1 large potato

1 tin of tomatoes, chopped

Other root vegetables,
    e.g. swede, turnip

1 cooking apple, peeled
    and chopped, or a few
    plums

Handful of dried fruit

Spices (DIY Curry Powder,
    p.131)

Chop onion and garlic and fry until soft.

Chop up the cabbage and tomatoes and dice the other vegetables and add to the pan along with the buckwheat, apple or plums, and dried fruit. Simmer until vegetables are soft, adding a little water if necessary if it's getting too dry.

Add spices (DIY Curry Power, see page 131) and continue to simmer for a few more minutes.

Leave to stand for a day to allow the flavours to develop. Reheat before serving.

Adapted from *Whole New Ways* published by Movement for Compassionate Living (out of print).

Thanks to Catherine and Dean Yates

BASIC POTATO AND TOMATO CURRY

*The perfect base for a vegetable curry that can be expanded
and improvised in so many ways.*

Cut the potatoes into fairly small chunks and parboil
for 15 minutes or so. Save the cooking water.

At the same time chop the onion and crush the garlic
and sauté in a good amount of oil until soft, moving
them around with a spatula so that they don't scorch.

Add the curry powder and continue to sauté for a few
more minutes, then add the tomatoes. Allow to simmer
for a few minutes, then add the potatoes, with a little of
their cooking water if the curry sauce is a little dry.

Simmer for 20 minutes or so, adding more of the
potato cooking water if the curry is becoming too thick
(but not too much or it will get too sloppy/watery),
then stir in the coconut. Simmer for a further few
minutes before serving.

Other items you could add include apple, banana,
beans, shredded cabbage, carrots, cauliflower, courgettes,
marrow, mushrooms, okra (add these fairly late or they
will tend to go slimy if over-cooked – most unpleasant!),
parsnip, peas, turnip, sultanas, sweet potato... Whatever
you want in fact! Serve on a bed of brown wholemeal
rice, or an alternative such as bulgur wheat or quinoa.

1 large onion

2-3 potatoes

2 tins of tomatoes

1-2 cloves of garlic, crushed

Curry powder (see above)

1-2tbsp desiccated coconut
(optional)

SPINACH AND CHICKPEA CURRY

2 medium carrots

1-2 tins of chickpeas

1 large onion

Lots of fresh, washed spinach leaves ('perpetual' spinach is easier to grow than 'true' spinach, which tends to easily run to seed in dry conditions, or use fresh chard)

A few fresh, very ripe tomatoes (or a tin)

Curry powder (see above)

A bunch of fresh coriander

A few garlic cloves

Fresh root ginger

Chop the onion and slice carrots into sticks. Finely chop the coriander. Crush garlic and grate the ginger and sauté all in a good amount of oil for 5 minutes or so until all ingredients are soft but not scorched.

Add the curry powder and continue to sauté for a few more minutes. Add tomatoes and a little water if necessary, i.e. if the ingredients are tending to 'stick' to the pan. Simmer for a while, then add the chickpeas.

Shred the spinach (use loads, it breaks down considerably whilst cooking) and stir it. Simmer for 20-25 minutes or so.

You could also add a few tablespoons of fruit chutney for flavour (see page 52).

MUSHROOM 'KORMA'

*This mild, slightly sweet curry is the perfect accompaniment to
the chickpea and spinach curry above. Try them together!*

Chop onion and gently sauté with the curry powder and
turmeric. Add soya milk and coconut cream.

Slice the mushrooms small and add to the sauce.

Add a little cornflour (a level teaspoon should be
enough – blend this to a paste in a splash of cold water
at the bottom of a cup, add a little more water, just
enough to enable you to pour it) then simmer for 10-15
minutes until sauce begins to thicken up – add a little
more soya milk if it gets too thick too quickly.

1 small onion
10-12 mushrooms
½ cup of soya milk
3-4 tbsp coconut cream
1tsp cornflour
Mild curry powder
1tsp of turmeric
Vegetable oil

CURRIED POTATOES

When we do a special curry meal we also add curried potatoes to the chickpea, spinach and mushroom korma; the three make a perfect combination especially if served with a good quality basmati rice!

1 onion

5-6 medium potatoes

1 bunch of fresh coriander

Curry powder

Sunflower oil

Cut the potatoes into pieces and boil in a large pan for 15-20 minutes until just soft. Drain and keep the cooking water.

Chop the onion and coriander and gently fry in a good amount of oil in a heavy bottomed pan, then add the curry powder.

Add the cooked potatoes, and a splash of their cooking water to stop them sticking to the bottom of the pan. Keep the potatoes moving in the pan with a spatula or wooden spoon, and add more of the water as necessary until they are starting to break down.

DHAL WITH SPROUTS (SEEDS AND BEANS, NOT BRUSSELS!)

Cook the lentils with enough water to cover them in a heavy pan until soft and set to one side. Careful you don't burn them, or that you use too much water and they go sloppy.

Chop the onion and carrot and fry gently in the oil until starting to soften. Add the curry powder and ginger and continue to sauté for a few more minutes. Add the lentils and simmer, stirring continually, adding more water if necessary.

Chop up the beet leaves and add to the mix along with the sprouts and the peas. Cook for another 10 minutes or so.

1 cup red lentils

A good handful of broccoli sprouts

A good handful of mung bean sprouts

A good handful of sea beet leaves (or use chard or spinach)

1 medium onion

1 medium carrot

A handful of peas

Coriander, chopped

A little ginger, grated

Medium curry powder

PULSE CHUTNEY

An Indian vegan recipe. Use fewer chillies if you do not want it so hot.

Soak the green mung beans overnight. Allow to sprout.

Mince the green chillies, fresh ginger and salt. Grind to a paste in a pestle and mortar or food processor. Season with lemon juice.

4 green chillies

50g (2oz) green mung beans

3.5cm (½ in) piece of root ginger

Lemon juice

Salt

VEGETABLE PAKORAS

From The Lemon Jelly Gardener's Cookbook, *a community project encouraging young children to grow their own food and eat healthily:* "This recipe is spicy but not too hot. You can change the amounts of chilli, coriander and cumin up or down a little bit. You should use an oil that is especially for deep-frying as these oils get hot enough to cook the pakora so they are nice and crisp and not soggy. Of course you do not have to use all these different vegetables and you can add your own favourites but we warn you peas are good for frying, cucumber is not."

1 medium carrot

½ small cauliflower

220g (8oz) gram flour

1 medium onion

1 small pepper

3 large potatoes

½ tsp chilli powder

1tsp coriander seeds

½ tsp ground coriander

½ tsp ground cumin

¼ tsp salt

Wash all the vegetables thoroughly. Peel and cut the potatoes into thin slices. Cut the cauliflower into little pieces like mini cauliflowers the size of a daisy. Chop the pepper and carrot into very small pieces about the size of big peas. Cut the onion into thin slices – the potatoes and the onion should be thin enough to be bendy so they can wrap around the smaller chunks of vegetables a bit.

Put all the raw vegetables and all the other ingredients into a big bowl, add water until the flour becomes a paste thick enough to cover the vegetables and stick to them without dripping off too much. It is best to do this by adding a bit of water at a time.

Heat up your oil in a deep fat frying pan to a medium heat. Scoop up a tablespoon of the mixture in the bowl and put it carefully into the frying pan. Cook the mixture until it is a golden brown colour and then put it onto some kitchen roll to drain off a bit of the oil.

Thanks to the Lemon Jelly Gardener's Project

Keep cooking spoonfuls of the mixture until it is all done. You can eat it as you go or keep them warm in the oven until you have a big plateful – be careful; they will be very, very hot when they first come out of the pan.

MARINADE

½ cup olive oil

½ cup lemon or lime juice

¼ cup water

¼ cup Dijon mustard

2tbsp maple syrup

1tbsp garlic, minced

2tbsp fresh basil leaves,
chopped

2tbsp ginger, grated

½tsp salt

½tsp freshly ground black
pepper

Whisk together all ingredients in a small bowl.

Will keep in a cool place for up to 7 days.

Sauces, Gravies, Spreads and Dips

Here is a selection of sauces that can accompany and enhance most of the recipes in this book, and spreads suitable for sandwich making, or for use as 'dips' or whatever.

TOMATO SAUCE

2 garlic cloves

1 small onion, or 2 shallots

1 tin of tomato puree

Splash of cider vinegar

½ tsp yeast extract, or 1 tbsp tamari (soy sauce)

A splash of oil

Herbs to taste, e.g. bay, oregano, basil, etc.

Finely chop onion and garlic, and gently sauté for a few minutes.

Add tomato puree, cider vinegar, herbs and yeast extract. Cook on a gentle heat for 5-10 minutes. Add a very small amount of water if it gets too thick.

Goes well with nut roasts, bean bakes and the like.

HOT SALSA

A good handful of fresh basil leaves

1 chilli

2 garlic cloves

1 onion

A handful of fresh parsley

1 medium green pepper

4 large juicy tomatoes

1 tbsp soy sauce

1 lemon, juice of

Finely chop all ingredients and blend together in a bowl.

Great as an accompaniment to salads, as a dip, etc.

SWEET AND SOUR SAUCE

Mix the flour to a smooth paste in the cider vinegar. Combine with other ingredients and bring to the boil in a saucepan. Simmer until tomatoes have broken down to a mush.

Serve over bean sprouts or stir-fried vegetables, or over steamed mixed vegetables, e.g. cabbage, celery, fennel, leeks, etc.

3-4 tbsp concentrated apple juice

1 tin of tomatoes

4-5 tbsp cider vinegar

150ml/¼ pint vegetable stock

1½ tbsp wholemeal flour

A little oil

GRAHAM'S GRAVY

Fry onion over a fairly high flame until caramelised. Add the vegetable water, and simmer for a few minutes, adding the yeast extract, wine and tomato paste. Continue to simmer for a few more minutes. Thicken with cornflour.

This gravy is quite improvised, and so bung any other leftovers in that you think might add interest; chopped mushrooms, peas, a mashed potato or two, whatever you fancy.

1 small onion

600ml/1 pint or so of vegetable stock - use the water from boiled potatoes or other veg

A little tomato paste

1 tbsp yeast extract

Splash of red wine or cider vinegar

2 tsp cornflour, stirred to a paste in a little water

VEGAN 'CHEESE'

Roughly equal parts of soya flour and vegan margarine (use soft margarine for a 'spread', hard for a 'cheese' that is sliceable)

A small amount of yeast extract

Heat the margarine in a small pan, when liquid and bubbling stir in the soya flour. Add a small amount of yeast extract – too much will dominate the flavour – I'd suggest a quarter of a teaspoon or less; use your own judgement.

When left to cool this makes an acceptable, if rather basic, cheese substitute. Adding a little crushed garlic, mixed herbs or chopped chives before cooling can liven up the flavour.

BEAN SPREAD

1 cup (or tin) of well-cooked beans, e.g. butter beans, field beans, haricot, kidney beans, etc.

1 small carrot

1 small onion

1tbsp tomato paste

A little vegetable oil

A dash of cider vinegar

Herbs to taste, e.g. basil, thyme, sage, oregano, etc.

Put all the ingredients together in a blender and blend to a smooth paste.

If you haven't got a blender, chop the onion and grate the carrot, combine all ingredients in a bowl and mash with a fork.

Chill for an hour or so before using as a sandwich spread or as a dip with crudités.

HUMMUS

In our house hummus really is the ultimate in dips, especially excellent with something like tortilla chips, in a bit of pitta bread with some olives and salad or with a baked potato. If you are having a party or taking some food along to a potluck or something, hummus can look pretty classy in a bowl with a little paprika and chopped parsley sprinkled on top. I dare say that by now you've got the message that we are pretty enthusiastic about hummus in our house.

Combine all ingredients in a liquidiser and blend to a smooth, white creamy texture. You may need to add a dash of water if it is too lumpy, but don't let it get too runny. You really can't overdo the amount of garlic you put in – personally I think nothing of slinging a whole bulb in, but it's really up to you!

Variations – add a little cumin, or maybe a red pepper or chilli if you like hot stuff. Alternatively you can make raw hummus by substituting sprouted for cooked chickpeas.

Important note: Hummus is not the same as humus (see page 80). Both are wonderful and sustaining, the latter however does not taste so good with falafels and salsa.

2 cups chickpeas, well cooked

A few cloves of garlic – as much as you like, the more the better (within reason - my friend once used 2 whole bulbs - that was a bit much!)

½ a jar of tahini (sesame seed paste)

Lemon juice - again use loads!

2tbsp olive oil (sunflower oil will do)

A little salt

CHAPTER 6

Main Crops and Staples

"A metaphor for resilience is the baking of a cake.
Before the oil age all the major ingredients of the cake,
the flour, eggs and so on, were produced locally and
only the icing on the cake was externally sourced.
Our present economy has turned this on its head.
For the great bulk of our needs we depend on supply
lines which reach across the world and are dependent
on an uninterrupted flow of oil. The tanker drivers'
dispute of 2000 showed how we are just three days
away from supermarket food shortages."

Rob Hopkins, *The Transition Handbook*

Zone 3

*Z*one 3 is concerned with thinking about the production and supply of our main crops and staple foods – those that are eaten regularly and in such quantities as to constitute the dominant part of our diets and which supply a major proportion of our energy and nutrient needs. Most of us don't have the land or resources to meet all of our own staple food needs, and so rely on agricultural systems over which we often do not have much direct control. Therefore any serious attempt to create sustainable food production and distribution systems will need to consider questions around food sovereignty and infrastructure, and how the permaculture ethics of Earthcare, Peoplecare and Fair Shares can be applied to these.

All Lost in the Supermarket?

Cheap post war food production policies and disconnectedness from the land have led us to overlook the true costs of what we eat and drink. In the UK, food production has increased by 100% since the Second World War, yet the farming labour force is dwindling and the quality of agricultural land is diminishing. In addition, the energy inputs to achieve that production have increased 1,600%. In other words, farming is actually about eight times less efficient now than it was in 1945.[22] Other hidden consequences of this cheap-at-all-costs/live-now-pay-later ethic include massive soil erosion, loss of biodiversity and wildlife habitat and the release of greenhouse gasses such as methane and carbon dioxide caused by excessive cattle farming and ploughing.

These problems are compounded by the rise of corporatism. Around 75% of our food is now purchased from the 'Big Four' supermarket chains consisting of Tesco, Sainsbury's, Morrisons, and Asda. In fact during 2005 it was reported that one in every eight UK pounds was spent in a Tesco store.[23] Although such corporations claim to represent value and choice, the reality is actually very different. The marketing mantra of 'Stack 'em high, sell 'em low' has huge global implications both environmentally and socially when the only accounting that is recognised is shareholder profit:

- Farmers are forced to accept low prices for their produce, with an average of only 10 pence in every pound spent in a supermarket going to the person who actually grew the food.
- Fruit and vegetables, especially those that are out of season, are often imported thousands of miles across the world by aircraft, burning vast amounts of fossil fuel and exacerbating climate change. What is more, the average 'food miles'

distance from field to plate has doubled in the last 20 years.

- Processed foods typically contain high levels of salt, sugar and fats. Excessive consumption is contributing to an obesity epidemic in the UK, including amongst children. Many supermarket foods also contain unacceptable amounts of pesticide residues.
- Intensive farming leads to the raising of animals for food in extreme confinement, with little or no attention paid to welfare. Other practices associated with factory farming include the routine administration of hormones and antibiotics, and chickens, sheep, cows and pigs subjected to de-beaking, tail docking, gestation crates and other barbaric practices that cause unimaginable stress and suffering.
- Packaging makes up nearly a quarter of household waste, and 35-40% of household waste ending up in landfill begins as a purchase from one of the big five supermarkets.

So is the future vision for our food supply an exponentially growing sprawl of superstores and convenience 'one stop shops' owned by an ever diminishing number of corporate brands and logos and patronised by an ever more alienated population of consumers? Or are there compassionate, community focused and environmentally sustainable alternatives that can continue to meet our needs when globalised supply chains begin to clog up or collapse?

Grow Your Own!

I have already touched on the small-scale food producing opportunities of the kitchen or back garden in the previous sections. Allotments are another possibility that offer a whole raft of additional benefits to growing fresh organic vegetables and fruit, from healthy exercise in the open air, community reconnection, socialising and stress relief, through to the preservation of what are often some of the only green spaces and wildlife habitats to be found within the centres of our towns and cities.

Despite the official position that local authorities have a statutory obligation to provide allotment sites if six or more ratepayers request them, the reality is that there can be large discrepancies regarding the availability of plots – sometimes there are lengthy waiting lists, whilst in other areas many plots are largely disused and overgrown. Many sites are also finding themselves under threat due to pressure from land developers, with numbers declining from 1.4 million during WWII to less than 300,000 by the start of the new millennium.[24] So be proactive – get in touch directly with your local allotment society, or, better still, take yourself on a tour round your nearest allotment site. Get chatting to the plot-holders and find out which are vacant. You might even be able to take over a plot and get to work straight away, paying the annual rent – usually around £20-30 per year – when it becomes due. Some societies will even let you off the first year's rent if the plot has been neglected for some time and requires clearing. Advice on growing some of the more common 'staple vegetables' is given in the previous chapter. In addition, there are plenty of books to help you get started; a few titles are to be found in the further reading section.

For most of us there are of course limits to how much food we can realistically grow ourselves, particularly when our lives are full of other commitments. In the case of our own family we seldom have to buy garlic, leeks or onions from the shops as the allotment supplies enough of these either fresh or from storage to keep us going all year round. Soft fruits practically come out of our ear-holes in the summer, as do courgettes, broad, French and runner beans, and tomatoes. In a good year we will have home grown potatoes available from summer to winter solstice, and plenty of other crops come and go throughout the productive season: apples, beetroots, carrots, celeriac, chard, cherries, herbs, plums, salad leaves and squashes to name just a few. Yet we are by no means anywhere near being self-sufficient. Peter Harper puts the limits of urban home scale food growing into a sensible perspective:

> "If you had enough land you might eventually succeed in providing most of your carbohydrates, eggs, and vegetables, but you would have little time or money to do much else. (It) will require total dedication from both you and your garden. Your lifestyle will necessarily be so unusual that you will cut yourself from 99% of your fellow citizens. If it isn't, your food growing is not making a large enough contribution to be worth while."[25]

What is more, such dedication to total self-sufficiency may actually be denying a livelihood to local commercial organic growers who are actually able to produce more efficiently. Aiming for a degree of self reliance (that is, having the skills, resources and confidence to be a part of a mutually supportive and resilient community) is probably a more realistic goal than striving for 100% self sufficiency, and changes to your diet and food-buying habits in order to bypass the supermarket monopolies may actually have a greater impact than trying to grow all of your own.

Going Beyond 'Sustainability' – Towards a Regenerative Agriculture

Sustainable agriculture is to some extent about putting the brakes on the cycles of dependence and degradation that are caused by oil based farming practices. Yet the term also begs questions about exactly what it is we actually want to 'sustain'. Sustainable farming practices reduce the harm done by artificial inputs like fertilisers and pesticides, but often maintain a 'business as usual' approach to the status quo, albeit with a little 'green' shading around the edges. Indeed many aspects of 'sustainability' have been very successfully co-opted by big business and the multinational corporations as the concept becomes increasingly mainstream. How often do we see mass-media advertising campaigns exhorting the consumer to 'do their bit for The Planet' by buying the latest eco-product? It could be argued that in some ways this is a good thing. It is at least raising awareness and maybe encouraging us to take what Joanna Macy terms 'holding actions' (see page 24) and mitigate the harm being done to our ecosystems. But simply not making things worse isn't enough any more. Where possible, we should support agricultural systems that are actively **regenerative**, in that they build soils, restore watercourses, and encourage biodiversity, while at the same time reduce dependency on outside inputs, and increase farm yields and economic viability. Or, in the words of RegenAG International founder Darren Doherty, leave things better than we found them.

Conventional thinking says that it takes a thousand years to create a few centimetres of soil. But under the right circumstances we can in fact build soils just as quickly as we can erode them, and at the same time sequester up to 40% of carbon emissions by adopting regenerative agricultural practices. The five essential requirements for rapid soil building are:

- Sun, air and water
- Biologically available minerals
- Living things IN the soil (plants and animals) and their by-products
- Living things ON the soil (plants and animals) and their by-products
- Intermittent and patchy disturbance regimes

Regenerative agriculture therefore encompasses a diverse portfolio of strategies that individually or together can rapidly build soils, communities and economic viability. Some techniques, such as encouraging livestock 'mob grazing' modelled on the behaviour of wild herds, are not within the scope of this book. Others, such as: minimising the usage of heavy machinery; harvesting water and practising effective irrigation; utilising long term cover crops and subsoil ploughing in order to avoid erosion and compaction; and developing viable local markets for produce, are well suited to stock free farming systems.

The walled garden at Tolhurst Organic.

Tolhurst Organic[26] is situated near the village of Whitchurch-on-Thames in south Oxfordshire and consists of 6.8ha (17 acres) in two fields and 0.8ha (2 acres) in the 500-year-old walled garden. For over 30 years the farm has been husbanded by Iain Tolhurst and his business partner Lin, and has had no grazing or other animal inputs added to any part of the farm for at least a decade. In addition to earning Soil Association accreditation, in 2004 Tolhurst Organic were the first growers to attain the Vegan Organic Network's 'Stockfree Organic' certification symbol. Ian argues that primary fertility needs to come from the use of well-designed rotations using grasses, herbs or other fertility building crops. He points out that even though many consumers assume that organic production relies on animal manures to support fertility, most farmers growing vegetable crops do not have livestock, and so become reliant on imported manures. Bringing manure in from another farm is depriving that farm of its own fertility and is expensive in terms or energy, plus uses fossil fuels and adds traffic and pollution to the local environment. Instead Tolhurst is developing a 'closed systems based' approach, aimed at building biodiversity in order to maintain fertility and naturally manage pest populations by encouraging predators:

> "Within our 17 acres of field vegetables we now have over 1,800m of hedgerow, which have completely changed the way that our crops interact with their local environment. The hedges are just a part of our biodiversity and habitat management: there are many other features that we have implemented on our fields to improve the chances for wildlife. We have had to give up small areas of land to do this, but it has enabled us to reduce the problems of pest attacks on our vegetables."

Other strategies used at Tolhurst Organic include the use of 'green manures' as winter cover crops, and the implementation in winter 2013 of an extensive agroforestry system. This involves planting around 1,000 mixed tree species (including some fruit trees) between vegetable cropping areas in order to create a multi-dimensional growing system. The whole project will be monitored over the forthcoming years to evaluate its advantages and disadvantages in terms of productivity, as well as looking at the effect on sequestering carbon into the soil. The farm also demonstrates its social and economic resilience by pro-active local marketing. Direct sales and a thriving box scheme are a crucial aspect of regenerative capacity building, offering a viable alternative to the financially precarious nature of so much modern industrialised agriculture.

Buy Local!

Indeed trade is one of the factors that pulls communities together, and spending our money with small growers as well as neighbourhood greengrocers and wholefood shops is one of the most powerful things we can do to support human scale social networks. Every time we spend a pound in the supermarket, 80p goes straight out of our community, swallowed up by the costs of transport, packaging and advertising or straight into the coffers of the faceless corporations. But when we use our money locally, investing in each others' skills and potential, we can have far more control over where our energy is used and what we are supporting. The same pound spent with a small business providing employment and using produce grown within the region largely stays within the community to be continually reinvested to produce wealth for all.

Farmers' Markets and Box Schemes

Recently described as "British farming industry's most high-profile shop-window", farmers' markets are currently enjoying a resurgence throughout the UK and US. A farmers' market is defined as one in which farmers, growers or producers from the local area (usually within a 30-50 mile radius) are present in person to sell their own produce to the public. All such products should have been grown, brewed, pickled, baked, or processed by the stallholders themselves.

Farmers' markets directly connect
producers and consumers
and cut food miles.

Box schemes too are an increasingly popular system whereby boxes of locally grown, seasonal fruits and vegetables are directly distributed to subscribers. Usually these are home delivered, or else are dropped off at a central point for customer collection.

In both cases, cutting out the middleman and maintaining face to face contact between producers and consumers creates a 'win:win' beneficial 'edge effect'. Customers are able to obtain fresh, high quality organic food at an affordable price. They can be confident of its origins, ask questions and get closer to the sources of local foods. Meanwhile, small independent growers are able to obtain a market for their produce that avoids dependence on the often crippling capriciousness of the corporate buyers, as well as getting valuable feedback from customers.

Growing Communities[27] in Hackney, northeast London was set up in 1996 by Julie Brown and other local residents who were concerned about a food production system that they saw as being vulnerable, wasteful and unhealthy:

> "We are working to create a more sustainable and resilient food system to meet the challenges posed by climate change and resource depletion. Oil, on which we depend for our food, won't last forever and will get increasingly expensive. Our health is suffering from processed food. I want to use community-led trading as a practical way to change from a system which is damaging to one that is more sustainable."

Starting from a small box scheme based in her garage in Stoke Newington, Julie soon made connections with farmers in or close to London and an organic wholesaler in Covent Garden Market that could supply fruit and vegetables all year round. The project now has over 600 members and employs 22 people, delivering to seven pick-up points in a converted milk float. Much of the produce is sourced from growing plots in and around Hackney, and the project is currently creating a 'Patchwork Farm' network where trained apprentices will grow food on small patches of land in back gardens, on church land and on estates. Growing Communities provides the land, tools, equipment and help with planting plans, and the apprentices gain transferable skills, and work to produce salad leaves and other vegetables that are fed into the box scheme. The aim is not only about generating more sustainable produce but is also to help people to generate an income from urban food production.

The project also runs a highly successful farmers' market in Stoke Newington that is committed to working with small-scale organic and biodynamic farmers from the areas closest to London. Most producers come from within 60 miles of Hackney, and include Ripple Farm in Kent, Wild Country Organics in Cambridgeshire, The Mushroom Table in Essex and Say It With Herbs in Hertfordshire. Growing Communities' Manifesto states that:

"Our experience has shown that urban communities are well placed to provide farmers and urban growers with many of the things they need, by establishing alternative trading routes for those farmers and growers. Which is why community-led trade and the Growing Communities approach have the potential to make a real difference here. Through community-led trade we can reach out and support those farmers now and in the future who struggle to farm sustainably and make a decent living. And in the process we can create sustainable and meaningful work for ourselves, while providing our communities with good food."

Subscription Farming and Community Supported Agriculture

'Tekai' is a Japanese term that means, 'putting the farmers face on food'. During the 1970s a group of women who were concerned about increases in food imports and a declining farming population initiated a direct growing and buying relationship between themselves and local producers. By the 1980s this concept of Community Supported Agriculture had spread to Europe and the USA.

Although produce is often distributed in a similar way, CSA requires a higher level of customer commitment than a box system. In the case of subscription farming, customers typically pay for a season's worth of produce, either upfront or by instalments. In this way they enter into a contract with the grower agreeing to share the risks of what the season may bring rather than buying a fixed amount of food. Although the grower will provide a list of crops and their expected yields, in a good year there will be plenty of produce, but in a bad year there may be less. In practice, risks are minimised by growing a wide variety of crops, and customers will usually get more than the worth of the financial share put in. The advantage for the grower is that they are guaranteed an income, as well as obtaining most of the money that they need for seeds, tools and other expenses at the beginning of the year. This reduces the need to borrow from (and pay interest to) the banks, which can be crucial for the viability of small-scale growers who do not have much capital.

An innovative variation on the CSA theme is the Rent-an-Apple scheme pioneered by Lathcoats,[28] a 55ha (135 acres) commercial fruit farm near Chelmsford, Essex. Facing increasing competition from supermarkets selling imported apples, the farm trialled a scheme in which they 'hired out' 47 apple trees for a fee of £10 each. Each customer was guaranteed 13kg (30lb) of apples equating to 77p/kg (35p/oz) – good value compared with supermarket prices, with the farm agreeing to make up any shortfall. Most customers lived within 15 miles of the farm, although a few came from as far as 35 miles away. Although not generating a huge amount of income in financial terms, the project has been considered a success in terms of publicity as well as the connections made with local people. Customers were encouraged to visit their trees throughout the year and those who watched their fruit develop tended to be more tolerant of imperfections. Project organiser Stephen Taylor compared the attitudes of farm customers: "The Pick Your Own scheme customers will reject fruit, throwing what they don't want onto the ground, with the rent-a-tree scheme they take it all home as they feel it is theirs."

Ethical Shopping and Fairtrade

In order to access the global market, small farmers and growers in the so called developing world are often forced to sell their produce for a pittance compared with 'developed' world prices. Supporting ethical and fair trade schemes are a way in which consumers can vote with their purses to ensure that such producers are able to get an adequate return for their goods, and that reasonable working conditions and human rights are respected throughout the supply chain. Fair trade products should meet stringent ethical and labour standards criteria that are regularly and independently audited. Probably the best known UK consumer guarantee is the Fairtrade mark, which can be found on over 250 products such as coffee, tea, fruit juice, wine, exotic fruit and so on.

During my permaculture courses I sometimes introduce an exercise designed to elicit discussion around issues of fair trade and ethical shopping. The ensuing debates are always lively and can sometimes become heated! There's a whole range of views and opinions on the subject, and it's true that from a purely 'earth right' perspective the issue raises some tricky questions. For example, fair trade does not automatically mean that produce is 'organic' (let alone veganic), and there are still 'food mile' issues associated with importation. Would land used to grow cash crops such as coffee or cocoa for export be better utilised growing food for direct human consumption by the people on that land? And how ethical really is the Fairtrade mark? Does it truly challenge the root causes of poverty and exploitation or is it more about assuaging 'first world' consumer guilt? Such questions have been highlighted in recent years by the controversial decision to award the Fairtrade mark to Nestlé's 'Partners Blend' brand coffee.[29] Nestlé have for several years been subject to a consumer boycott campaign for their unethical marketing of baby milk formula in the developing world, as well as other alleged human rights abuses. Colombian trade unionist activists have continued to be extremely critical of the corporation and have labelled their Fairtrade endorsement as 'a joke'. So is this an example of Fairtrade selling out, or are they in fact opening up a dialogue with Nestlé, offering them a way to 'come in from the cold' and clean up their act? I have my own ideas but will leave you to decide for yourself...

The ideal long term permacultural vision may be of a resilient UK that can feed itself from its own resources, but how many of us at the present time are actually prepared to do without, say, bananas, chickpeas, chocolate or olive oil? It could also be argued that the international exchange of goods and skills is as old as humankind itself, part and parcel of the spirit of adventure that has driven our development as a species and informed our naturally gregarious and eclectic nature. Since ancient times, countless merchant routes and spice trails have led to cultural and genetic cross-pollinations that have enriched human diversity, moving us away from tribalistic attitudes that can be insular and parochial.

So whilst growing our own and sourcing from local producers are positive steps that massively increase our self reliance and resilience, it's likely that there will always be a place for imported goods and international trade. However, perhaps these need to once again become the 'extras' rather than 'staples' of life – the icing on the top of the cake rather than the main ingredients of the cake itself. In addition, it seems only fair that when we do use imported goods, we remember the third permaculture ethic of 'Fair Shares' and ensure these are sourced from suppliers that are paying attention to both environmental and human rights issues.

If you do use imported goods ensure they are sourced from suppliers that are paying attention to both environmental and human rights issues.

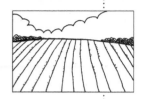

A Staple Diet

Cereal grains have been cultivated as a staple human food throughout the world since Neolithic times, some 10,000 years ago. The most popular types of grain such as barley, corn, oats, rice and wheat can be used in several forms, including wholegrains, pastas and noodles, couscous and flours. Cereals can be dried, stored, transported and processed with ease, and are a readily available source of a large fraction of the needs for energy-rich carbohydrates and other nutrients. However, while many fruit, nut and forage providers are long-lived perennial plants, all of the major grain crops are annuals or short-lived perennials grown as annuals, the cultivation of which causes huge environmental damage through soil erosion and compaction. Agricultural scientists such as Wes Jackson of the Kansas based Land Institute have for a number of years been researching the development of perennial versions of various grain crops. These include kernza, a relative of wheat that can be used in a lot of the same foods, yet can make a root system ten times the size of its annual counterpart. These roots improve the plant's resilience against pests and diseases and better collect water and nutrients, binding soil together so it doesn't wash away. Soil disruption caused by ploughing is minimised, as is labour, tractor fuel, and seed costs. Such perennials, when combined with the greater use of tree crops such as nuts, fruits, legumes and leaf protein (looked at in more depth in the next section of this book), could combine grain production with more regenerative practices, potentially reversing the damage caused by current fossil fuel driven farming.

Wheat

Historically wheat has been the largest and most important grain crop in the world, having been cultivated since at least 5,000 BC. The wheat kernel is comprised of the outer husk of bran, and wheatgerm, the nutritious seed from which the plant grows. Wheat is very important nutritionally as it is a source of complex carbohydrates, protein, vitamins and minerals. It is most nutritious when unprocessed and in its whole form. It is an excellent source of dietary fibre and is rich in B vitamins and vitamin E, as well as iron, selenium and zinc. However some people are intolerant to the wheat protein known as gluten, and some studies have related its consumption with weight gain and other health problems. Furthermore wheat is usually grown as a monoculture, and has been responsible for turning vast areas of the planet's soil into desert. For these reasons, as with rice, it will be important to increase the diversity of the cereals, grains and other staples that we rely on if we are to transition to a more ecologically harmonious and resilient future.

Bread

Up to 98% of the bread that is sold in supermarkets and bakeries (including most shop-bought 'wholemeal' bread) is manufactured by the 'Chorleywood Process'. Developed in 1961, this is a high speed mechanical mixing process that allows fermentation times to be drastically reduced using various chemical 'improvers', hydrogenated fats and anti-fungal agents. This is an intensive, low labour system aimed at maximising efficiency and profit at the expense of the consumer. Chorleywood bread is about as far removed from the real thing as it is possible to get, so maybe it's time to reclaim the staff of life – support those bakeries that use traditional methods, or better still make your own kitchen part of the campaign for real baking and Liberate the Loaf!

The best bread consists of four simple ingredients, flour, yeast, salt and water, plus a little molasses. Below is the basic recipe that I still use, adapted from the Lifespan Co-operative's booklet *Breadmaking* that I bought from a wholefood shop over 30 years ago! There are of course many other books available on the art of bread making, but in my opinion this simple little pamphlet contains all you need to know, and is worth tracking down if you can find it. Another classic book on the subject is *The Tassajara Bread Book* by Edward Espe Brown, a virtual Zen prose poem on an ancient art that is at the heart of community and life itself.

BREAD RECIPE

1.3kg (3lb) wholemeal bread (or 'strong') flour

1tsp dried or fresh yeast – fresh is best, but not so easy to find in the shops these days

470ml (1 pint) lukewarm water

1tbsp molasses or unrefined sugar

½tsp salt

Dissolve the molasses or sugar in the lukewarm water, and then stir in the yeast. It's important that the water isn't too hot as this will kill the yeast, nor too cold as it will remain dormant.

Leave for 10 minutes or so until the yeast becomes active – a froth will appear on the surface of the liquid – if it doesn't you will need to start again with a fresh batch of yeast.

In the meantime put half of the flour in a large mixing bowl. Slowly stir in the yeast liquid with a fork, combining thoroughly to make a mixture with the consistency of thick porridge. Set the bowl aside in a warm place and cover with a tea towel.

After about 20 minutes or so the mixture will have doubled in size. Add the rest of the flour along with a little salt, making sure it is all thoroughly mixed together.

Flour your hands to prevent the mixture sticking to them too much, and knead vigorously for at least 20 minutes or so – the longer the better. To knead effectively, the dough is put on a floured surface, then pressed and stretched with the heel of the hand, folded over, and rotated through 90 degrees. This process forces the gliadin and glutenin proteins in the flour to combine and form chains of gluten that form a network, trapping the carbon dioxide given off by the yeast in thousands of tiny pockets in the dough that then cause it to 'rise'.

Although time consuming, kneading dough is a very satisfying and even therapeutic activity that is all about putting us physically in touch with the food we eat in a very literal sense. The process is repeated until the dough has a smooth, elastic quality.

Form into a loaf shape and leave to rise for about 40-50 minutes on a greased tray. When it has risen, some bakers like to 'prove' the loaf by punching it flat and giving it a second kneading for 20 minutes or so, then allowing it to rise again, although others feel that this is not necessary. I guess it all depends on how much time you have available.

Bake for 40-50 minutes in an oven at about 180°C (350°F) or gas mark 4. You can tell when your loaf is ready by taking it from the oven and gently tapping the underside; it should have a hollow sound and a feel that you will quickly learn to recognise by experience.

The above is a basic fool proof 'pattern' for bread making, yet within this there is infinite scope for variation and experimentation. Try substituting half of the wheat flour with soya, rye, acorn, potato, quinoa, spelt or barley flours, or add ground nuts, chopped onions, grated apple, sun dried tomatoes, poppy seeds, chilli peppers, olives or maybe a handful of dried herbs. Don't add these until the initial mixture has risen however, or the action of the yeast may be inhibited. For a really nice fruit loaf, add a tablespoon of mixed spice, plus about three handfuls of dried fruit such as raisins and sultanas.

A BASIC PASTA SAUCE

'Keep it simple' is the rule of the best Italian pasta chefs, and good advice to follow!

1 medium onion

1 tin of plum tomatoes

1 tube tomato paste

2-3 cloves of garlic

Soy sauce

Sunflower oil

Mixed herbs, e.g. oregano, thyme, basil, parsley

Pasta

Pasta is usually made from wheat flour, and is another interesting way of incorporating the grain component to a vegan diet. It comes in many types including cannelloni, fusilli, lasagne, penne, ravioli, spaghetti and tagliatelle. Note that a large quantity of boiling water (preferably with a splash of vegetable or olive oil added) should be used to cook pasta in order to reduce starch and prevent stickiness.

Gently fry onion, garlic and herbs in oil for a few minutes. When soft add tomatoes, tomato paste and soy sauce, add a splash of water if the sauce gets too dry/thick.

Simmer for 5 minutes then add mushrooms and sweetcorn. Simmer for a further 20-25 minutes.

Serve over any type of pasta.

This basic sauce can be expanded on and experimented with: add mushrooms, sweetcorn, green or red peppers, courgettes, bean sprouts, chopped spinach, olives, etc.

SPAGHETTI BOLOGNESE

Crush the garlic and chop the onion. Gently fry with the herbs. Add tomatoes and tomato paste and simmer for a few minutes.

Scrub and grate the carrots, and stir into the sauce and continue to simmer. If it starts to get a bit stiff add a good splash of red wine to moisten the mixture.

Chop mushrooms and pepper and add, simmering for 20-30 minutes.

In the meantime add the spaghetti to a large pan of boiling water (a splash of olive oil will help to prevent the spaghetti sticking to itself) and cook for 10 minutes or so until it is 'al dente' (i.e. cooked yet still firm to the bite). Drain with a colander and distribute onto plates.

Add another good splash of red wine to the Bolognese sauce about 5 minutes before removing from the heat, then pour over the spaghetti and serve.

5-6 large carrots

8-10 mushrooms

1 large onion

1 green pepper

1 tin of tomatoes

1 tube of tomato puree

Lots of oregano, basil, thyme, bay leaves, etc.

3-4 garlic cloves

A good splash of red wine

Sunflower oil

Wholemeal spaghetti

LASAGNE

1 medium onion

A good handful of mushrooms

2 cups soaked split peas

2-3 fresh tomatoes

½ tube tomato paste

A couple of garlic cloves

1tsp yeast extract

Splash of cider vinegar

Mixed herbs, e.g. basil, oregano, marjoram, thyme, tarragon

A few strips of uncooked wholemeal lasagne

Boil the split peas until soft.

Meanwhile fry the onion and garlic with the herbs and then mix in with the cooked split peas, adding the tomato paste, yeast extract and a dash of cider vinegar to make a creamy sauce.

Boil the lasagne strips in water for 5 minutes or so.

Grease an oven dish and make alternate layers of chopped tomatoes and mushrooms, lasagne and the sauce. Finish the top layer with sliced tomatoes to stop the last layer of lasagne from drying out.

Cook in a medium hot oven for 40 minutes or so.

A BASIC PASTRY RECIPE

Stir oil and water into the flour with a fork until stiff. If pastry is too dry add a little more oil and water – if too soggy add more flour. When you can roll out the pastry on a flat surface, lightly dusted with flour, without it either sticking or breaking up, it's the right consistency. The amounts given here are approximate for a good-sized pie that will feed a family of 4.

Use a greater proportion of oil to water if you want a 'shorter' pastry.

For variations bung in some ground nuts or sesame seeds, or substitute half the wholemeal flour for a white flour (gives a lighter texture) or soya flour, rye flour, millet flour, gram flour, etc. or mashed potato to make 'gnocchi'.

4-5 cups of wholemeal flour

Equal parts of sunflower oil and water (about half a cup full of each)

CARROT PASTRY

An interesting change for pies etc. – use 280g (10oz) mashed carrots to 340g (12oz) wholemeal flour, 140ml (5fl. oz) oil and 3tbsp water and a little salt. Use as normal pastry – very easy and light to handle.

LENTIL PIE

2-3 medium carrots

1 large onion

5-6 mushrooms

2 cups of fairly traded red
   lentils

½ tube of tomato paste

2-3 garlic cloves

1tbsp yeast extract

Herbs to taste, e.g. sage,
   oregano, thyme, parsley

Pastry (page 163)

Cook lentils until soft (don't use too much water or they'll be too runny, but at the same time don't let them burn).

Chop up onion, garlic and carrots and gently fry them in a pan with the herbs for 5 minutes or so, then add the lentils and mushrooms. Stir in the yeast extract and the tomato paste.

Meanwhile roll out half of the pastry and place in a greased pie tin. Place in a medium oven and bake for 5 minutes or so.

Remove and add in the filling. Use the other half of the pastry to make a lid for the pie. Don't forget to make a few holes in the lid to let the hot air out. Cook in a medium heat oven for 20-30 minutes until the pie has a nice brown crust.

If you've got a little left over pastry you could roll it into thin strips and use it to make a simple design to decorate your pie.

Serve with, say, potatoes, steamed mixed vegetables, roast parsnips and gravy.

VEGETABLE PASTIES

Parboil the potatoes, drain and dice into small, fingernail-sized pieces along with the carrots and onion.

Fry onion in a pan with the herbs or curry powder. Add tomato paste and a very small amount of the water the potatoes were cooked in, just enough to keep the mixture moist.

Add the other veggies and continue to cook in the pan for 10-15 minutes. Mind this filling mixture doesn't get too dry and burn, or on the other hand get too sloppy due to adding too much water.

To make pasties, roll out pastry on a surface dusted with flour to prevent it sticking and cut into circular shapes using a side plate or saucer as a guide. Dollop a little of the filling into the middle of each circular shape, taking care not to put too much in each. Fold over and seal closed with a little water.

Cook in a medium heat oven for 15-20 minutes or so.

Perfect for packed lunches and picnics!

2 carrots

1 small onion

½ cup of peas

1-2 medium potatoes

½ cup sweetcorn

1tbsp tomato paste

Dried mixed herbs or curry powder

Pastry (page 163)

PUNK PIE

VEGGIE PIE

PEACE PIE

FREEDOM PIE

VEGETABLE WELLINGTON

This dish makes a majestic centrepiece for a dinner!

1 onion

Tomatoes, chopped, or
   tomato paste

Mixed seasonal vegetables,
   e.g. parsnips, carrots,
   leeks, potatoes, celery,
   kale, broccoli, etc.

2 garlic cloves

Wholemeal flour

Ground hazelnuts

Oatmeal

Herbs to taste
   (e.g. marjoram, thyme,
   parsley, etc.)

Finely chop onion and garlic, and fry until soft. Add ground hazelnuts, wholemeal flour, oatmeal, chopped tomatoes and herbs.

Knead into dough, then roll out onto a large sheet of greaseproof paper to an oblong shape.

Chop and steam mixed vegetables; when beginning to soften (but not over cooked), place these on the centre of the pastry and fold into a parcel. Seal the ends and decorate with the remaining pastry. Brush with a little oil and bake in a moderate oven for 30 minutes or so until browned.

Serve with gravy or tomato sauce and greens.

Adapted from *Whole New Ways* published by Movement for Compassionate Living (out of print).

Thanks to Catherine and Dean Yates

PUMPERNICKEL

Dissolve the yeast
in the water in a
large bowl. Add the
remaining ingredients.

Bake 35-40 minutes at
180°C (350°F).

2 cups rye flour

1tbsp dry yeast

1 cup soya or oat milk

1 cup warm water

2tbsp molasses

1tsp caraway seeds

2tbsp hulled pumpkin
    and sunflower
    seeds

1tbsp salt

2tbsp oil

SAVOURY RYE BISCUITS

Combine ingredients
together and roll out
flat to about 1cm
(0.25in) thickness, or
very thin for crackers.

Bake in a hot oven
at 200°C (400°F) for
about 15 minutes.

Variation – add 1tsp baking powder or
cream of tartar and 1tsp yeast extract for
'cheesy' biscuits.

12oz mashed potatoes

12oz rye flour

Oil

1tsp salt

Spelt

Spelt is an ancient grain that
is the ancestor of modern
wheat varieties. It has never
been modified, and is basically
identical to that which was
introduced into the UK by the
Romans 2,000 years ago. Spelt
flour can be used for bread
and pasta making, but has a
more digestible form of gluten
than that found in wheat, and
is therefore more suitable for
those who have intolerances.

Rye

Rye thrives in cold climates
and poor soils. It grows well in
Scandinavian countries, Russia,
Eastern Europe as well as in
the UK. It is high in fibre, and
a good source of vitamin E
and some B vitamins as well
as protein, iron, phosphorous
and potassium. Although rye
contains gluten, this is in a
different form to that found in
wheat, and therefore produces
coarser heavier breads such as
pumpernickel.

Oats

Oats are a cereal that do well in cool temperate conditions, and do particularly well in Scotland. They have much to commend them as an alternative to the wheat that tends to dominate most people's diets in the UK, having a higher energy value and greater proportions of protein, iron and calcium. Whole oats are unprocessed with the nutritious bran and germ remaining intact. Oat groats are the hulled whole kernel, whilst rolled (porridge) oats are made from groats that are heated and pressed flat. These are used in breakfast cereals such as muesli and for making flapjacks and cookies, and can also be used for crumbles or to bind nut roasts, etc. Oat flour can be made on a home scale by grinding porridge oats in a coffee grinder or food processor. This is gluten free, which makes it suitable for those who are gluten intolerant. However it needs to be combined with wheat flour for making leavened bread.

MUESLI

Soak a cupful of coarse oatmeal combined with a handful of raisins and other dried fruit in apple juice overnight.

The following breakfast time, add slices of apple, chopped nuts, sunflower and pumpkin seeds. Alternatively oat flakes can be used instead as these do not require soaking.

CRUMBLE MIXTURE

2 cups of porridge oats
Sunflower oil

To make a crumble topping combine the above ingredients in a large bowl, mixing in the oil with your fingers until the texture is neither too dry nor too stodgy, but just... er... crumbly!

You could also add ground nuts or sesame seeds, or for a sweet crumble, e.g. apple or rhubarb, mix in some raisins or some unrefined sugar.

LEEK AND CAULIFLOWER CRUMBLE

Chop leeks and fry over a gentle heat until tender.
Add soya milk.

Chop cauliflower and other veg, add along with
the herbs. You could also bung in other veggies, e.g.
sweetcorn, broccoli, courgettes, etc. Cook for 10-15
minutes or so.

Pour into a large heatproof oven dish and cover with the
crumble topping. Cook in a medium heat oven for 30
minutes or so.

Serve with roast potato, roast parsnips and carrots, fresh
peas and gravy. A marvellous winter meal, I guarantee
you won't be able to move for at least an hour after
munching this lot!

2-3 medium carrots

1 cauliflower head

2 largish leeks

A good handful (10-12) of
mushrooms

1 cup soya milk

1-2tbsp good quality soy
sauce, e.g. Shoyu or
Tamari

Herbs, e.g. sage, rosemary,
etc.

Crumble topping (page 168)

VEGAN HAGGIS

*Haggis is a traditional Scottish dish that combines oatmeal flour with
ingredients even most omnivores might not want to think about too closely,
this however is an absolutely delicious vegan alternative.*

½ cup fine oatmeal

2 cups cooked beans,
  e.g. kidney, haricot,
  butter, or a tin of cooked
  beans

¾ cup (110g/4oz) brown or
  green lentils

2 large carrots, finely grated

4-6 mushrooms, sliced

1 large onion, chopped

1tbsp vegetable oil

1tsp ground spices,
  e.g. cumin, paprika,
  turmeric, etc.

1tbsp soy sauce

2 garlic cloves

Salt and pepper to taste

Put the oatmeal in a bowl and cover with water. Let it
stand for at least an hour. Drain thoroughly.

Cook lentils until soft, then drain.

Chop the onion and sauté in oil until soft. Finely chop
the carrots and mushrooms and add to the onions, and
cook for a little longer.

Mash the cooked beans and stir in along with the
lentils, oatmeal, spices, soy sauce and crushed garlic.
Add a little more oil if it looks too dry.

Transfer to an oven dish and bake at 175°C (350°F) for
30-40 minutes.

Serve in the traditional way with mashed potatoes,
'neeps' (swedes and turnips mashed together) and gravy
(see page 141).

POLENTA

A traditional Italian staple, polenta is made from coarsely ground cornmeal, and can be used as an alternative to pasta, rice or potatoes. When left to cool it will have a firm cake-like texture that can be sliced then grilled, fried or baked. Polenta on its own has quite a bland flavour, thus can be flavoured with seasonings, or served with a tasty sauce such as tomato sauce (see page 140), or alternatively served as a desert accompanied by jams, agave syrup etc.

6 cups water

1tsp salt

1¾ cups yellow cornmeal

2tbsp oil

Bring 6 cups of water to the boil in a large heavy based saucepan. Add salt. Gradually whisk in the cornmeal, adding just a little at a time by letting it run slowly between your fingers. Be careful not to allow lumps to form.

Reduce the heat to low and cook until the mixture thickens, stirring frequently for 15-20 minutes. Remove from heat, stir in the oil, place in an oven dish and allow to cool.

You could also stir in a selection of vegetables before the polenta begins to set, e.g. bean sprouts, cooked beans, carrots, celery, garlic, mushrooms, peas, chopped peppers, onion, etc. and maybe a splash of soy sauce for flavouring.

Corn

Corn was introduced to Europe by the Spanish and Portuguese from South and Central America, and quickly became a staple crop. Corn requires more heat and sunshine than wheat, and tends to do better in the more southerly parts of Europe. It is still widely grown in Mexico and the southern states of the USA. Corn is believed to be the only grain that contains vitamin A. It is also the source of some B vitamins, vitamin C and iron. Corn products include flour, meal and wholegrains.

Rice

Rice is the second most widely cultivated grain in the world, and a staple of China, India, Southeast Asia, Africa and Latin America. Rice is grown in more than 100 countries, with a total harvested area in 2009 of approximately 158 million hectares (390 million acres), producing more than 700 million tons annually (470 million tons of milled rice). About 90% of the rice in the world is grown in Asia (nearly 640 million tons). Rice requires a hot climate to grow, and is very difficult to cultivate in the cool temperate UK. However, some gardeners report success growing small amounts experimentally under glass. According to Plants For A Future, wild rice (*Zizania aquatica*) has been observed to thrive in ponds at Kew Gardens in London, and may have some potential to be cultivated outdoors in parts of the UK such as the Isle of Wight, Norfolk and Cambridgeshire in the future. Nevertheless, at the present time, the UK is entirely dependent on fossil fuel depleting imports for its rice supply. Furthermore the bacteria in water-logged fields where rice is grown are a major source of methane emissions, thus it is important that we consider alternatives to its over-use as a staple food.

Barley

Barley is believed to have first been cultivated by the Egyptians around 5,000 years ago, and was the main bread grain of the Greeks, the Hebrews and the Romans. It was also widely used in Europe as human food until the Middle Ages. It is however low in gluten, and therefore suitable only for making unleavened bread. However this does make it more suitable for those whose diets are gluten intolerant. Barley is a low sodium food, with useful quantities of zinc, potassium, iron, copper and sulphur. It can be bought as 'pot barley', or, with its valuable outer layers removed, as 'pearl barley'. The former has a higher nutritional value, but does require longer cooking, needing to be soaked for several hours then simmered in plenty of water for an hour or so.

Barley grows well in a wide range of climates, being able to withstand both near drought and cool damp conditions. Nowadays barley is mainly used as a livestock feed, especially in intensive cattle and pig units.[30] Used to feed humans instead it could be a valuable staple crop well suited to the UK climate. Fermented germinated barley gives malt, a valuable sweetening agent that is used in the fermentation of beer and malt vinegars.

Used in soups, stews and casseroles, barley has a pleasant flavour and a chewy consistency that many find enjoyable. Barley can also be substituted for rice as an accompaniment to many dishes.

1.Wheat 2.Barley 3.Rye 4.Oats

BARLEY RISOTTO

1½ cups pearl barley

1 large carrot

2-3 stalks of celery

2 garlic cloves

A handful (6-8) mushrooms

1 large onion

1 cup fresh or frozen peas

Any other vegetables you have around

Oil

500ml (1 pint) of vegetable stock

Good splash of white wine

Herbs to taste, e.g. thyme, marjoram

Slice onion, crush garlic and chop the vegetables into small pieces. Heat stock and put to one side.

Sauté the barley in oil in a heavy pan until turning light brown. Add the vegetables and continue to cook on a low heat until the vegetables are beginning to sweat.

Add a good splash of white wine and continue to cook until the barley absorbs this. Add the stock a little at a time until it is absorbed but not too dry.

Serve with a green salad and a nice glass of white wine (if there is any left).

POT BARLEY AND LEEK BAKE

2 leeks

230g (8oz) pot barley

3-4 tomatoes

500ml (1 pint) water

1tbsp rye or wheat flour

1 cup of vegetable stock

1 tbsp oil

Herbs and seasoning to taste

Simmer pot barley for around 45 minutes until most of the water is absorbed.

Meanwhile, chop leeks and fry in oil, stir in flour and stock and simmer to thicken. Add cooked pot barley.

Put in baking tin. Cover with sliced tomatoes and cook in a medium oven for 30 minutes or so.

Buckwheat

A member of the Polygonacae family, which also includes sorrel and rhubarb, buckwheat is a highly nutritious gluten free grain substitute that can be grown on a small-scale, such as in a medium-sized garden. It does well on rough land and poor soils, maturing in 10-12 weeks. It grows to a height of up to 60cm (24in) with red stems and masses of pink flowers that attract hoverflies, the larvae of which feed prolifically on aphids. As well as yielding a useful edible crop, it has bacteria in its roots that fix nitrogen from the air, and can also be used as an overwintering 'green manure' that can be forked into the soil or used for compost.

The triangular seeds can be sprouted and eaten raw or cooked and used in a variety of ways. They are high in proteins and have a good balance of amino acids. They also contain rutin, which is used to treat atherosclerosis (hardening of the arteries).

Cooking

Unprocessed buckwheat can easily be toasted. For a moderate sized portion, put 2 flat tablespoons in a lightly oiled pan and toast over a medium heat for around 10 minutes, shaking the pan occasionally. Transfer to a pot and add boiling water, simmering over a moderate heat for 15-20 minutes until all the water is absorbed. Do not stir but shake occasionally to avoid sticking. The grains can then be used in a variety of ways in easily prepared but nutritious meals.

For breakfast try adding raisins, grated apples and groundnuts as an alternative to muesli.

Buckwheat has little flavour of its own, so can be used in the same way as rice or other grains as an accompaniment for main meals or salads, or can be flavoured with yeast extract or herbs, etc. It can also be used in roasts (see page 227), burgers (see page 183), or in stews, casseroles, etc.

Buckwheat can also be ground into flour, which can be bought from many wholefood shops, or processed on a small scale in the kitchen.

BUCKWHEAT CROQUETTES

60g (2oz) buckwheat

1 small onion

2 small potatoes

A handful of fresh mint

A little vegetable oil

1tsp yeast extract

Herbs to taste

Pre-cook buckwheat (see page 175). Chop onion and mint finely. Boil the potatoes and mash well. Mix all ingredients thoroughly.

Shape into croquettes and place on an oiled baking tray. Bake for 45 minutes or so or until brown and crisp in a moderate oven 150°C (300°F).

BUCKWHEAT CASSEROLE

1 cup buckwheat

1 small onion

2 cups fresh peas

2 small peppers

2 large potatoes

4-5 large tomatoes

Vegetable oil

1tsp yeast extract

500ml (1 pint) water

Herbs to taste

Pre-cook buckwheat (see page 175). Chop onion and peppers. Slice potatoes and tomatoes. Put ingredients in layers in a casserole dish.

Dissolve yeast extract in hot water and pour over ingredients. Bake for 60 minutes at 150°C (300°F).

BUCKWHEAT PANCAKES

Mix 3 parts wholemeal wheat flour to 2 parts buckwheat flour. Add water and a very small amount of oil and salt, and mix to a batter consistency. Pour into a hot oiled pan. Turn down when pancake is set and cook slowly. Turn. Delicious as a savoury dish, or with lemon and syrup, e.g. agave or maple.

Quinoa

Originating in South America in the mountainous region of The Andes, quinoa is a member of the Chenopodium family that also includes chard, spinach, beets and goosefoot. The Inca peoples called it 'The Mother of all Grains' cultivating it as a staple for hundreds of years before it was almost wiped out by the Spanish invasion of the 16th Century, along with the rest of that civilisation. Today it is considered a 'superfood' by many due to its superior nutritional value. It is a complete protein, containing all nine essential amino acids as well as iron, lysine, riboflavin (vitamin B2), magnesium and manganese, and has a very high fibre content, and is therefore ideally suited to a vegan or vegetarian diet.

Quinoa has been observed to grow well in cool temperature regions, and has huge potential as a possible staple that could be grown in the UK as an alternative to wheat or imported and environmentally damaging rice. Another advantage is its coating of bitter tasting saponins. This makes it unpalatable to birds, and so it requires less protection than most other grain crops. Quinoa is also very suitable for growing on a small scale in the garden, the multi-coloured seed heads providing visual interest within any edible polyculture, or even in an ornamental setting. The leaves can also be used as a spinach substitute. Seed is now easily obtainable from a number of suppliers (see page 288).

The quinoa that is sold in the shops has usually had the bitter saponins removed, although this is easily done with home grown seed by soaking for a few hours then draining off the water. Simmer for a few minutes in a fresh amount of water, then put into a sieve and shake under a running tap.

The recipes below are adapted from the Movement for Compassionate Living booklet Recipes from New Leaves.

SAVOURY QUINOA

1 cup quinoa

1 medium onion

1 tin of tomatoes

2 cups water

Oil

1 tbsp yeast extract

Herbs to taste, e.g. thyme, marjoram, basil, sage, etc.

Simmer quinoa until texture changes, i.e. the seeds become crescent shaped and the water has been absorbed. Make sure it doesn't stick – add more water if necessary.

Finely slice onion and sauté in oil until golden brown. Chop tomatoes and add to cooked onion, stirring in the yeast extract. Add quinoa and herbs and mix well.

Bake in a medium oven for 15-20 minutes. Can also be used as a stuffing, e.g. for stuffed marrow or peppers, etc.

QUINOA BURGERS

Mixture as above

1 cup porridge oats

Combine mixture above with oats to make firm consistency. Shape into burgers and bake for 15-20 minutes in a medium oven or fry.

QUINOA SAUCE

Finely grind half a cup of quinoa in a coffee or nut grinder. Make into a smooth paste with water. Add a small cupful of vegetable stock or yeast extract dissolved in hot water. Pour into a well-oiled saucepan and simmer until it thickens, stirring constantly. Served with a variety of vegetables this provides the high protein part of the meal very quickly and easily.

QUINOA SHORTBREAD

Grind quinoa flour, oats and sugar in a coffee grinder or food processor.

Combine margarine and sugar and mix well with other ingredients.

Press into a baking tin, flatten and smooth well. Bake in a low oven at 150°C (300°F) for 45-50 minutes or until brown on top.

Cut into sections and leave to cool before removing from the tin.

115g (4oz) soft margarine

60g (2oz) fairly traded fine brown sugar

30g (1oz) fine quinoa flour

30g (1oz) fine oatmeal or porridge oats

30g (4oz) fine wholemeal flour

QUINOA AND RAISIN PUDDING

Simmer quinoa seeds and the raisins in the water until seeds are crescent shaped. Fold in grated walnuts and serve hot or cold.

2tbsp quinoa seeds

3tbsp raisins

60-85g (2-3oz) walnuts

250ml (½ pint) of water

Beans and Pulses

These are the edible seeds from plants of the legume family and include beans, lentils and peas. They represent a rich source of protein as well as fibre, folate, iron, manganese, magnesium, phosphorous, potassium and most B vitamins in the vegan diet. Soya beans are the most nutritious of all the beans, although they do not do well in the UK at the present time. Some growers have attempted to breed varieties more suited to this climate but success has been limited. Broad, field, French and Hunter beans crop more reliably even in the home garden or allotment, and can be dried for storage. Dried beans need to be boiled before they can be eaten, although cooking times can be reduced by soaking them for a few hours beforehand which helps to soften them. Cooking times can also be greatly reduced by using a pressure cooker, taking only 15 minutes or so rather than the times shown below:

Aduki beans	30-45 minutes
Black eyed beans	1-1½ hours
Borlotti beans	1-1½ hours
Broad beans	1-1½ hours
Butter beans	1-1½ hours
Chickpeas	1½-2½ hours
Flageolet beans	1 ½ hours
Haricot beans	1-1½ hours
Kidney beans	1-1½ hours
Lentils	15-20 minutes
Mung beans	25-45 minutes
Pinto beans	1-1½ hours
Soya beans	2 hours

Note also that most beans can be sprouted (see page 40), although kidney beans must be boiled for at least 15 minutes before they can be consumed as they contain a substance that can cause severe food poisoning.

BEAN LAYER PIE

Boil and mash potatoes in a large pan. Chop onion and fry in oil for a few minutes.

Chop tomatoes, celery and pepper and add to onion. Cook together for another few minutes.

Place layers of well-cooked beans and vegetables in an ovenproof dish, add seasoning and herbs to taste. Cover with the mashed potato and bake in a moderate oven – 170°C (325°F) for 30 minutes or so.

A couple of cups of cooked beans (see page 180)
2 celery sticks
1 large onion
1 small green pepper
2-3 large potatoes
3 medium tomatoes
1tsp dried herbs
2tbsp oil
1tbsp chopped parsley

BEAN AND VEGETABLE CASSEROLE

2 cups cooked beans

Sliced or chopped
vegetables, e.g. leeks,
onions, carrots, swedes,
celery, parsnips,
cabbage, spinach,
tomatoes, sweetcorn,
cauliflower, mushrooms,
courgettes, turnips,
peppers, etc. Use
whatever is in season
or you happen to have
around

3-4 garlic cloves, chopped

A handful of uncooked
wholemeal pasta shells
or broken spaghetti

2-3 large potatoes

Herbs, e.g. bay, rosemary,
thyme, sage, etc.

Coriander seeds

Tomato paste

1tbsp of yeast extract

Splash of cider vinegar

Nearly fill a large casserole dish with a combination of beans, pasta, and raw, mixed vegetables (not the potatoes) and herbs.

Add yeast extract, tomato paste and cider vinegar to a pint of boiling water to make a stock.

Thinly slice the potatoes and arrange them to cover the other vegetables and beans, then pour the stock over the potatoes, ensuring that all are moistened by the stock.

Cover the dish and cook in a high oven for about an hour so that the vegetables will cook in their own juices and the stock.

Remove the cover and return to the oven for another 20-30 minutes until the potatoes on top of the casserole are brown and crisp.

Serve with steamed greens and bread to mop up the juices!

A BASIC LENTIL BURGER RECIPE

The secret of making good burgers is all about getting the right consistency –
not too sticky and gloopy, but not so dry that they crumble and fall apart.

Boil lentils until soft – make sure they don't burn!

Finely chop the onion and mushrooms and stir into the lentils along with the tomato purée, soy sauce and curry powder.

Remove from heat and add the oats, stirring in to make a mixture stiff enough to shape into burgers without them either falling apart or sticking. Fry in a pan until golden brown.

You want it served in a wholemeal roll with fried onions, chipped roast potatoes and organic tomato sauce? You got it!

The above quantities make quite a bit of burger mixture: you can either pig out (if you'll excuse the speciesist term!), invite some friends round to share them with or make a few burger shapes up for freezing – separate them with pieces of greaseproof paper to prevent them sticking together.

2 cups of fairly traded red lentils (you could also use other pulses such as split peas or mashed beans, etc.)

1 cup porridge oats

1 small onion

A few mushrooms

A good splash of soy sauce, or 1tbsp or so of yeast extract

1tsp of either curry powder or dried herbs, depending on the flavour you want

2tbsp tomato purée

Vegetable oil for frying

PARSNIP AND SPLIT PEA BAKE

1 large parsnip

110g (4oz) split peas
(dry weight)

1tbsp grated nuts or
sunflower seeds

1tbsp oil

Cook split peas and drain well. Boil parsnip until very soft.

Mash peas and parsnip together to a creamy mixture. Stir in seeds and oil.

Bake for 35 minutes at 175°C (340°F).

BLACK-EYED PEAS AND KALE

A tasty side dish – serves 4

1tbsp olive oil

2 garlic cloves, chopped

1 medium onion, chopped

A tin of tomatoes, chopped

Cooked black-eyed peas,
or use a tin

¼ - ½ tsp cayenne pepper

1 bay leaf

A good handful of fresh kale

Salt and pepper to taste

Sauté the onion and garlic in the oil over medium heat for several minutes. Add tomatoes and their juice, peas, cayenne and bay leaf and simmer, covered, for 15 minutes.

Add kale and simmer, uncovered, until kale is tender but still green, 5-10 minutes.

Season to taste with salt and freshly ground black pepper.

BROAD BEAN PATTIES

Shred the chard and chop the onion, mash the beans and combine together with the oats and curry powder until you have a stiff mixture.

Shape into patties and fry in a hot pan (or under a grill) until golden brown.

A couple of cups of broad beans (fresh or cooked)

A good handful (8-10 leaves) of chard or perpetual spinach

1 small onion

A handful of porridge oats for binding

A dash of curry powder

HOME-BAKED BEANS

Chop and fry onion and leek, grate apple and parsnip and stir into pan along with the tomatoes, cider vinegar, herbs and spices.

Place beans in a heatproof dish and pour the mixture over these, making sure they are well covered – add a little water if necessary.

Bake in a low oven for 45-60 minutes.

2 cups cooked haricot beans

1 apple

1 leek

1 onion

1 parsnip

1 tin of tomatoes

1 bay leaf

1tbsp cider vinegar

1tsp crushed coriander seed

1tsp ground cumin

1tsp mustard seeds

CHAPTER 7

Towards a Tree Based Culture

"I picture village communities of the future in valleys protected by trees on the high ground. They would have fruit and nut orchards, live free from disease and enjoy leisure, liberty and justice for all living with a sense of oneness with the earth and all living things. The accomplishment of this will assure, not only the perpetuation of the forests through intelligent use, but also the regeneration of the very spirit of mankind."

Richard St Barbe Baker, the 'Man of the Trees'

In permaculture design, Zone 4 is usually considered to be semi-managed, semi-wild land that is used for pasture, or for coppicing, timber production and reforestation. The management and design strategies employed here tend to be more broad scale and longer term in scope, and are more focused on longer term regeneration of the land. In this book I will use the concept of Zone 4 to look at the possibilities of a future in which the production of our food, energy and other important materials is derived from perennial plants such as trees rather than from unsustainable annuals and animal products.

Fields or Forests?

Permaculture utilises the 80:20 principle. This means that we aim to put in all the hard work at the beginning of a project, ideally devoting 80% of our efforts to designing and setting up robust and durable systems, and 20% into harvesting yields and providing a little maintenance once those systems are well established. The current agricultural situation directly reverses this equation – think of the effort expended in the cultivation of annually grown monoculture cereal crops – all that yearly ploughing, sowing and weeding of vast prairie-like fields; all those chemical additives that need to be put on the land to counter fertility lost to erosion; all those pesticides that have to be manufactured, transported and sprayed on a regular basis...

On the other hand, the regenerative productive systems that will characterise low carbon, human-scale and compassionate communities make far more use of permanent crops such as the perennial grains mentioned in the last chapter, but also trees that yield edible nuts, fruits, beans and leaf protein that will become our staples of the future, as well as medicines, building materials, fuels and fibres. Choosing, planning and planting suitable edible and useful trees is a considerable investment of time and energy, and it may often be several years before they begin to yield. However, once established, tree crops require relatively little attention apart from picking their fruit and nuts, or being pruned every few years. Indeed, for the vastly greater part of the million or so years that humans have walked the earth, tree crops and other vegetation have been amongst our primary sources of sustenance. Of course, population levels are now far higher than when our hunter-gatherer ancestors subsisted on a diet consisting largely of fruit, seeds, roots, leaves, fish and the occasional wild animal. Nonetheless, with careful research and selection of species, as well as the visionary implementation of long term re-afforestation projects, trees can not only meet virtually all our material needs but have the potential to help reverse the damage wrought by 10,000 years of plough based agriculture, accelerated by the last 200 years or so of oil based destructoculture.

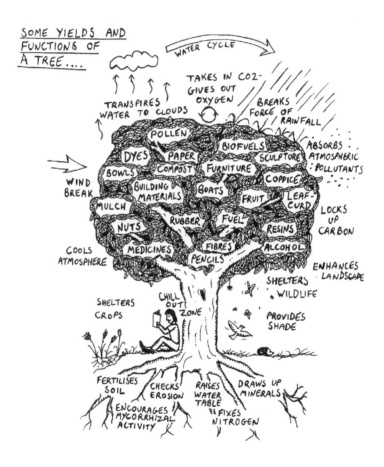

Trees provide many yields and products that are useful to peoplekind,
as well as regulating energy transactions on a planetary scale.

On both local and global scales, the benefits of trees and forests on all life processes are innumerable as they modify and transform the elemental forces of sunlight, wind, soil and rainfall. The immense and inconceivably complex networks of their root systems and the microorganisms and fungi they interact with catch and cycle nutrients, stabilise and build fertile soils, reduce erosion and counter the spread of deserts. Transpiration through the immeasurably vast collective leaf surface area of the forest canopy pumps out oxygen and cleanses the air, powers the world's water cycles and regulates entire climatic systems. Trees also absorb carbon dioxide from the atmosphere and lock carbon into their cell tissues, thus they could play a major role in halting and reversing the threat of climate change. The amounts of land required for such a task would of course be huge (estimates suggest that around 200 million hectares, or 500 million acres, of reafforested land would make a 'significant difference to global warming'),[31] but not beyond the efforts of a concerted mobilisation of human energy and ingenuity, particularly if we are able to make the evolutionary shifts that would enable us to transcend our old addictions to unsustainable lifestyles.

The Coming Age of the Tree

We can't know what a future tree based culture will look like any more than our ancestors would have been able to envisage the world after the advent of the plough or the internal combustion engine. But Kathleen Jannaway's visionary publication *Abundant Living in the Coming Age of the Tree* perhaps offers some glimpses of how things could be:

> "Trees of carefully selected species can be grown in most habitable areas of the world to meet human needs locally in a sustainable manner. Apart from the enormous saving of the fuel, labour and materials that now transport goods backwards and forwards across the world, such local resources will facilitate the functioning of self-reliant village communities. Such communities will be large enough to provide sufficient reserves of human skills and enlightenment for the whole to function smoothly, and small enough for each individual member to feel that he or she has an essential part to play in the whole, that her or his contribution is valuable and valued. Face to face democracy will function, with decisions affecting the village community reached by consensus.

> "Food will be produced locally in small fields protected by hedges. Within each

village, each garden will have its trees, especially fruit and nut bearing trees. Extensive forest will serve groups of villages. They will be large enough for their function as maintainers of environmental health not to be damaged by their use for supplies of wood. Trees will be sensitively felled in a sustainable yield system, no clear felling. Much of the wood will go to the village to be made, by wise and joyful craftsmanship, into articles that will last. The rest will be used in the forest industries. Waste wood will be used as fuel for the industries and for any heating and lighting in the villages that cannot be provided by such means as solar panels and sensitively sited wind or water mills.

"As nearly all food will be produced locally and eaten fresh, the enormous amounts of energy and resources now used for processing, packaging and transport will be saved. Similar economy will be achieved by goods being made by local craftsmen and in local industries. Nourished by health giving foods, enjoying the security of being members of a mutually caring group, with a proper balance of worthwhile labour and creative leisure, people will be free of many of the frustrations and fears that, in our present culture, erupt into ill health, crime and violence. A new world order will develop through the recognition of the need for unity in diversity. It will evolve according to the same principles as inspire the villages: that physical needs must be met in an environmentally sustainable manner, that spiritual growth must be nurtured by freedom, mutual respect and service, and opportunities for creative expression.

"A vision such as that suggested above is so at variance with present values and practices and with dominating social, religious and political institutions that it may be regarded as the idle fancy of impractical dreamers. Yet it accords with much of the ethos of tribal societies that have flourished for many generations and with the teachings of Buddha, Jesus, Gandhi, Lao-Tse and many others. As it becomes ever more obvious that the 'practical' men are leading humanity to extinction at an ever increasing pace, the 'impractical' visions will come to be recognised as viable and desirable alternatives."

Obviously such a world would be radically different from anything so far seen in human history, and would mean totally rethinking our diets, resource base, economic values and how we use land. Indeed our landscape would be completely transformed from that with which we are familiar today, with open fields of grains and pasture replaced by woodlands, forests and orchards intermittently broken up by clearings for annual crop production and human settlements such as villages, towns and small cities. Far fetched? Perhaps, but as the old proverb reminds us, 'without vision the people perish...'

The Renaissance of Wood

The march of industrialisation and the mechanisation of woodland management, combined with greatly increased importation of timber products from the Far East, has caused a huge decline in the size and quality of British woodland since the middle of the 20th century. But the tide is turning. Modern day stewards of the forest such as Ben Law, Mike Abbott and Ele and Anthony Waters are part of a new generation who are actively reviving traditional crafts and skills such as coppicing, charcoal burning and green woodworking, proving that these can be economically viable ways of creating livelihood in the new millennium. At the same time 'low impact', off-the-grid communities such as Stewards Wood in south Devon are demonstrating how people and the forest can co-exist harmoniously. There are even signs that mainstream organisations such as the Forestry Commission, previously often seen as the 'villains of the piece', are becoming more enlightened in their attitudes as policies aimed at restoring deciduous tree cover begin to replace those that have seen our forests degraded into mono-cropped deserts of Sitka spruce over the last 100 years or so.

Mighty oaks from tiny acorns grow, and we can all make a contribution to the coming age of wood in the here and now – in fact probably the easiest way to establish a woodland is simply to put a fence around some land and leave it to its own devices. In just a few years the process of succession will return it to a natural forest as ground cover weeds give way to brambles and gorse, then pioneer trees such as birch and ash, followed by 'climax' species including oak, beech and chestnut. However, many of us may want to speed up this process, or have more control over the species that we wish to grow, in which case we will have to plant the desired trees ourselves.

Community Woodlands

New woodlands have been created by community groups such as the Pentiddy Woodland Co-operative. In 2001 the group purchased 3.32ha (8.2 acres) of low-grade agricultural land on the edge of Bodmin Moor that was in danger of being sold for housing development. Over the next two years this was planted up with over 6,500 trees, transforming an expanse of poor quality grazing land into a vibrant and abundant forest, freely open to the public for walking, picnicking, learning and relaxing. Remarkably, this was achieved with absolutely no capital by making creative use of the range of grants available for improving biodiversity and public access to woodlands, setting up a tree sponsorship scheme supported by the local community, and by nurturing a co-operative relationship with the local council in order to raise the funds to buy the land and pay for tree stock. Despite the hard work involved, project director Ele Waters sees the project as a potential inspiration for others:

> "When you hear of the mass destruction of the world's woodland environment at a rate of 15 million hectares per year, to have created a 3.32 hectare area of woodland in two years seems somewhat pathetic, but when you remember that ours is just one project of one community of one county of one country on this wonderful globe, it helps to put things into perspective.

> "One thing that has been made very clear to us through this experience is that money, time and people do not need to be seen as limiting factors. All of this was achieved without a penny of capital, very few really committed individuals, and less than two years from the idea to the launch.

> "In the words of a great song by the group Seize the Day, I'm sure we'd all love to see more people, "taking back our fields and our oceans and the clean air, so we can breath again". It's not impossible. The land, money and people power is available, and it's great to hear that more and more communities are taking up the challenge."

Orchards

Many schools, local authorities, parish councils and community groups are creating new community orchards in previously underutilised urban spaces. Butterfield Green in Stoke Newington, north east London, consists of 34 half-standard fruit trees including apples, cherries, hazelnuts, medlars, pears, peaches, plums and quinces, planted in an area of public open space between a main road and park during the winter of 2007. It is managed and maintained by The Shakespeare Residents Association in partnership with Hackney Council and Growing Communities, a local social enterprise project dedicated to growing food in urban areas. There have been tree and orchard care events including Apple Days, planting, mulching, pruning and grafting demonstrations, school events and bird and bat watching. Each tree has been adopted by a local resident who assumes responsibility for its watering and aftercare, and fruit harvests are free to local people. Project coordinator Maggie Chattaway explains the social benefits:

> "The orchard is proving popular locally and has had a bringing together effect on the local community, involving all sorts of people who have never been involved in growing things before."

Older orchards that have been neglected for the last few decades are also enjoying a renaissance as more and more people begin to appreciate the value and importance of re-localising our food links, starting to think in terms of 'food yards' instead of 'food miles'. St Laurence Orchard in Southend-on-Sea is one of many throughout the land currently being restored and recognised as an invaluable community asset, in this case by Growing Together, a charity supporting people with mental health needs through horticulture. Project Manager Ron Bates spoke about the beneficial connections that orchards can make between people and nature:

> "It's an amazing environment. It's an ecology. We've got the first indicators such as these holes in the old trees that are used by woodpeckers and later by starlings, robins, all sorts of birds. For the first time this year I heard whitethroats here. So nature is always changing, it's an on-going process. And we come and help to manage it – giving people skills in pruning the older trees, looking at their shape and space. Joining in with the harvesting... Offering the experience of just a place that is very tranquil. It is literally a breathing space, people enjoy coming here and working here. The locals keep an eye on it, and there are apple days, invitations to blossom days, bug days. People and nature maintain and use this space, giving it life and meaning."

While we need to protect and promote our orchards, it is vital that they should not be seen as static museum pieces. Nor should they become part of the ever-burgeoning 'Heritage Industry', to be 'experienced' like just another theme park attraction. Rather we need to reinstate them as living, evolving ecosystems, inevitably changing and adapting to meet the needs of an ever-shifting future, with economic as well as cultural and environmental importance. There are still many commercial orchards in Essex, where they enjoy a relatively warm and dry climate. Assisted by apprentice grower and permaculturist Ben Lambert, Andrew Tann continues to make a good living growing over 150 varieties of apples in his 7ha (15 acre) orchard near Colchester.[32] Most of these are sold directly by mail order, with different mixes of apple varieties available from August to January. Nottingham based permaculture designer and proprietor of Cool Temperate Tree Nursery,[33] Phil Corbett, has been experimenting with the idea of 'coppice orchards', using 'own rootstock' trees to combine the fruiting yields of traditional orchards with the timber production of conventional woodland management systems. Martin Crawford, founder of the Agroforestry Research Trust in Dartington, south Devon, reminds us of the need for longer term planning:

> "In the face of climate change not all varieties of apples will continue to thrive well in their indigenous homelands. They may well be good varieties and some will adapt to changing conditions better than others, but gradually their optimum locations are moving northwards as climate zones shift. So Devon apples will soon be of more value in Wales, whilst apples from north-west France will be valuable in Devon."

Forest Gardening

Despite the name, which perhaps implies that they require large amounts of space, forest gardens can be a way of incorporating edible and useful trees and bushes into our home gardens, even in an urban situation. Indeed even those with no gardens at all can adapt the basic principles of forest gardening – I have seen them on allotments and in communal open spaces on inner city housing estates, and even mini-forest gardens planted in containers and tubs on tower block balconies!

The forest gardening concept was pioneered in the UK during the 1970s by Robert Hart, who examined the interactions and relationships that take place between plants in natural systems. In particular he looked at deciduous woodland, the climax ecosystem of a cool temperate region such as the British Isles, as well as the abundant food producing 'home gardens' of Kerala in southern India. He observed that unlike many cultivated gardens, nature does not neatly compartmentalise her landscapes with ornamentals growing in one place, vegetables in another and trees in yet a third location. In the woodland, several plants such as standard and half standard sized trees, shrubs, climbers and ground cover occupy the same area of space, each 'stacked' to find its own requirements within its particular 'level' in the system. Replicating the layers of the wild plants of the woodland on a miniature scale with fruits, herbs, vegetables and other plants that are useful to peoplekind, Robert developed an existing small orchard of apples and pears into an edible landscape consisting of seven dimensions:

1) A 'canopy' layer consisting of the original mature fruit trees
2) A 'low-tree' layer of smaller nut and fruit trees on dwarfing rootstocks
3) A 'shrub layer' of fruit bushes such as currants and berries
4) An 'herbaceous layer' of perennial vegetables and herbs
5) A 'ground cover' layer of edible plants that spread horizontally
6) A 'rhizosphere' or 'underground' dimension of plants grown for their roots and tubers as well as subterranean fungi that yield via their fruiting bodies and move nutrients between plants via mycorrhizal associations
7) A vertical 'layer' of vines and climbers

The seven layers of the forest garden.

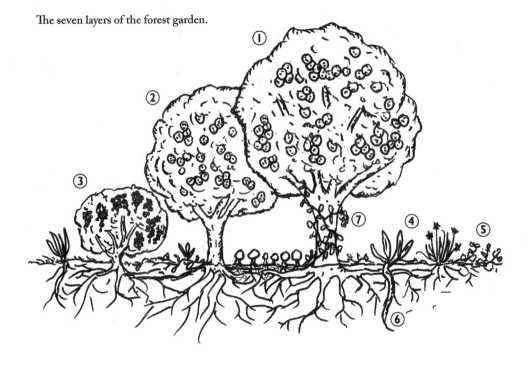

Reflecting on the productivity of the low maintenance, self-fertilising system that he had created, Robert wrote that:

"Forest gardening offers the potential for all gardeners to grow an important element of their health-creating food; it combines positive gardening and positive health... The wealth, abundance and diversity of the forest garden provides for all human needs – physical needs through foods, materials and exercise, as well as medicines and spiritual needs through beauty and the connection with the whole."

I had the good fortune to visit Robert's place in Shropshire a few years before his death in 2000. Stepping into the forest garden felt like entering another world. All around was lushness and abundance, a sharp contrast to the dust bowl aridity of the surrounding prairie farmed fields and farmlands. At first the sheer profusion of growth was bewildering, like entering a wild wood. We're not used to productive landscapes appearing so disorderly. But it didn't take long for the true harmony of nature's systems to reveal themselves, and for the realisation to dawn that in fact it is the agri-buisness monocultures, with their heavy machinery, genetic manipulation, erosion, high water inputs, pesticides and fertilisers that are in a total state of maintained chaos. Whereas hectares of land may produce bushel after bushel of but one crop, genetically degraded and totally vulnerable to ever more virulent strains of pest and disease without the dubious protection of massive chemical inputs, a garden of just 0.1ha (one eighth of an acre) such as Robert's can output a tremendous variety of yields.

Inspired by the example of Robert, and more recently the work of Martin Crawford of the Agroforestry Research Trust and others who have learned lessons from both Robert's successes as well as those things that did not work so well, forest gardening has now become an international movement. Literally thousands have been created in community spaces, private gardens and school grounds both in the UK and around the world:

"Obviously, few of us are in a position to restore the forests. But tens of millions of us have gardens, or access to open spaces such as industrial wastelands, where trees can be planted and if full advantage can be taken of the potentialities that are available even in heavily built up areas, new 'city forests' can arise..."

Robert A. de J. Hart

Creating a Forest Garden

Having an understanding of a few basic ecological and design principles enables us to work through the process of combining fruit trees and bushes and other (mainly) perennial species in order to create our own highly productive edible landscapes...

Aims and Objectives – What Do You Want?

What are the desired outcomes from your forest garden project? Deciding these at the outset will be very helpful in working out what to plant and the kind of management regime you might decide to adopt. Some possible outputs and products might include:

- Edible yields, including fruit (apples, cherries, currants, gooseberries, grapes, medlars, pears, plums, raspberries, etc.), vegetables (Good King Henry, hops, horseradish, Jerusalem artichokes, perennial onions, Turkish rocket, etc.), herbs and salads (lemon balm, lovage, ramsons, sorrel, young tree leaves, etc.), nuts and seeds (almonds, hazels, sweet chestnut, etc.), mushrooms and fungi (lion's mane, oyster, shitake, etc.), beverages (birch sap wine, cider, elderflower cordial, nettle beer, etc.).
- Non-edible yields, including medicinal plants (balms, eucalyptus, periwinkle, St Johns Wort, woundwort, etc.), fibres (nettles, New Zealand flax, etc.), craft and basketry materials, poles and canes (bamboo, coppiced hazel, willow charcoal, etc.), building materials, firewood and so on.
- Other yields, including educational, income stream/livelihood, research data, wildlife habitat, parties and celebrations, relaxation, aesthetic and spiritual yields, the list is endless...

What Have You Got?

Map the existing site and collect information. Finding out as much as possible about your site will give you a clear picture of its limitations and potential resources before you start to think about what will and will not work. Whether your site is shady or sheltered, has a northerly or southerly aspect, is prone to frosts or flooding, its prevailing winds etc. will have a major bearing on what trees and shrubs will be suitable or likely to thrive, (see 'Survey Stage' check list on page 55).

Designing the Boundaries

If starting from scratch on exposed land (for example an area of pasture or open field that was previously used for cereal growing), your first priority will be to establish some form of shelter from wind and frosts. Creating a hedgerow shelterbelt of hardy trees and shrubs around your site will provide protection for higher value specimens such as fruit or nut trees whose blossom may be susceptible to damage by late frosts and cold winds that can seriously affect yields. The height of the hedge should be at least one eighth of the size of the area to be protected and needs to be dense in composition in order to provide full protection. Hedging trees and shrubs should be planted at least a year or so before more delicate species go in in order to allow time to get established. Choose multifunctional species that provide wildlife benefits, edible crops or other yields, e.g. crab apple, field maple, hawthorn, hazel, *Rosa rugosa*, as well as nitrogen fixers such as alder, broom, elaeagnus, etc.

Potential Resources and Obtaining Stock

Research species that fulfil your criteria (i.e. will do well and are suitable and appropriate to your site conditions, including nitrogen fixers and less usual specimens); some sources of information are provided in the appendix. Create a 'wish list' of plants, although this may well need to be edited down! Investigate potential suppliers – support independent and specialist local nurseries where possible. However, buying plants can be expensive so think about other ways you might be able to beg, borrow or steal stock – where could you obtain seeds, cuttings, grafts or other plants cheaply or for free? Avoid false economy however; sometimes 'bargains' that end up being sold off cheaply by commercial garden centres or 'budget stores' can be of poor quality. Draw up a timescale for the implementation of your project; this will usually be over a period of a few years rather than trying to achieve all of your aims at once.

Designing the Canopy/Layout of Larger Trees

Top fruit (e.g. apples, pears, gages and plums) and nut 'canopy' trees will form the backbone of your forest garden, and are the single most important part of the design. These will determine the positioning of all other elements; therefore particular care should be given when considering their location. Most fruit trees are grafted onto rootstocks that will control their height and cropping potential. Take into account the tree's predicted mature size, including canopy spread – it can be hard to visualise just how much space an apple tree grafted onto an M25 rootstock will take up in 10 years' time when putting a two foot tall sapling

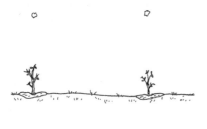

Year one

Year three

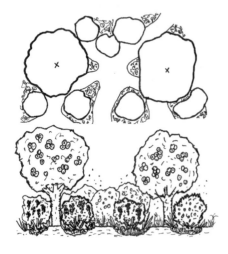

Year five

into the ground! Also bear in mind their long term needs for moisture, soil fertility and light. It can be tempting to try and fit in too many trees, particularly when there seems to be so much empty ground between them at this stage, but in the long run this will result in overcrowding and nutrient deficient trees competing for sunlight, water and space. In general aim to put larger trees at the north of the site and smaller ones towards the south and ensure that newly planted trees are well mulched for the first few years while they are becoming established.

Fitting in the Shrubs and Bushes

Smaller trees such as apples and pears on dwarfing rootstocks as well as shrubs and fruit bushes including black, white and red currants, gooseberries, Worcester-berries, etc. can be fitted into the spaces between the canopy trees. A planting plan for these can be created at the same time during the design process, or can be decided later on. Similarly you may wish to plant the shrub layer at the same time as the canopy specimens, or it might make more sense (and be more financially viable!) to wait a year or two. Be sure to incorporate some nitrogen fixing shrubs such as elaeagnus, sea buckthorn or Siberian pea tree into the shrub layer in order to help build and maintain soil fertility, and to encourage the presence of mycorrhizal fungi by adding inoculant spawn (these can be obtained in powder form) to any planting holes.

Designing the Ground Layer

Once the placement of the main canopy trees and shrubs has been decided, it is time to start thinking about the design of the understorey. In addition to providing leafy salad and vegetable crops such as Turkish rocket, sweet cicely, lovage and perennial onions, one of the main functions of the lower levels of the forest garden is to create a living mulch with spreading plants such as wild garlic, Nepalese raspberry and wild strawberries. These keep the ground covered for as much of the year as possible, and prevent less desirable invasive species such as bramble, nettles and grasses from taking over. They also maintain soil moisture and prevent compaction through exposure to drying sunlight, heavy rain, etc. Nitrogen fixers like clovers, trefoil and vetches and deep rooted herbaceous plants such as comfrey and sorrel accumulate minerals and nutrients in their leaves that help to build fertility in the garden. Aromatic plants such as feverfew, lemon balm, mint and tansy are said to promote health in the garden due to the anti-fungal properties of the essential oils they exude during the growing season. The design of the ground cover and herbaceous layers of your forest will determine whether it is going to be a high or low maintenance endeavour, depending on its complexity. Therefore I would suggest that if you don't have a lot of time it's probably not a good idea to plant more than a few species during initial establishment phase, instead adding more as the system evolves in later years.

To Bee or Not to Bee?

An eighth possible 'layer' to consider in the forest garden system is the animal component. Many insects, birds, amphibians and mammals will of course arrive in this thriving ecosystem of their own accord. If you have the opportunity you may also want to consider bringing in bees to improve pollination rates. As well as performing a number of useful functions within the forest garden ecology, you will also be providing these currently threatened species with a source of food and a relatively safe habitat – at present bees are disappearing due to the use of neonicotinoid pesticides and other industrialised agricultural practices. Contrary to commercial honey production, natural beekeeping is about working with, rather than suppressing and manipulating, the bees intrinsic behaviours; "Giving to the bees" as opposed to "taking from the bees". The Natural Beekeeping Trust[34] encourages "bee guardianship" - keeping bees for the bees' sake rather than for their honey - with an apicentric approach guided by the wisdom of the bees themselves. To me this fits well with both veganic and permacultural principles.

Maintenance and Access

Access for maintenance and harvesting of produce is important, so do not forget to design in paths that are wide enough to comfortably accommodate both yourself as well as wheelbarrows and any other equipment you may need to get in and out. There is a myth that forest gardening is a 'no work' system. I'm afraid this isn't really true, although it is certainly less, and maybe even more enjoyable, work than much of what conventional food production entails. Certainly a forest garden is tolerant of periods of neglect that would be disastrous in an annual vegetable garden. Once established, the chief tasks on the forest gardener's maintenance schedule are harvesting produce, some annual pruning, plus what Robert Hart preferred to describe as a little occasional 'editing' of any vigorous plants that are getting out of hand.

Fruits of the Forest Garden

Apples

Britain's temperate climate means that we produce some of the best tasting apples in the world. Ranging from the aromatic rich complexity of Cox's Orange Pippin to the dry yet sweet/sharp nutty balance of Egremont Russett, these are living celebrations of local distinctiveness and symbolise deep connections with our food-growing past. The national fruit collection at Brogdale[35] near Faversham in Kent includes specimens of some 2,200 apple varieties that have been grown in this country, and lists hundreds more – Beauty Of Bath, Braintree Seedling, Chelmsford Wonder, Crawley Reinette, Kentish Fillbasket, Merton Knave, Norfolk Biffen and Vicar of Beighton among them.

Today we live in an age where we are told that we have more choice than our forebears could ever have imagined. Yet supermarket demands for uniformity, the ability to store and travel well, and freedom from blemishes have ensured that only some five or six apple varieties can now be found stacked on their shelves. Golden Delicious and Granny Smiths, textured like cotton wool and with even less flavour, are air freighted around the planet to be sold individually packaged in malls and motorway service stations, but what now has happened to the Ball's Bittersweet, Puckrup Pippin, the Red Ribbed Greening, the Scarlett Pearmain or Slack-ma-Girdle? Growing our own gives us the opportunity to keep these old local varieties alive.

APPLE AND PARSNIP SOUP

2 cooking apples
1 large onion
2-3 large parsnips
1tsp thyme
Vegetable stock
A splash of vegetable oil

Chop the onion and parsnips and gently sauté for a few minutes with the thyme in a heavy-bottomed saucepan. Add vegetable stock and a pint or so of boiling water.

Peel and core apples, chop and add to the boiling water. Simmer for 15-20 minutes until all ingredients are soft.

Blend in a liquidiser until smooth.

APPLE CASSEROLE

2 large cooking apples
2 large celery stalks
1 large parsnip
4-5 tomatoes
1tbsp oil
150ml (¼ pint) stock
1tsp yeast extract
A handful of sunflower
    seeds

Cut apples and parsnip into cubes, slice celery and halve tomatoes. Sauté tomatoes in oil.

Put in layers in a casserole dish, sprinkling with sunflower seeds.

Dissolve yeast extract in stock, and pour over vegetables, adding a little more water if necessary to make sure the vegetables are covered.

Cover with a tight fitting lid. Cook in a slow oven for 45-60 minutes.

SAVOURY APPLE MOULD

Sauté tomatoes in oil until soft. Chop apples and stew in stock until soft.

Mash tomatoes and apples together with soy sauce. Bring to boil then simmer gently while tapping in the agar. Simmer for a minute or so longer.

Chop nuts and add to the mixture. Pour into an oiled basin and place in fridge or a cool place to set for at least an hour.

Turn out and garnish with parsley and pieces of tomato or red pepper. Serve with salad and potatoes.

2-3 large cooking apples

1 cup nuts, e.g. hazels, walnuts, almonds, etc.

1 tin of tomatoes

300ml (½ pint) of stock

1tbsp oil

A splash of shoyu soy sauce

2tsp (heaped) agar

APPLE AND POTATO PIE

Prepare equal quantities of raw potatoes, apples and onions, all peeled and sliced, the apples sliced less thinly

Oil a pie dish and cover with a layer of sliced potato, sprinkle with celery salt and cover with a layer of sliced onion. Then add a layer of apples. Repeat until dish is full, finishing with potato.

Add 300ml (½ pint) of vegetable stock and cover with lid or greaseproof paper. Cook in a medium heat oven for 30 minutes or so, then remove cover and cook in a hot oven for a further 15-20 minutes.

2 cooking apples

2 large onions

2 large potatoes

300ml (½ pint) vegetable stock (page 126)

Celery salt

APPLE, PEAR AND QUINCE TART

For the pastry:

2-3 cups of wholemeal flour

2-3 cups of soya flour

½ cup seeds, e.g. linseed, pumpkin, sunflower, etc.

½ cup water with half cup of vegetable oil

Filling:

3-4 large cooking apples, or any other apples you have around. Windfalls that are a bit damaged are fine.

3-4 large pears

2-3 quinces

1 handful of dried fruit, e.g. raisins

1tbsp (or to taste) of unrefined sugar

Place all flour and seeds in a mixing bowl, and slowly stir in the water and oil mixture with a fork until firm pastry dough is formed.

Divide pastry in half, and line a pie dish with one half. Place in a medium heat oven for 10 minutes or so until partly baked.

Meanwhile peel and core the fruit, discarding any damaged parts. Chop up into small pieces and place in a pan, covered with water to prevent oxidisation (quince in particular tends to go brown in air very quickly).

Drain off the water so that there is only a very small amount left at the bottom of the pan, add the sugar and dried fruit and simmer gently until the fruit is beginning to soften and break down. Remove from heat and spoon into the pie case.

Roll out the remaining pastry, and cut into thin strips. These are then laid across the top of the fruit to form a 'lattice'.

Return to oven and bake for a further 20-30 minutes until the pastry is cooked and the fruit is browning on top.

Any left over pastry can be used to make a few jam tarts.

SPICY APPLE AND FIG CRUMBLE

Simmer all ingredients in wine at a low temperature until soft.

Place in an ovenproof dish and cover with crumble topping. Bake in a medium oven for 40-45 minutes.

5-6 cooking apples

1 cup chopped dried Fairtrade figs

A handful of raisins

Mixed spice

2tbsp unrefined fairly traded sugar

A generous splash of white wine

Crumble topping (page 168)

INSTANT APPLE SAUCE

Bring to boil and simmer until thickened.

300ml (½ pint) apple juice

2tsp arrowroot

APPLE AND FRUIT OAT BISCUITS

115g (4oz) porridge oats

85g (3oz) wholemeal flour

1 cup currants

1tsp (levelled) baking powder

170g (6oz) grated apple

A little oil

A little water

A little sea salt

Mix dry ingredients together well. Add apple, oil and water and mix to a stiff consistency.

Scatter spoonfuls on to an oiled baking tray, spread out and flatten them out evenly. Bake in a medium oven for 35 minutes or so until evenly browned.

Thanks to the late Kathleen Jannaway

AMANDA'S EASY WINDFALL APPLE AND GINGER JAM

Approx 1.8kg (4lb) windfall apples

Approx 1.3kg (3lb) organic vegan sugar

2tsp ground ginger

Lemon juice

Collect windfall apples. Peel, core and chop them into a preserving pan of cold water, adding a splash of lemon juice. They may go brown, but this doesn't matter once they are cooked.

Drain, then cook with a little water in the pan until they started to go 'mushy'. Add organic vegan sugar and ground ginger, and boil for about 15 minutes. Skim off the scum with a large, flat slotted spoon.

This recipe produced about 8 jars.

Thanks to Amanda Baker

Cider

Fermenting into alcohol is what apples do – unlike wine and beer, they don't even require the addition of sugars or yeasts – those that occur naturally in and on the fruit being quite sufficient to get them brewing once fallen from the tree. It's best to use a mixture of apple varieties for cider making, as well as any damaged or bruised apples that can't be stored. The fruit should be well washed, then roughly chopped and crushed into a pulp. For small amounts you can do this in a food processor, or else by using a bucket with a special fruit pulping drill attachment. The apple juice should then be extracted from the pulp using a fruit press, and poured straight away into sterile demijohns. Fit an airlock to exclude unwanted microorganisms. Fermentation will begin within a few days from the wild yeast on the apples, and should take a couple of weeks. Siphon the cider from its lees (the sediment that collects at the bottom of the demijohn), and continue to ferment for another couple of weeks. When fermentation is finally finished siphon into sealed sterile bottles and store in a cool dark place for a few weeks to mature. Cider pressed in October should be ready for drinking by the Winter Solstice season, and should keep for a year or two.

Pears

Pear trees closely resemble apple trees, although they have shinier leaves and a more upright growth habit. Trees tend to be very vigorous on their own roots, and are usually too large to be pruned, maintained or harvested easily. For this reason they are generally grafted onto quince rootstocks, which produce smaller compact trees that are easier to look after. Pears are much more fragile than apples, and do not tend to store as well. They also tend to be eaten raw more often than they are cooked. Varieties include Anjou, Comice, Conference, and Forelle.

PEAR CAKE

100g (3½oz) wholemeal
organic flour

1 large dessert pear

50g (1½oz) soft brown
sugar

4tbsp sunflower oil

2tbsp golden syrup

1tsp baking powder

½tsp bicarbonate of soda

Peel and grate pear, then combine with the flour, sugar,
bicarbonate of soda and baking powder.

Add the oil and golden syrup and beat all the
ingredients together with a small amount of water if
necessary to keep the mixture moist but not too wet
and sticky.

Put mixture in a cake tin and bake at 190°C (375°F) for
25-30 minutes until cooked through and brown on top.

SPICED PEARS

1kg (2lb) firm pears

Boiling water to cover

500ml (¾ pint) cider vinegar

250ml (½ pint) water

400g (1lb) sugar

Cinnamon

10 whole cloves

Piece of root ginger

Peel and cut up pears, removing the cores. Cover with
boiling water in a pan and simmer gently until nearly
tender then drain.

Boil the remaining ingredients together for 5 minutes.

Pack pears tightly into hot sterile jars, cover with boiling
syrup and seal.

QUINCE JELLY

1.8kg (4lb) fully ripe quinces
3.4 litres (6 pints) water
Sugar

Wash and finely chop quinces. Simmer for about an hour with 2.2 litres (4 pints) of water.

Strain through a jelly bag when tender, and put the extract to one side.

N.B. Do not squeeze the cooked quinces or you will get cloudy jelly, simply allow the juice to drip through the jelly bag for a few hours, overnight if necessary.

Return the pulp to the pan and simmer with the remaining 1.2 litres (2 pints) of water for a further 30 minutes. Strain again.

Combine the extracts and measure. Add 450g (1lb) sugar to each 550ml (1 pint) of extract.

Return extract to pan and bring to boiling point. Boil rapidly until setting point is reached. Skim off any scum, and pour into heat-sterilised jars.

Quince

Quinces have distinctive golden yellow skin and alluring fragrance although the flesh is astringent and sour when raw. When cooked however, quince is a delicious and distinctive addition to many dishes, both sweet and savoury, and can also be made into a very tasty jelly due to its high levels of pectin. Quinces are frequently used as a rootstock for grafting pears, to which they are closely related.

Plums

Plums have juicy, acidic flesh covered by a smooth skin, usually covered with a dusty white wax bloom that helps to prevent damage to the fruit from rainfall. There are many varieties of plums with a huge range of flavours, shapes, colours and sizes, usually grown on rootstocks such as St Juien A and the newer Pixy, which produces a smaller tree with a mature height of only 3-4.5m (10-15ft). Trees can also be grown on wild plum or Myrobalan rootstocks, although these tend to be too large and vigorous for an ordinary garden. Dessert plums are sweeter, and can be eaten raw on their own. They include varieties such as Victoria, Purple Pershore, Laxton and Opal. Culinary plums such as Czar and gages are rather more tart in flavour and are better suited for cooking in pies and cakes, although the trees tend to have greater tolerance of poor growing conditions. Damsons and bullaces are wilder relatives of the plum, and produce tart, spicy fruits that are mainly used for cooking.

DRIED PLUMS

450g (1lb) firm sugar plums or plums (other stone fruit works well too but you will have to adjust times for larger fruit like peaches or pears)

½ cup orange juice or apple juice

½ cup water

Halve the fruit and remove stones. I found that with sugarplums, the best place to cut them in half was along the seam which made the stone easier to remove.

Combine fruit juice and water in a container. Place the fruit overnight in this mixture tossing to coat. I actually left these for more than a day, baking them the next evening.

Arrange plums on a wire metal cake cooling rack and place overnight in a very low temperature oven. The longer they are left the drier they will be; 10 hours is a good time to produce prunes that are chewy but moist.

N.B. Firm fruit is better to dry than softer, over-ripe fruit.

PLUM PUDDING

Traditionally eaten at Yuletide, plum pudding should be prepared at least several weeks ahead in order for the wonderful rich flavours to fully develop and mature. In fact I usually make two of these every other October or November time, with one to be eaten the following year

Combine all ingredients in a large mixing bowl, with enough orange juice to ensure that the mixture is firm and moist but not too wet and sticky. Cover with a tea towel and leave to stand overnight.

The following day add a little more moisture if necessary – more juice or spirits, and pack tightly into a well greased pudding basin.

Cover with greaseproof paper and steam for 8 hours (or 2 hours in a pressure cooker). A further good steaming of around 2 hours (30 minutes in a pressure cooker) on the day will bring out the flavours still more.

For a final touch, douse with a good splash of brandy and set light to it immediately before serving!

1 cup chopped pitted prunes (page 212)

1 cup currants

1 cup raisins

1 cup sultanas

1 cup groundnuts, e.g. hazels, walnuts, almonds

3 cups wholemeal fresh breadcrumbs

1 cup porridge oats

300ml (½ pint) orange juice

230g (8oz) fairly traded Demerara sugar

1 cup vegetable suet

2tsp mixed spice

A good splash of brandy

A good splash of sherry

Cherries

Due to their size and vigour, growing varieties of cherry tree suitable for the smaller garden has been impractical until relatively recently. In recent years, however, dwarfing Colt and Inmil rootstocks have been introduced, along with self-fertile sweet varieties such as Stella and Sunburst. These developments mean that highly productive yet compact trees can now be maintained at 4.5-6m (15-20ft), or even smaller if trained as pyramids. Sweet cherries have soft juicy flesh that ranges in colour from pale yellow to near black, and are eaten fresh. Sour cherries such as Morello and Nabella may be white, pink or red, and are usually used for cooking, bottling, wine-making, and also for jams, although cherries are very low in pectin so it can be difficult to achieve a set unless combined with a higher pectin fruit such as redcurrants or lemons.

SOUR CHERRY COMPOTE

2½ cups cherries
2 lemons, juice of
6tbsp sugar
½ cup water
½ tsp powdered vanilla

Remove stones from cherries with a stoner.

Combine water, sugar and lemon juice in heavy medium saucepan, add vanilla powder. Bring to boil, stirring until sugar dissolves. Boil for further 6-7 minutes until thin syrup forms.

Reduce heat and add cherries. Stir for 1 minute, then simmer for a few more minutes.

Allow compote to cool and store in fridge. Will keep for about a week.

RAW CHERRY AND NUT ENERGY BARS

Combine ingredients in food processor and roughly blend for a few seconds to form a solid ball, but not too smooth. Add a drop or two of water if necessary.

Press mixture firmly onto a baking tray lined with greaseproof paper. Place in fridge or cool place and slice into bars.

1 cup dried cherries with stones removed

½ cup dried cranberries

½ cup flaxseed meal

2½ cups ground mixed nuts

½ cup raisins

1 tbsp agave syrup drops

1 pinch sea salt

2–3 tbsp raw hemp seeds (optional)

Soft Fruits

Other fruits and berries that you might consider for the forest garden (or any other garden for that matter) include climbers such as grapes, loganberries and blackberries. However, be aware that some varieties of grape need to be grown under glass, and even outdoor varieties require a lot of sunlight in order to ripen properly and so will probably only be suitable for a sunny south facing edge. Blackberries can be very vigorous and will become rampant given half a chance. Some modern thornless varieties are less vigorous than their wild counterparts, so could be more suitable where space is limited. The flavour of freshly picked strawberries is incomparable, but they do require a lot of sun, more than might be available deeper in the forest garden, although they may do well on sunny south facing edges. They also take up a lot of space all year round for a relatively short productive season. Wild strawberries make good ground cover however, although their fruits are very small and fiddly. Blackcurrants and redcurrants are very high in vitamin C although may need some protection from marauding birds! Jostaberries and worcesterberries are blackcurrant and gooseberry hybrids, and can yield large amounts of very tasty fruits from July to November.

FOREST GARDEN
FRUITS

GRAPE WINE

In theory, grapes should contain enough natural sugar to ferment into a wine of about 12-14% alcohol by volume. However due to our cool temperate climate, this is unlikely to be the case with UK grown grapes, so the addition of extra sugar to this method may be necessary.

Take 5.5-7kg (12-15lb) grapes and crush by hand into a food grade plastic bucket – it's a good idea to put latex gloves on as the acid content of the grapes can cause skin irritation. This should provide about a gallon of juice – you can top up with a carton of grape juice if it's a bit under.

Add a wine yeast and nutrient, and stir thoroughly. Use a clean plate to keep the grape skins under the surface of the liquid to prevent oxidisation.

If using dark grapes and a red wine is required, strain the juice off the skins into a demijohn after about 10 days. For a lighter coloured wine strain off a few days earlier.

Fit airlock and ferment for 5-6 months.

'HEDGEROW' SALAD

2 apples, chopped

1 pear, chopped

Fresh seasonal bush fruits, e.g. blackberries, blackcurrants, gooseberries, loganberries, raspberries, redcurrants, whitecurrants etc.

A little lemon juice to prevent apples from oxidising

A handful of chopped nuts and seeds, egg, walnuts, hazels, sunflower or pumpkin, etc.

Combine and serve cold.

Goes well with vegan cream.

FRUIT PUDDING

1 cup mixed berries, e.g. blackberries, blackcurrants, gooseberries, loganberries, raspberries, redcurrants, whitecurrants etc.

¼ cup concentrated apple juice

2½ cups sweet cider

¼ cup rye flour

½ tsp salt

1 tsp oil

Pinch of nutmeg

Heat cider and bring to the boil. Sift flour and salt into the boiling cider and simmer, stirring constantly.

Add fruit when the liquid begins to thicken. Simmer for 1-2 minutes, then remove from heat and stir in other ingredients.

Eat hot or chilled.

RASPBERRY BUNS

Mix flour, sugar and salt. Add oil, fruit and soya milk
to make a moist cake mix, adding a little water or fruit
juice if necessary.

Make into bun shapes and place on a greased baking
tray. Make an indentation on the top of each bun and
fill with a generous blob of jam.

Cook in a medium oven at 180°C (350°F) for 20-30
minutes.

225g (8oz) self-raising flour

110g (4oz) unrefined sugar

4 tbsp vegetable oil

A good splash of soya milk

A large handful of dried
fruit (e.g. sultanas,
raisins, etc.)

Raspberry jam

A pinch of salt

RASPBERRY AND APPLE PIE

Use really ripe soft raspberries that are almost 'on the
turn' – this should then provide enough natural sugar to
eliminate the need to add any additional sugar.

Peel and chop the apples, and stew for 10 minutes or
so in the raspberries. There should be no need to add
any water – the juices of the berries should be sufficient
liquid needed to cook the apples.

When berries are fully broken down and the apples are
fairly soft, place in the pie dish. Bake for 20-30 minutes
in a medium heat oven.

In the autumn substitute blackberries for raspberries
in this dish, or you could try other soft fruits, e.g.
gooseberries, loganberries, blackcurrants, etc.

3-4 large apples

1kg (2lb) very ripe
raspberries

Pastry (page 163)

CIDER FRUIT SALAD

2 cups dried fruit, e.g. apple
    rings, apricots, dried
    plums, etc.

500ml (1 pint) cider
    (page 209)

1 tsp cinnamon

Sprinkle cinnamon onto dried fruit, and soak overnight in the cider.

Eat the next day served with nut or soya cream.

CUT AND COME AGAIN FRUIT CAKE

30g (1lb) dried fruit (raisins,
    sultanas, currants, etc.)

110g (4oz) fairly traded
    unrefined sugar

110g (4oz) vegetable
    margarine

225g (8oz) self-raising flour

½ tsp mixed spice

1tsp vinegar

Warm water

Mix all dry ingredients together. Melt margarine and mix well with an equal amount of warm water. Add to dry mixture. Stir well, adding more water if necessary. Add vinegar and mix well again.

Turn into a well-oiled baking tin and bake at a low heat, 130°C (250°F) for 3½-4 hours.

From *Recipes from New Leaves*.

Thanks to Edna Waterhouse

Some Less Usual Species

The above are perhaps the 'staple' fruits for the UK climate – we know that they grow well in the by and large (at the moment!) cool temperate conditions of these islands and will crop fairly reliably. Therefore we should perhaps consider these as the 'backbone' of our forest garden species selection if self reliance is one of the desired outcomes of our project. However it may also be worth experimenting with some of the more unusual fruit trees and bushes, for example, those that may be considered 'exotic', or that are perhaps not always thought of as having edible or useful yields:

Amelanchier

This is a shrub that rarely grows more than 2-3m (7-10ft) tall in this country and so is relatively easy to protect from the birds, producing very sweet and juicy Juneberries. Once established, this plant will often produce suckers and can in time form thickets. Despite the name, the fruit actually ripens around the middle of July. This fruit is a bit smaller than a blackcurrant and has a sweet apple flavour.

American Hawthorn

The native British hawthorn (*Cratageus monogyna*) has edible berries that can be made into a tasty jelly, although they are very small and fiddly, and its main use is as a hedging plant. More worthwhile as a food plant is the American hawthorn, *C. arnoldiana*. This bears fruit the size of a large cherry with a delicious sweet flavour that ripens in August.

Cornelian Cherry

Cornelian Cherry is a deciduous shrub that can reach 5m (16ft) or more in height. It is wind tolerant and can be used as a hedging plant. It produces yellow flowers in midwinter and produces fruit that ripens in late summer. Must be fully ripe or it is very astringent and not very palatable.

Elaeagnus

There are many varieties of this fruit bearing shrub that are highly useful in the forest garden due to their nitrogen fixing properties:

Elaeagnus cordifolia. A shrub growing to about 4m (13ft) tall and wide, it is probably not hardy in the colder areas of the country. This produces the largest and earliest fruits.

Elaeagnus macrophylla. Grows about 3m (10ft) tall and wide. Not hardy in the colder areas of the country. Selected cultivars have very good-sized fruits.

Elaeagnus x ebbingei. A very common hedging plant, it can crop prolifically when given suitable conditions.

Goji Berry

The goji berry or wolfberry is the fruit of *Lycium barbarum*, an easy to establish shrub reaching up to 3m (10ft) high. The red fruits that are eaten fresh or dried and are very nutritious, are said to have health promoting properties. The young shoots and leaves are also edible, usually cooked as a vegetable and have a minty cress flavour.

Japanese Wineberry

A favourite of forest gardening pioneer Robert Hart, this is a deciduous shrub that can grow up to 3m (10ft) tall. Closely related to raspberries, it has biennial stems, new stems being produced each year that flower in their second year and then die. The orange or red fruit is about 10mm in diameter and is produced in late summer. It is very juicy and has a very nice raspberry flavour.

Mulberry

Easy to grow trees that produce regular crops of long blackberry-like fruits of good flavour widely used in pies, tarts, wines, cordials and tea. The fruit of the black mulberry, native to southwest Asia, and the red mulberry, native to eastern North America, have the strongest flavour. Most varieties start fruiting after 2-3 years, and can grow up to 10-15m (33-50ft), although are frequently more compact.

Sea Buckthorn

A nitrogen fixing deciduous shrub that produces small orange fruit with a sharp lemon flavour and a very high nutrient content that may have cancer-fighting properties. It suckers freely so is not suitable for places where space is at a premium. Sea buckthorn is a light-demanding species: it will not fruit well in the shade; it is however very tolerant of wind, and makes a valuable hedging plant in maritime conditions.

Nuts and Tree Seeds –
The Staples of Tomorrow

Nuts are expensive to buy in the shops, but invaluable in ecological terms, that is, the yield of their nutrients compared to the amount of space they take up, and the benefits to the environment of the trees that bear them. They could in fact provide the bulk of our dietary carbohydrates and proteins, with the potential to largely replace annual cereals as our staple crops. Nut trees do take several years to begin cropping, therefore we need to plant as many as we can now as a long-term investment in this future food source. Thus far nut trees have not been widely grown in the UK, however there are several varieties that are or have been grown in temperate regions for food purposes such as almond, beech, chestnut, hazel and walnut, as well as a number of other high yielding species that may well prove worthwhile researching and developing through selective plant breeding.

Almonds (*Prunus amygdalus*)

Almonds prefer a deep, well-drained soil, and as with the walnut, is early flowering thus susceptible to crop damage caused by an early spring and late frosts, and can be prone to peach leaf curl. They can be open grown in the south of England, or against a wall further north. It is advisable to select named varieties of sweet almonds to ensure an edible crop. Many trees yield bitter almonds, which are poisonous to humans.

Beech (*Fagus sylvatica*)

Older beech trees can produce huge quantities of 'mast' every three or four years, although these nuts are very small and fiddly and probably not worth the effort to process as a food on a home scale. Husked, cleaned and ground they can be used as a coffee substitute, or pressed for a high protein oil, yielding up to 85mm per 0.4kg (3.5in per 14oz). Beech is commonly grown in public parks and woodland, but is also worth considering if planting up a new woodland. The trees produce excellent timber and a valuable fuel wood.

Hazel and Cob Nuts (*Corylus spp.*)

Hazels grow wild in most parts of Britain, including the uplands. Yields of selected varieties of cobnuts and filberts such as Butler, Corabel, Ennis, Kent Cob or Webb's Prize Cob can be prolific, and can store for years. Richard Mabey writes that, "weight for weight, hazel nuts contain 50% more protein, seven times more fat and five times more carbohydrates than hen's eggs".[36] Fruiting begins after 2-3 years. Flowering in early spring, the nuts ripen in September. Hazels prefer a light soil that is not too rich, and can be grown as small trees, bushes or hedges. They will tolerate some shade, but do better when grown in full sun, yielding up to 2 tons per acre. They are, however, susceptible to predation by squirrels who will strip trees bare given half a chance, so protection is required if growing commercially or on a wider scale. Hazels are also very suitable for coppicing on a relatively short rotational basis for poles that have many uses.

Monkey Puzzle (*Araucaria araucana*)

The monkey-puzzle is often seen as an ornamental tree in suburban parks and gardens, yet according to Ken Fern of Plants for a Future, it is a tree that has huge potential for development as a food-producing tree in a cool temperate climate. Indeed it has long been a staple food of the indigenous people of southern Chile from whence it originates, and that shares a similar cool maritime climate to the UK. It produces good-sized nuts of a high nutritional value. However there is a drawback in that male and female specimens need to be grown together in order to produce a crop. Trees grown from seed may take 30 years or more to flower, and it is not possible to tell the sex of the tree until this time. Ken suggests we start planting them as soon as possible!

Sweet Chestnut (*Castanea sativa*)

The sweet or Spanish chestnut is common in woodlands and plantations. 'Wild' trees may yield nuts of good quality. However for a reliable crop of large nuts of good quality it is better to plant a named cultivar or hybrid such as 'Bouche de Betziac', 'Marigoule', 'Marlhac' or 'Marron De Lyon' which can be obtained from specialist nurseries. Grafted trees should begin producing in 4-8 years. As yet there are no dwarfing rootstocks for chestnuts, but their size can be controlled by coppicing them every 10 years or so. Unlike most other nuts, chestnuts are low in proteins and fats, but are high in carbohydrates. The nuts can be ground into flour and will keep for some years if properly dried.

Walnuts (*Juglans regia*)

Walnuts prefer full sun, and a deep, well drained soil and can be grown on higher ground in milder areas in southern England where there is less chance of late frost damage to the female flowers. They are susceptible to blight in cool wet springs and can also suffer from leaf spot. Varieties that are fairly resistant to these diseases include Corne du Perigord, Fernette, Franquette, Mayette and Ronde de Montignac. Research and selective breeding may lead to hardier cultivars that will do well in other areas of the country, in the meantime we are largely reliant on imports from European countries. The trees can grow quite large – up to 30m (100ft) – but can be kept small or grown as bushes. Walnuts require pollinators, although some varieties are partially self-pollinating. Grafted trees from nurseries should start to crop after 5-10 years. Walnuts are mildly allelopathic, that is, their roots exude a chemical that can restrict the growth of other plants in their vicinity, therefore they may not be good companions of other trees that you might be considering growing nearby.

A BASIC NUT ROAST RECIPE

Nut roasts are great as a basic meal to fill you up and keep you warm on a cold winter's day served with steamed vegetables and a hearty gravy, or are sound in summer with a salad.

Chop the onion, crush the garlic and lightly sauté on a medium heat in a small pan until soft. Add the herbs, tomatoes and yeast extract and simmer for a few more minutes then remove from the heat.

Stir in the grains, nuts and breadcrumbs to make a firm mixture. Add more grains, nuts and breadcrumbs if it's a bit runny to stiffen it up.

Place in a greased oven tin and cook in a hot oven for 20 minutes or so.

Variations – Like all the recipes in this book – use your imagination! Add any vegetables that are in season or that you can get hold of, but chop them fairly small – apple, cabbage, carrots, celery, mushrooms and peppers. Substitute curry powder for the herbs (see page 131), or mashed beans (broad beans, field beans, kidney beans, etc.) instead of (or as well as) the nuts or rice. A handful of porridge oats will do the job of binding instead of the breadcrumbs. Add a dash of cider vinegar or red wine or maybe a handful of raisins for an interesting flavour. Use chestnuts as the principal ingredient to make a delicious winter solstice or Christmas celebrational dish.

1 large onion

2 cups nuts, chopped, e.g. hazels, walnuts

1 cup brown rice, cooked or an alternative grain, e.g. quinoa, millet, bulgur wheat, etc.

Wholemeal breadcrumbs (about a crusts' worth)

1 tin of tomatoes or a few very ripe fresh plum tomatoes

1-2 garlic cloves

1tsp yeast extract

Dried mixed herbs, e.g. rosemary, oregano, thyme, sage, etc.

STUFFED PEPPERS

Nut roast mixture
(page 227)

6-8 mushrooms

4 red or green peppers

Olive oil

Make up the nut roast, adding some chopped mushrooms to the mixture.

Slice the tops off of the peppers and remove their seeds. Fill peppers with the roast mixture and replace the tops.

Baste with olive oil and bake in a hot oven for 20-30 minutes until peppers are cooked.

Serve with home made tomato sauce (see page 140).

CABBAGE LEAF DOLMADES

Nut roast mixture
(page 227)

6-7 savoy cabbage leaves

Olive oil

Blanch savoy leaves for 2-3 minutes in boiling water, then immediately rinse in cold water. Lay flat and dollop a little of the cold nut roast mixture into the middle of each leaf.

Fold the leaf around the mixture to create a small 'parcel'. Pin them together with a cocktail stick to prevent them falling apart.

Drizzle with a little olive oil and serve cold.

If you grow grapes in your garden you could substitute vine leaves for the cabbage leaves.

NUT STUFFED AUBERGINES

Cut aubergine in half lengthways. Scrape out and finely chop most of the flesh.

Mix in with grated nuts, half the oil and well-chopped lovage mixed with a little water and yeast extract.

Brush aubergine shells inside and out with the rest of the oil and place in an ovenproof dish. Fill shells with aubergine flesh and nut mixture.

Bake for 40 minutes in hot oven.

1 large aubergine

2-3 fresh lovage leaves

1 cup mixed nuts, e.g. walnuts, hazels, etc.

1tbsp oil

1tsp yeast extract

CARROT AND NUT SAVOURY

Grate carrots and chop onion and nuts finely. Mix ingredients well and put in a dish with a weight on top.

Leave for 30 minutes or so and serve with baked potato and salad.

Alternatively, fry onion lightly in oil and add other ingredients, mix well and bake for 30 minutes or so at 175°C (350°F).

2 large carrots

1 cup nuts, e.g. hazels, walnuts etc.

1 small onion

1 small handful porridge oats

1tsp yeast extract

A splash of oil

Herbs to taste

RAW NUT BUTTER

Grind a handful of nuts (almonds, hazel, walnut, etc.) moistened with a little oil (e.g. hemp) in a food processor. Use with sweet or savoury spreads, or flavour with a little yeast extract and fresh mint or other herbs.

RAW NUT CREAM

Grind nuts finely and whip with a little cold water to the desired consistency. Serve on fruit.

RAW NUT BALLS

A handful of nuts

A handful of porridge oats

½ tsp yeast extract

½ tsp dried basil or more fresh

1 tsp boiling water

1 tsp oil

A little sea salt to taste

Roughly chop nuts and grind with oats. Mix in the basil.

Mix yeast extract with a teaspoon of boiling water, add oil and stir into the mixture, setting aside a teaspoon of the nut mixture.

Shape into 4 balls. Roll into reserved nuts. Leave in a cool place for about 10 minutes.

Serve with salad.

RAW ENERGY NUT LOAF

Adapted from a recipe in Ronnie Worsey's excellent little Salad Scoffer *booklet, available from Active Distribution.*[37]

Finely chop onion, ginger and garlic and grate celery and carrot. Finely chop nuts and sunflower seeds using a blender. Add in tahini and soy sauce.

Combine all ingredients together and mix well. Place in a loaf tin and refrigerate for a couple of hours before serving.

Serve cold with a salad, or can be warmed through if you prefer.

Thanks to Ronny Worsey

2 cups mixed nuts,
    e.g. walnuts, almonds,
    hazelnuts

1 carrot

1 stalk celery

2 garlic cloves

1 small onion

1 small piece of root ginger

½ cup sunflower seeds

1tsp cumin

3tbsp tahini

1-2tbsp soy sauce

1-2tbsp oil, e.g. olive oil,
    hemp oil

WALNUTS AND HARICOT BEANS

Chop onions and cook slowly in oil in a pan with a lid until soft.

Finely chop the walnuts, mash the beans and stir into the cooked onions with the yeast extract.

Heat through and serve garnished with parsley.

110g (4oz) walnuts

110g (4oz) well cooked
    haricot beans

110g (4oz) onions

Splash of oil

POTATO AND WALNUT TART

1 large onion

450g (1lb) potatoes

A splash of oat or soya milk

2–3 large fresh tomatoes

110g (4oz) shelled walnuts

1tbsp yeast extract

Boil and mash the potatoes with a splash of milk, stirring in the yeast extract. Use half the mash to line an oiled deep tart dish.

Put in layers of finely sliced onion, tomatoes and roughly chopped or ground walnuts. Spread the rest of the potatoes on top.

Bake in a medium hot oven for 45 minutes or so or until potato top is brown and crisp.

WALNUT AND POTATO SAUSAGES

A quick and easy 'fast food...'

1 cup walnuts

1 handful porridge oats

2 medium potatoes

Yeast extract

Herbs to taste

Cook potatoes, mash them and leave to cool down.

Finely chop the walnuts and stir into the mashed potatoes with the yeast extract and herbs. Mix well, adding a little porridge oats if necessary to make a firm mixture.

Shape into sausages and cook in an oiled pan until crisp and golden. Don't use much oil as the walnuts have a lot.

Oaks and Acorns

The two main species of oak in Britain are the English or penduculate oak (*Quercus robur*) and the sessile oak (*Quercus patraea*). The history of these species can be traced back to the earliest colonisation by trees of the British Isles from the European mainland following the end of the last Ice Age around 10,000 years ago. By 5,500 BC the majority of the country was covered by virgin forest, much of it dominated by oak, lime and hazel. The oak provides habitat for some 256 animal species, and its use to humankind is unprecedented. It provides the highest quality timber and gives a slow burning sustainable fuel. Acorns have long been utilised as a source of fodder for pigs, goats and chickens, however their potential as a high value food source for humankind has been largely overlooked in the UK. Acorns have in fact been a staple food in many parts of the world for hundreds of years and have significant nutritional content.

Richard St. Barbe Baker, 'Man of the Trees' and founder of the International Tree Foundation,[38] once described oaks and sweet chestnuts as 'corn trees'. They are high in carbohydrates and are 7% protein, and can be ground into gluten-free flour, or used in any recipe requiring nuts. Acorns have a high tannin content that makes them bitter to taste. This can however easily be removed by soaking for eight hours, changing the water after four hours. Cooking then converts any remaining tannins to dextrose. Personally I find the texture of acorns to be somewhat glutinous, and they are best combined with 'lighter' lower fat nuts or other foods.

ACORN ROAST

170g (6oz) leached acorns

A handful porridge oats

1 small onion

A splash of oil

A little water

1tsp yeast extract

1tsp mixed herbs

Grind the acorns and add a little water. Finely chop onion and lightly fry in oil.

Melt yeast extract in the hot oil and add herbs to taste.

Bake for 15-20 minutes in a medium hot oven.

ACORN AND CARROT TART

Filling:

110g (4oz) leached acorns

2 large carrots

1tsp yeast extract

Herbs to taste

Pastry case:

225g (8oz) wholemeal flour

1tsp baking powder

A splash of oil

A little water

Grind acorns and grate the carrots, mix together with yeast extract and herbs, adding a little water if necessary to maintain a moist texture.

Mix flour and baking powder, then mix oil and water and stir into the flour to make a smooth mixture. Roll out and spread in a baking tray or dish.

Spoon in the filling and bake for 20 minutes or so in a medium heat oven until the pastry is browned.

Serve topped with sliced tomatoes.

SAVOURY ACORN COOKIES

Grind acorns and mix with flour to a smooth consistency.

Dissolve yeast extract in hot water. Add oil and mix well.

Drop dessert spoonfuls of the mixture onto a baking tray. Flatten to about 1cm (0.25in) thick, and bake for 15 minutes or so in a medium heat oven, or longer if a more biscuit-like consistency is preferred.

110g (4oz) leached acorns
110g (4oz) wholemeal flour
55g (2oz) oil
85g (3oz) water
1tsp yeast extract

1. Green leaves

2. Pulp

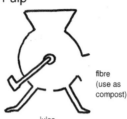

fibre
(use as
compost)

juice

3. Strain

Leaf Protein

Leaf curd, especially made from the leaves of trees such as beech, hawthorn, lime and chestnut, could take over from cereals as a major worldwide food staple. Plant leaves are the most abundant source of protein on earth. However thus far they have been largely untapped as a source of human sustenance due to the fact that their high indigestible fibre content makes it impossible for us to eat sufficient quantities. Instead we feed ruminant cattle on vegetation, converting plant protein into fibre-free meat and milk. This is a hugely wasteful process as animals are only around 8-15% efficient at turning plant matter into the food that humans eat. However in recent years methods have been developed that use simple technologies to successfully extract the protein rich juices from leaf fibre, which is then heated to just below boiling point so that the nutrients coagulate and can be strained off. The resulting curd, which resembles cottage cheese, can be dried as a powder. It is practically tasteless and can be added to any sweet or savoury food to greatly add to its nutrition value. Leaf curd yields at least three times as much high quality protein per acre as cereal crops, and 10 times as much as animals. It is also rich in iron, calcium, unsaturated fats and beta-carotene that the body can convert into vitamin A.

In principle, any green leaves (provided they are not poisonous) can be used for the extraction of leaf nutrient.

4. Heat juice to 90 °C

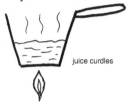

juice curdles

5. Strain

to separate 'curd'
from 'whey'
(liquor)

6. Press

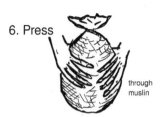

through
muslin

Making leaf curd is a simple process.

Find Your Feet (FYF), a voluntary charity founded during the early 1960s, has been exploring the potential of leaf nutrient to address human hunger using simple grinding machines that can be used on a small scale that are not reliant on complex technological fixes. The first long term feeding trials of this cheap and easy to extract curd took place in Coimbatore in India. Nursery school children were fed supplements in addition to their normal diet, and were observed to have marked improvements in height and body weight growth as well as blood quality, and marked decreases in anaemia and night blindness. Leaf nutrient is now being routinely added to the diets of children in projects in Sri Lanka, Mexico, India and Ghana with consistently positive results. FYF report that there has been some criticism of leaf curd due to its 'green colour and uninteresting flavour', yet how interesting is a spoonful of wheat or cornflour on its own? Trials have shown that there are no lasting objections to this 'new' food when it is incorporated into existing crops.[39]

CHAPTER 8

Walking on the Wild Side

"The human spirit has a primal allegiance to wildness, to really live, to snatch the fruit and suck it, to spill the juice. We may think we are domesticated but we are not. Feral in pheromone and intuition, feral in our sweat and fear, feral in tongue and language. This is the first command: to live in fealty to the feral angel."

Jay Griffiths, *Wild*

Zone 5

T oo often we can forget that we are a part of, not apart from, the forces of nature. Zone 5 is the place where as permaculturists we let go of 'design' and instead learn to simply observe. Exploring the wild edges of our landscapes, experiencing the shifting energies of the changing cycles of the seasons reconnects us with our world, and can teach us many lessons about how it functions, as well as yielding an abundance of wild delights.

Well, You Don't Know Where They've Been, Do You?

A few years ago I used to regularly cycle through a local park on my way to the care home for adults with learning disabilities where I worked at the time. As I pedalled past a neglected corner of the park one day I noticed a thicket of cherry plum bushes heavily laden with perfectly ripe, golden fruits just ready for the picking. These were delicious and succulent, melting in the mouth as they released their natural sugars and flavours, like sunshine in a tangible form. It took me not more than a few minutes to harvest enough to fill a couple of carrier bags which I stashed in my panniers before going on my way, leaving plenty more for other foragers and the wildlife to share. Once at work I rinsed them and set them out in bowls, encouraging everybody to help themselves. Whilst the residents at the home were more than happy to tuck in, none of the staff would touch them. When I asked why not, one of my colleagues wrinkled her nose and replied: "Well you don't know where they've been, do you?" The irony made me laugh out loud. Unlike the catering-sized tins of industrially processed, artificially flavoured and coloured 'fruit salad' in the kitchen store cupboard or the over-sized and over-waxed, blemish-free apples, bananas and oranges sitting in the fruit bowl on top of the day room TV, I knew **exactly** where my cherry plums had come from! Although amusing on one level, this exchange also crystallised for me the sense of alienation and separation from our natural world that characterises the attitudes of so many of us in this age of oil-reliant, sanitised industrialisation.

So often we see the world beyond our 'Best Before' packaged supermarket food, manicured suburban lawns and glass-plated shopping malls not as a source of wonder and abundance, but as a dark, tangled and threatening place, filled with poisonous berries and toadstools, beasts, bugs and 'bad' bacteria. Since the 1600s the mechanistic view of nature as separate and 'other', propounded by Descartes, Francis Bacon and their contemporaries, have informed Western culture's

relationship with the world. Nature is a force that needs to be constantly kept in check and tamed, its untidy, primal potency subdued lest it should break free and undermine the fragile edifices of 'civilisation' that we have so meticulously constructed around us.

In the UK there is probably no remaining truly pristine wilderness, that is, land that has never been touched or altered in any way by the hand of peoplekind – pretty much every square yard of these small islands has been managed at some point or other over the last few thousand years. The sheep grazed 'wild' moorlands of the Scottish Highlands were until the Bronze Age part of the mighty Caledonian Forest, covered with a diversity of trees including aspen, birch, juniper, oak, rowan and Scots pine. And even what we often consider to be our 'ancient' woodlands, are but remnants of mighty forests that once covered the length and breadth of these islands and were once parcelled up into plots and highly managed for food, fuel, construction materials and other economic uses.

Yet despite our hubristic attempts at a 'command and control' approach, exemplified in this modern era by herbicide sprayed road verges and concreted patios, wild nature always has a way of creeping back into even our most domesticated human habitats. Neglected corners of municipal gardens that local authorities can no longer afford to maintain; disused railway lines and embankments; urban waste grounds colonised by feral volunteers like buddleia, ash and bramble. These unmanaged interstices in our otherwise formalised urban landscapes have an intrinsic worth that is often unappreciated and overlooked as we go about the hustle and bustle of our daily human business. For those who are prepared to develop keener observational skills however, there are abundant rewards to be gained... The foraged yields of these often temporary and transient zones include not only opportunistic harvests of cherry plum, wild garlic, sea beet or blackberries, but also chances to observe the interactions of plants, animals and fungi within uninterrupted ecosystems. Wilderness is the big classroom where those of us who would design with nature can contemplate and learn the lessons about how she actually functions. We can then bring back and apply these insights to our own productive systems. Indeed it was Bill Mollison's observations in the rainforests of Tasmania during the late 1950s that led him to develop the origins of the permaculture concept. He noted the complex interactions between browsing marsupials and a relatively small number of plant species, concluding that it was the synergy between the components of the ecosystem, rather than the number of species, that gave the system both its flexibility and stability.

Just as it is important for us to take opportunities to visit wild nature, so too can we invite her into our otherwise managed places. If you are lucky enough to have access to woodland, why not fence off part of it, and allow the processes of succession to continue unchecked just to see what happens? Or maybe leave part of your lawn un-mown and let it become a wild meadow area? Even the smallest garden can make space for a small log pile in the corner that can become the domain of the beetles, centipedes, toads and spiders.

Food for Free

There is an abundance of wild foods available in the UK for those who can make the effort to look around for them. Woodlands and hedgerows yield fruits, nuts, roots, fungi and herbs, but even urban areas have their 'waste grounds', parks and footpaths where rosehips, blackberries or mushrooms might be found – use your knowledge of the local environment. Sea beet, one of my personal favourite green vegetables, grows prolifically in spring and autumn along the sea walls by the Thames Estuary where I live, while in the town centre there used to be a walnut tree a few seconds walk from one of the largest 'superstores' in the area. Unfortunately it has now been cut down to make way for a cinema multiplex, but before this I used to regularly pick several pounds of nuts from the ground around it with no effort at all. Yet most other passers-by failed to even register it on their way into the store, no doubt to buy expensive nuts that had been imported from half way across the planet! Around the corner from our house used to be a long closed down hospital that had been boarded up with 'Keep Out!' signs around it. Many local people including myself and my children used to climb through gaps in the fences to scrump the hundreds of apples that fell every year, and were otherwise left to rot on the floor of the small orchard in its grounds. Some might call that trespassing, but personally I feel that to have wasted such abundance would have been the criminal act!

Once you have trained your eye and broadened your knowledge, the potential cornucopia of nature's larder can sometimes be a little overwhelming. I don't consider myself an expert forager by any means, but I do remember once walking along an urban footpath on the way to visit a project with a group of permaculture course students. One of them casually asked me which plants in front of us there and then would be OK to eat. I stopped to look and was amazed to realise that almost every plant in our field of vision at that moment – all typical of any footpath or roadside verge – was edible or useful. More often than not these are overlooked, even by myself: Brambles (blackberries and growing tips for salads); burdock (edible roots); chickweed (for salads or stir fries); common mallow (for salads or as a green vegetable); cow parsley (for salads and stir fries – be careful not to mistake cow parsley for the poisonous fool's parsley or poison hemlock); dandelion (coffee from the roots; leaves in salads or stir fries; flowers for wine); fat hen (for salads or spinach substitute); goosegrass (a 'spring tonic' tea); hedge garlic (for salads); nettles (for soups and beer); plantain (for salads or as a vegetable); yarrow (for salads); a crab apple (for crab apple jelly, chutneys or cider); a couple of elder shrubs (for elderflower cordial or elderberry wine) and an oak tree (acorns for roasts or acorn flour).

A Few Foraging Dos and Don'ts

- Do use your common sense when gathering wild foods – avoid picking specimens close to roads – they may have been contaminated by pollution from traffic.
- Do make sure you can properly identify the fruit, leaves or mushrooms that you've found. Use several features to be sure (check leaf, flower, berry colour and shape, season, and so on). Use a clear guidebook, or better still, go out with a more experienced person to give you guidance.
- Do wash your harvest well, wherever you have collected it.
- Don't allow children to pick or eat wild food unsupervised.
- Don't eat an unhealthy looking plant or fruit – if it appears burnt, bruised or has any sign of mould, for example.
- Do keep a sample of any mushroom, berry or leaf aside so it can later be identified if you do have a stomach upset.
- Don't take more than you need of any plant, and ensure that there is enough of the plant left to reproduce, and also enough for the wildlife and other foragers.
- Do remember that under the 1981 Wildlife and Countryside Act, it is illegal to uproot any wild plant without the permission of the owner or occupier of the land. It is also illegal to pick, uproot, collect the seed from, or sell, any of particularly rare or vulnerable species.

Burdock
(*Arctium lappa*)

Widespread and common throughout the UK on woodland edges, roadsides and wasteground. Has large, broad, heart shaped leaves, flowering between July and September, followed by prickly burrs that are often caught on clothes and the fur of animals. Young leaves can be used in salads or as a spinach substitute, and stems can be steamed like asparagus. The rather tough black roots are also edible, normally in a finely chopped form.

Chickweed
(*Stellaria media*)

Chickweed is an annual plant that grows abundantly on cultivated land from late winter/ early spring onwards, and is commonly considered a 'weed'. Despite this, it has a valuable function in providing a ground cover, protecting otherwise bare soil from erosion by wind and heavy rain, and is easily dug in as a fertility building 'green manure'. It is also edible, having a mild flavour that provides plenty of 'bulk' for your salad dishes during the spring before most of your cultivated salad plants begin cropping, and is free of charge and labour!

CHICKWEED SALAD

1 large bunch chickweed

A handful of chopped
3 cornered leeks
or Welsh onions

2 crisp apples, cubed

4 tbsp fairly traded olive oil

4 tbsp cider vinegar

Wash the chickweed, chop coarsely and mix with the 3 cornered leeks and apples in a serving bowl.

Dress with the olive oil and cider vinegar.

DANDELION SALAD

Combine a handful of young dandelion leaves with other green leaves, e.g. Little Gem lettuce, rocket, etc., cherry tomatoes, lemon juice and freshly ground black pepper.

DANDELION COFFEE

Dig up roots in autumn, when they are at their fattest. Do not peel but scrub well and dry thoroughly, preferably in the sun, then roast in an oven until brittle. Grind and use in the same way as coffee.

Common Mallow (*Malva sylvestris*)

A widespread plant often found by roadsides and on wasteland, it has large broad leaves that can be gathered from summer onwards. These have a bland flavour and rather glutinous texture, and can be used in stews and salads, or else deep-fried as a kind of 'wafer'. Prepare by dropping them a few at a time into a pan of hot sunflower oil. They will become flat, then curl at the edges and become almost translucent green. Carefully remove brittle leaves from pan with a spoon and drain on paper towels.

Dandelion (*Taraxacum officinale*)

Growing almost anywhere practically all year round, all parts of this very common and well known plant are edible. The roots can be used as a coffee substitute or root vegetable, the young leaves can be used in salads or as a green vegetable, and the flowers can be made into a surprisingly delicately flavoured wine. A word of caution however – a traditional English name for the dandelion is 'Piss the Bed' – it can be a very powerful diuretic!

Fat Hen (*Chenopodium album*)

A common and widespread plant of cultivated soils and waste grounds.
It has greyish green, diamond shaped leaves, with tiny pale green flowers
clumped in spikes. Young leaves are edible, and can be used in salads or as
a spinach substitute in much the same way as its close relatives, Good King
Henry (*Chenopodium bonus-henricus*) and orache (*Atriplex spp.*). Fat hen is
high in dietary fibre, as well as iron, protein and vitamins A, B and C.
The seeds are also highly nutritious, and in the past have been ground into
flour and added to gruels.

Garlic Mustard (*Alliaria petiolata*)

An upright plant growing up to a metre or so in height, common in
hedgerows and the woodland edge. Unlike wild garlic or ramsons (*Allium
ursinum*), garlic mustard is not related to the onions, but is in fact part of
the cabbage tribe, and has only a faint garlic scent and flavour. Can be used
in salads, sauces or as a potherb in the early spring, although the leaves can
become bitter after flowering, usually in April or May.

Hairy Bittercress (*Cardamine hirsuta*)

A diminutive yet widespread self-sown wild plant commonly found all
year round on bare cultivated ground. "It's not hairy and it's not bitter!"
is the comment of most people who try this for the first time, in fact it
has a pleasant nutty, peppery flavour, and is a nice little addition to the
salad bowl.

Nettles (*Urtica dioica*)

Probably **the** best-known wild plant growing in the UK, mainly because of its unpleasant sting that we all learned to avoid as children! Many people dismiss the common nettle as a 'weed', going to great lengths to try to get rid of it from their gardens. Yet it is in fact one of the most useful and multifunctional plants I can think of. In the past, the coarse fibres of its stalks have been used for cloth making, and during the Second World War hundreds of tons of nettles were gathered in the UK for dyeing army uniforms. Nettle is an indicator of fertile soil, and is a 'dynamic accumulator' that takes up many minerals with its roots. The plants can then be either added to compost, or rotted down in rainwater to make a nutrient-rich liquid fertiliser. It also provides a wonderful wildlife habitat, providing a home to a number of butterfly species that feed on its leaves. Nettles are useful as a food until around mid June, when they become rather too coarse to be palatable. Use gloves to gather young nettles and wash them well. They have high iron content, and can be used as a spinach substitute, juiced or used in soups and stews, etc. Nettles can also be used as the basis of a refreshing herbal tea, or made into nettle beer.

NETTLE SOUP

Wear gloves to wash and roughly chop the nettles and spinach.

Chop onion and sauté together with the herbs until onion is soft. Add nettles, spinach and stock and simmer.

Cut potatoes into small pieces and add to the soup along with more water. Continue to simmer until potatoes are soft, then put through a blender until smooth.

Simmer for a little longer before serving with a little freshly ground pepper on top.

A good carrier bag full of freshly collected nettles

A good handful of fresh spinach

1 large onion

2 large potatoes

500ml (1 pint) of vegetable stock

Oil

Herbs to taste

Freshly ground black pepper

NETTLE BEER

A carrier bag full of freshly
collected loose nettle
leaves

2 lemons

450g (1lb) Demerara sugar

30g (1oz) cream of tartar

4.5 litres (1 gallon) water

Beer yeast

Boil the nettles in a large pan for 20 minutes or so.
Strain the liquid onto the sugar and cream of tartar in
a large sterile plastic bucket.

When cooled to around 36°C (96°F) add the juice of
the lemons plus the yeast. Cover and leave to ferment
for 3-4 days.

Strain and bottle in strong bottles, e.g. with 'Grolsch'
style stoppers, as this is pretty lively!

Nettle beer is essentially a summer drink, and is very
refreshing although it doesn't keep well. It can have a
rather murky appearance, but you'll soon get used to that!

NETTLE AND SPINACH PESTO

*This is a variation on the classic basil sauce that is stirred into freshly cooked
pasta, but also goes well as a filling for baked jacket potatoes or even on toast!*

A good handful of 3 cornered leeks (leaves and bulbs)

A generous handful of wild garlic (or 2-3 garlic cloves)

A handful of nettles (use gloves to protect your hands
when you pick them!)

A handful of young spinach or chard leaves

A good handful of basil

A handful of shelled walnuts

Splash of olive oil

Gently wash the leaves, then
finely chop all ingredients
together, preferably in a blender.

SEA BEET AND TOMATO SOUP

If you can't obtain sea beet around your way try substituting Swiss chard, although the flavour isn't quite the same or as strong.

1 onion

1-2 garlic cloves

A good couple of handfuls
of fresh sea beet leaves

10 or so large, very ripe,
almost squashy tomatoes

1 handful of fresh lovage

A little cornflour

Splash of red wine

Fairly traded olive oil

Chop onion finely, and gently sauté in olive oil in a large pan. Meanwhile liquidise the tomatoes, sea beet and lovage and add to the pan. Simmer for 20 minutes or so, adding a little water if necessary.

Mix a spoonful of cornflour to a smooth paste in a cup and stir in if you feel that the soup needs a little thickening. There's no need to add any stock to this soup as the lovage has a strong, savoury flavour. You might want to add a splash of red wine shortly before removing from the heat, but it's not compulsory. Home made elderberry is good.

Serve with a good hunk of garlic bread.

Sea Beet (*Beta vulgaris*)

Sea beet grows prolifically on the sea walls and footpaths by the Thames estuary where I live. It also grows as a 'volunteer' on my allotment where I've used seaweed collected from the Thames as a mulch material, although I've not had so much success establishing it when I've tried deliberately planting seeds that I've collected. It's the ancestor of cultivated beets such as beetroot and chard, and has a strong, quite salty flavour that really does go well with the tomatoes. The best times for harvesting sea beet are the spring and early autumn, when it has a second flush of fresh leaves.

Blackberries (*Rubus fruticosus*)

Blackberries are found pretty much anywhere in September, and are probably the most commonly foraged wild plant in the UK. The berries can be used in jams, fruit pies (they are in season at the same time as apples and perfectly complement each other), fruit salads, to flavour vinegars or can be made into wine.

Blackthorn (*Prunus spinosa*)

A common shrub of woodlands, hedgerows and scrub, it has vicious spines and white flowers that appear before its oval leaves. Sloes are its small round fruit; these darken from September onwards and resemble small plums. Although they may look juicy and tempting, you will only ever try them once, as they are so sour, they actually feel like they are sandpapering the roof of your mouth off! They do however make a delicious liqueur when steeped in alcohol for a few weeks. Collect a pound or so after the first frosts when their skins have softened, or if picked earlier, prick each berry with a pin to allow the liquid to penetrate (or you could always cheat and put them in the freezer for a couple of days), then put them in a large jar. Cover with enough spirit of your choice (e.g. gin, brandy or whisky) and a couple of tablespoons of sugar, seal and leave to mature for three months or so, shaking occasionally.

Dog Rose (*Rosa canina*)

A widespread shrub of hedgerows, woodlands and waste grounds, this wild rose bears attractive pale pink or white flowers from June to July, followed by bright red, egg shaped hips. These contain more vitamin C than any other known fruit or vegetable, around 40 times more than fresh oranges. During the Second World War when supplies of citrus fruit were cut off, Britain was able to supply its young children with vitamin C obtained from rose hips converted into syrup. It is vital however that when using rose hips the seeds are removed beforehand, as these can cause quite nasty irritation in the throat, and are in fact used as an itching powder!

BLACKBERRY AND APPLE COBBLER

Wash the blackberries. Stew for five minutes with the apple and a splash of water. Place fruit in an ovenproof dish.

Mix dry ingredients apart from the raisins. Rub in oil until mixture resembles breadcrumbs. Add raisins and enough water to form a firm dough. Roll out to about 2cm (1in) thick and cut into 4cm (2in) circles.

Top the fruit mixture with the scone rounds. Bake in a medium oven at 180°C (350°F) for about 30 minutes.

170g (6oz) blackberries
220g (8oz) apples
55g (2oz) raisins
280g (10oz) wholemeal flour
55g (2oz) rolled oats
4 tbsp oil
Water to mix

RAW BLACKBERRY AND HAZEL CAKES

Roughly chop hazels. Mash berries and raisins together with oil. Add chopped nuts and enough oats to make a firm mixture.

Form into little balls and roll in ground porridge oats.

A good handful of blackberries and raisins
1 handful of hazelnuts (or other nuts)
½ cup porridge oats
A little oil

ELDERBERRY WINE

1.3kg (3lb) (about a carrier
bag full) of ripe, washed
elderberries

1.5kg (3lb 5oz) sugar

4.5 litres (1 gallon) water

Wine yeast and nutrient

Elder (Sambucus nigra)

Despite the rather unpromising appearance of the elder bush during the winter months, and the unpleasant smell of its leaves when they appear at the beginning of the year, the elderflower blossom that forms around May or June is pleasantly fragrant. This can be eaten straight off the bush, or else made into a refreshing summer cordial by steeping them in diluted apple juice, or a lightly alcoholic 'champagne'. Elderberries appear later in the year and can be made into a jelly or else added to jams such as apple or blackberry. They can also be made into a red wine, but don't eat the berries raw – they are a powerful emetic!

Mash berries in a large mixing bowl. Boil water and pour over crushed berries.

When cooled to about lukewarm (no hotter – this will kill the yeast), add the yeast and nutrient.

Leave for about three days, stirring a couple of times a day, then strain off the liquid from the waste pulp onto the sugar.

Transfer this to a dark demijohn, as this helps to retain the colour which may be lost if a clear jar is used. Fit an airlock and leave for several months until fermentation is complete.

Siphon into clean bottles. The longer you leave this wine the more mature it will be.

ELDERFLOWER CHAMPAGNE

Select the best looking clusters of elderflower blossom, preferably on a bright sunny afternoon. Discard any that are looking a bit old – these won't be fresh and will smell 'mousey'.

Bring 4 litres of water to the boil and pour into a scrupulously clean plastic fermenting bucket. Top up with a further 2 litres (4 pints) of cold water. There are now 6 litres (1.3 gallons) of water in the bucket.

Stir in the sugar, then add the blossom, trimming away as much of the stem as possible. Add the white wine vinegar plus juice and zest of 4 lemons. Stir well and cover with lid.

After a day or two the mixture should be fermenting; if it isn't, add a sprinkling of wine yeast. You shouldn't need to though as the blossom has its own natural yeast.

Ferment for 4-5 days before straining off the liquid. Decant into strong bottles – those with 'Grolsch' style stoppers are ideal. Strong bottles with good seals are essential due to the build up of carbon dioxide during fermentation – which is what gives the drink its champagne-like fizz!

Stored in a cool dry place this should keep for several months – I drank a bottle I made three years ago the other day and it was still fine. Summer in a bottle!

A carrier bag full of elder blossom, i.e. around 15-20 good sized heads

700g (1lb 9oz) sugar

4 lemons

2tbsp white wine vinegar

6 litres (1.3 gallons) water

ROWANBERRY JELLY

900g (2lb) rowanberries
A handful or so of crab
apples or lemon juice
Sugar
600ml (1 pint) water

Rowan
(*Sorbus aucuparia*)

A small, tough native tree with smooth bark bearing clusters of orange-red berries from August to November, capable of growing at a higher altitude than any other British tree. These should be picked as soon as they are soft enough to be squashed between the finger and thumb. Pick clusters whole, and strip from the stalks with a kitchen fork. The berries can be used to make a liqueur in the same way as sloes, or can be made into a jelly with a rather tart and smokey flavour that would make a good accompaniment to festive dishes such as a chestnut roast, although they do require additional pectin to help set.

Boil rowanberries and crab apples in water and simmer until pulpy.

Strain through a jelly bag and add 450g (1lb) sugar for each 600ml (1 pint) of juice, and boil and skim until setting point is reached.

Pour into sterile jars and seal.

Mushrooms and Fungi

The key word when gathering mushrooms and fungi from the wild is **caution**! The majority of fungi are harmless, if not especially palatable. However some of the most deadly specimens have an unfortunate tendency to look like some of the tastiest ones! For example the fairy ring champignon common on many lawns between April and November, could easily be confused with the lighter coloured but deadly poisonous *Clitocybe rivulosa*, and the delicious edible morels have a close resemblance to the deadly *Gyromitra esculenta*, or False morel. Even the common Field mushroom could be easily confused with the Yellow Stainer (*Agaricus xanthodermus*) if cautions were to go unobserved. In fact the latter mushroom is the most common cause of poisoning through misidentification, although thankfully its effects are short-lived, if unpleasant, rather than fatal. When mushroom hunting always take along at least two good quality field identification guides, and cross reference their illustrations and descriptions. Pick only those specimens that satisfy **all** the criteria of both guides. Pick only sound specimens and don't pick them too young – not all of their identifying characteristics may have yet developed – or too old as they may have begun to decay. Avoid picking on wet days, and be especially wary of specimens that may be maggot-infested. If you know somebody who has experience in mushroom and fungi hunting that is prepared to give you guidance – all the better!

Cep (*Boletus edulis*)

Also known as the penny bun, this brown, bun-shaped mushroom has a spongy, yellowy cream underside rather than gills. It is commonly found in woodland from mid-July and has a slightly nutty flavour. Only the youngest specimens should be used. Ceps have a texture and flavour that some describe as meaty, and are best sliced complete with stems and simmered in olive oil for 10 minutes and dressed with a splash of sherry or red wine.

Chicken of the Woods (*Laetiporus sulphureus*)

Is a sulphurous yellow bracket fungi found on the sides of living or dead trees including beech, oak, chestnut, yew and less frequently cherry and other hardwoods. The flavour and texture closely resemble that of chicken, which many consider delicious, but I must confess it is a little too close to the real thing for my own palate, and I'm not overly keen myself.

Field Mushrooms (*Agaricus campestris*)

Probably the mushroom that most people will recognise, and commonly found in grasslands and pasture between August and November. It is however easily confused with the poisonous yellow stainer, so be completely sure of it before picking. The best way of picking field mushrooms is to gently twist them away from their base. Discard any that show evidence of tunnelling from insects, as these are likely to be infested with maggots. For a simple preparation idea, slice and simmer in olive oil, and serve with a little lemon juice and a sprinkling of freshly ground black pepper.

Giant Puffball (*Lycoperdon giganteum*)

Commonly found in pastures and under hedges between August and September, the giant puffball is the largest wild food to be found in the UK, resembling a large white football. The flesh is pure white throughout, and very tasty. To check whether they are still fresh enough to eat, cut a slice from the top or side – if it has begun to turn yellow, do not bother to pick it. They are not poisonous in this state but can cause indigestion. The easiest way to prepare puffballs is to slice them thickly and gently fry in olive oil with a little crushed garlic.

Horse Mushrooms (*Agaricus arvensis*)

These are very similar to the field mushrooms above, and found in the same places and months. They are however considerably larger.

Shaggy Inkcap (*Coprinus comatus*)

Common on waste ground from June to November, this mushroom thrives on nitrogen rich soil and has an almost cylindrical cap that is covered with woolly scales. The stem is white and has a small ring around it. Its flesh is jelly like when cooked, and is good casseroled for around 25 minutes in a dish with a little mustard and garlic.

WILD MUSHROOM BHAJI WITH ALFALFA SPROUTS

Chop mushrooms into small pieces. Chop onions and sauté in oil for a few minutes. When starting to soften, add garlic and spices.

Cook for another few minutes then add mushrooms and alfalfa sprouts. Mix together and cook gently for a few more minutes.

Wild mushrooms, e.g. field, oyster or others, or use shop bought mushrooms if unavailable

2 large onions

2 cups alfalfa sprouts

A little oil

1tsp tumeric

½ tsp chilli powder

1 garlic clove

WILD MUSHROOM AND COURGETTE FLAN

Around 220g (8oz)
   field, oyster or other
   mushrooms - you can
   of course also use shop
   bought mushrooms!

1 large courgette

2 garlic cloves

1 medium onion

1 cup of porridge oats

Splash of olive or other oil

1 cup of water or stock

Tamari soy sauce

Herbs to taste

Pastry (page 163)

Make a pastry as described on page 163 and roll out to line a large pie dish.

Chop onion and garlic, slice courgette and mushrooms and gently sauté in oil with the herbs until onions are translucent.

Mix oats with water or stock and add to pan with the soy sauce and simmer until the mixture thickens.

Pour mixture into the pastry case. Bake in a medium heat oven 180°C (350°F) for 20 minutes or so.

Serve with a foraged salad and boiled fresh potatoes.

CHAPTER 9

Coming Full Circle –
The Power of Community

"If more of us valued food and cheer and song above hoarded gold, it would be a merrier world."

J. R. R. Tolkien, *The Hobbit*

P roviding the physical, emotional and spiritual sustenance for the individual that allows them to both meet their basic needs as well as develop to their fullest human potential, is fundamental to any ethically centred permaculture design process. And yet a forest doesn't simply consist of healthy trees that happen to be growing close to each other, it is actually so much more, an amazingly complex ecological web of nutrient exchanges and mutually beneficial mycorrhizal interactions between each tree's root systems, branches, leaves and canopies. So too human communities are made up of individuals who have beneficial connections with each other, and the health and well-being of every person is crucial if our future is to be truly based around values of compassion, sustainability, equity and social justice.

Everyone's a Winner!

Our currently dominant destructoculture reflects a scarcity paradigm – the 'story' we are encouraged to buy into right from birth is that life is a struggle and that there isn't enough to go around. This 'survival of the fittest' ethos is steeped in a history of conflict, exploitation and subjugation, whether inflicted against the natural world or our fellow human beings. Permaculture on the other hand is about switching to a new paradigm of abundance. We recognise that it is the tendency of nature to grow and proliferate. Look at the lushness and greenery to be found in a healthy woodland, or the way that wild plants, 'weeds', will rapidly colonise vacant land or even the cracks in the pavements. No shortages to be seen there! This isn't to say that the earth's resources are infinite or inexhaustible, rather that as a species we need to become more intelligent and creative about how they are utilised if all Earth Citizens are to enjoy clean air and water, good quality food, comfortable shelter and meaningful work and leisure. As Gandhi once put it, "there's enough for all our needs, but not for all our greed".

Earlier in this book we looked at the idea of symbiosis and co-operation in natural systems, exemplified by mutually beneficial 'guilds' such as the Native American 'Three Sisters' plantings of corn, squash and beans, or the 'stacked' structure of the woodland edge which is the basis of the forest garden. Even more powerful are the guilds that we can create between **people**, especially when we actively seek opportunities to mutually assist one another rather than behave competitively. LETS schemes, wholefood bulk-buying groups, credit unions, skill sharing workshops, Community Supported Agriculture and veggie box schemes, car-share clubs, co-housing and eco-village projects, ethical investment funds, healing and therapeutic self-help groups and many other social and economic alternatives, are all working examples of the "I'm OK, you're OK" co-operative relationships that can be developed between individuals and communities when we learn to recognise, harness and value each others' skills and strengths. Synergy – literally 'working together', is that forging of a whole that is greater than the sum of its parts, utilising and enhancing the 'edge effect'. And as we all know, it's at the edges where the interesting things happen...

Communities in Transition

The Transition movement is probably one of the most successful examples of permaculture principles at work on a wider community scale. The concept originally emerged from work permaculture designer Rob Hopkins had done with the students at Kinsale Further Education College in Ireland when writing an 'Energy Descent Action Plan' for the locality. This looked at across-the-board creative adaptations in the realms of energy production, health, education, economy and agriculture, producing a 'road map' to a sustainable future that was unanimously adopted by Kinsale Council in 2005.

Climate change and peak oil can cause us to feel confronted by overwhelmingly huge forces that we cannot do anything about. Responses such as despair, anger or denial are perfectly understandable in the face of such enormous global challenges. The central message of Transition, however, is that this state of mind is not the place to start from if we want to create positive alternatives. Indeed, by shifting our mind-set we can actually recognise the coming post-cheap oil era as an opportunity rather than a threat, and design our future low energy societies to be thriving, resilient and abundant. This is somewhere much better to live than our current alienated consumer culture based on greed, war and the myth of perpetual growth.

Using consultation and consensus building methods, Transition is about bringing all sectors of local communities, including individuals, families, businesses, local authorities and the voluntary sectors together, to collectively vision the future that we want to see: What would a society that is no longer dependent upon cheap oil and gas look like? How will such low energy communities house and power themselves? How will we meet our food and health needs? What will our transport look like? Where will business and economics fit in? What about education, arts and culture?

Rob subsequently rolled out the Transition concept to Totnes in Devon before it became an almost viral movement as communities from Lewes to Brixton began to consider how they might become more resilient and sustainable by, for example, localising food production (food yards, not food miles!), developing renewable energy sources, building with natural materials, enhancing regional economies (LETS, local currencies, etc.) and promoting distinctive 'cultures of place'. Transition is now a global movement. The Transition Model isn't about having a central blueprint or waiting for our 'leaders' to come up with the solutions that will save us, but is instead essentially 'bottom up', encouraging us to take responsibility and get up and do it ourselves and has now become an international movement. Transition initiatives around the world are creating and supporting a huge range of projects that are helping to build local self reliance and independence from oil based infrastructures:

- Transition Brixton, Totnes, Lewes, Stroud and others have launched their own currencies in order to boost local economies and build mutual support systems amongst independent businesses by encouraging shoppers to source goods and services from their own area.
- Transition Streets is a project originating in Totnes that supports neighbourhoods in coming together to explore ways to make easy changes to how they use energy, water, food, packaging and transport, saving an estimated £700 annually for each of the 500 or so participating households.
- Transition Kensal to Kilburn, in partnership with Transport For London, have created a food producing community allotment on the platform at Kilburn Underground Station in west London.
- Many Transition groups run regular seed swapping and skill sharing days where people are able to teach each other the arts of baking bread, wine making, fruit tree pruning, beekeeping and so on.
- Transition Fujino in Japan responded to the devastating 2011 tsunami and the Fukushima nuclear disaster by setting up a community energy company, with

the intention of powering their whole valley using renewable energy.

- Transition Monteveglio in Bologna, Italy have very successfully collaborated with their local council to produce a ground-breaking resolution committing them to deep sustainability and resilience-building.

Nurturing Health

When a small group of friends and activists decided to initiate a Transition project here in southeast Essex, we agreed that one of our most appropriate roles would be around networking – enabling links and connections to be made between the many existing positive initiatives in the area. From the start therefore, Southend in Transition has had a commitment to publicise, honour and celebrate the good work that is already being done around the town – the thriving local allotment scene; sustainable building and food growing projects in local schools, as well as the households, businesses, faith groups and organisations that are doing their bit to develop local empowerment, self reliance and resilience.

In conjunction with Milton Community Partnership (MCP), Southend in Transition (SiT) initiated the Fruit and Veg Together Co-op to provide local residents in one of the most economically deprived parts of the town with affordable fresh organic produce. Initially piloted in 2008, with twelve participants who each agreed to pay £3 a week for a bag of fruit and £3 for a bag of vegetables sourced from an organic wholesaler, the scheme now has over fifty members who use it on a regular or less frequent basis. One of the many positive outcomes of the co-op is the community dimension of collectively buying and picking up food. Project founders, Eleanor King and Louise Harris, have noticed many conversations about food growing, healthy eating and home cooking amongst those collecting produce. Although produce supplied by the scheme has far less of a carbon footprint than that available from nearby supermarkets, Eleanor was keen to further reduce the 'food miles' associated with transporting it from the wholesalers in Cambridgeshire (the nearest that will accept the Healthy Start vouchers used by many subscribers) to 'food metres' by encouraging more home growing. In the summer of 2010, MCP

and SiT received funding from NHS South East Essex to set up Nurturing Health, a project aimed at empowering residents to cultivate their own fruit and vegetables. This has paid for the production of a colourful leaflet designed to encourage families to turn their gardens, balconies and patios into productive spaces, plus a 'Top of the Crops' booklet and website[40] that provides more in depth information.

Feedback from the Fruit and Veg Co-op highlighted that health and affordability are the primary concerns of many households in the area. This therefore has been the emphasis of Nurturing Health, whilst at the same time linking it to a wider picture that includes positive visioning of a post-peak oil society. Co-ordinator Matt King explains:

> "We believe that fresh, locally grown food is fundamental to a healthy life. But what we eat can also affect the wider world... Climate change is a reality and we need to begin to adapt to a world in which oil is running out. But the future can be positive, as we transition to locally resilient and self-reliant households and communities. Imagine stepping out your front door to collect herbs from the pot on your doorstep, gathering tomatoes from the windowsill and salad from the tub out the back... Sharing a verge of land with your neighbours, where small nut trees grow and gathering blackberries from the hedgerow by the railway line... Cycling to the community orchard to get cooking and eating apples. Our children will know where their food comes from, how to grow it and consequently will waste much less of it."

The project also provides practical help, including giving fruit trees and bushes to community hubs to help them set up 'flagship' demonstration gardens, as well as a programme of horticultural reskilling events. The first of these, at which children were shown how to plant broad beans in paper pots, was held at a local festival. Another workshop last autumn saw the planting of a 'micro-orchard' in the tiny courtyard of the church hall. Representatives of a number of local schools also attended and got their hands dirty, as well as an opportunity to think about ways of turning their own playgrounds into edible landscapes.

Breaking Bread and Sharing Soup

Gathering over a meal is one of the most ancient forms of community process, as people sharing food appreciate each other at a profound level. Nourished bodies and relationships pave the way for better collaboration and higher quality work. Indeed I've often observed that during permaculture workshops and gatherings much of the real learning and creative thinking doesn't take place in 'formal' session time, but during the conversations and exchanges of ideas that happen while preparing and sharing communal meals.

Southend Soup[41] is a community connection and microfinance initiative that has shared food at its heart. Local activist Sherry Fuller set up the project after she'd heard about a similar idea in Detroit on a radio programme. The idea is simple, as their publicity leaflet explains:

> "On arrival, people donate a minimum of £3 (or more, if they wish) to buy soup, bread, a drink, and a vote. People mingle and get to know one another, sharing food, stories and laughter. People with good ideas get about five minutes (with a short time afterwards for questions) to talk about what they want to do, and how they'll use the money. Ideas are submitted in advance. Everyone in the room votes for the idea they want to see happen. If people feel inspired by the idea, they can also offer to help make it happen. The idea with the most votes wins the night's takings."

The first Southend Soup event took place in October 2013, raising £130 for Southend in Transition's Community Allotment project, not a huge sum, but enough to pay for shed roofing materials, weed control fabric and some much needed tools, and with enough left over to make a donation to the other project that had put in a bid that evening. But this evening was about much more than the money raised. As one attendee commented:

> "It provided a forum for friends and strangers to come together, ideas were exchanged, the air was electric with creativity, inspiration, and laughter. Children played on an old piano; whilst soup was served, slurped and savoured. It felt like everyone had chipped in one way or another. Some of the bread rolls had been donated by Gilberts, a local bakery. People had supplied the ingredients for the soup; loving hands had prepared the soup. People with full bellies, and warm hearts helped to clear away and wash up. All this in a way that can only happen when people eat together."

Southend Soup is always vegan, so that everyone can eat it. As Sherry explains, "we want to be as inclusive as possible. It also helps that vegan food is wholesome, ethical, tasty and made from ingredients that people can grow themselves; or grow with friends!" What is more, cooking only with non-animal based ingredients entails a much lower risk of cross contamination of food, and is far more straightforward from a purely logistical point of view as storage and preparation precautions are minimal.

It's also good practice (and a legal requirement) to make sure that anybody who is preparing food for members of the public to consume has appropriate training in basic health and safety procedures. This might feel like a bit of an onerous bureaucratic hoop to jump through, but really it's just common sense. Food Hygiene Certification courses are not expensive to attend (and can even be taken online), and are certainly a worthwhile investment when weighed against the liability costs of causing an outbreak of food poisoning due to being inadequately trained!

Feeding the People!

Probably the simplest way of providing food at a social gathering is the potluck. Often it's requested that those coming along to permaculture courses and events bring vegan or vegetarian food to share. This has been known to cause a little anxiety among some participants beforehand. What should they bring? What if there isn't enough to go round? What if everybody brings the same thing? Yet in all the years I've been teaching I've never failed to see a banquet conjured up, with people contributing all manner of wonderful ingredients that somebody or other will magically transform into an incredible selection of culinary delights! Usually two or three people will be nominated to take responsibility for the actual food preparation as more than this can cause chaos in the kitchen area. There are always plenty of jobs for other people to do, such as organising foraging expeditions to knock up an accompanying salad, or co-ordinating trips to the nearest store for wine and beer supplies! Potlucks are all about creativity and improvisation. On one occasion the course organisers forgot to bring plates, but the permaculture principle of seeing solutions instead of problems came into play by simply picking some large Swiss chard leaves from the vegetable garden that not only served as improvised plates, but could be eaten afterwards, thus saving on washing up!

Cooking by the Fire

There is something particularly special about cooking and eating by an open fire, especially when accompanied by story telling, good conversation or maybe some improvised songs played on a few musical instruments. Perhaps it is the rituals of gathering the materials and lighting the fire, or the warmth, the crackling flames, and the smell of wood smoke on your clothes and in your hair. Or maybe it taps into deep ancestral remembering of the experiences of security and community that we have shared at the hearth for so many thousands of years.

The trick to cooking with fire is to make one that is not too hot rather than having a roaring blaze. Ideally the wood used should be between 2.5-5cm (1-2in) in diameter, with the aim of creating a thick bed of coals suitable to cook on. Large heavy bottomed pans are a must, which should be suspended above the fire rather than coming directly into contact with it. Ideally use a tripod, the height of which can be adjusted according to the intensity of the heat source. Alternatively some form of grate can be set above the flames by raising it on bricks on either side of the fire pit. Always be aware of safety issues when working with fire, especially when children (or alcohol!) are around. Be sure that a responsible person is supervising at all times, and that there is a 'safe zone' around the fire pit of at least a metre distance all round. It can be a good idea to create a ring of stones around the fire pit in order to create a physical and psychological barrier. If moving around, people should always walk (and not run!) outside of this circle rather than inside. Have a bucket of water (not plastic as this might melt!) to hand at all times just in case of emergencies. Always make sure any fires are fully extinguished before leaving them alone.

Soups and stews improvised with whatever veggies, beans and other ingredients such as pasta, lentils, etc. happen to be about, always make for good hearty outdoor fayre. A Dutch Oven (basically a large heavy cast iron cooking pan) is a worthwhile investment if you can afford it or are likely to be doing a lot of outdoor cooking, but it can also be fun to improvise. Here is a selection of other campfire favourites that children in particular will always enjoy, especially if they are involved with the preparation:

Biscuit Tin Oven

Place three pebbles in the bottom of a metal biscuit tin. Place a metal plate on the pebbles then place the item you want to cook on the plate. Position at the edge of the fire, with twice as many embers on the top of the metal box as on the bottom. You could try pizza – make a quick dough with flour, water and oil, maybe adding a little yeast to help it rise. Roll flat to about 1.5cm (0.5in) thickness. Spread tomato paste and add toppings; sliced onions, courgettes, mushrooms, sweetcorn, olives, peppers, whatever you fancy. Cooking like this is very quick so be warned, check your food regularly!

JACKET POTATOES

Wrap potatoes in silver foil and place in fire embers, or at the edge of the fire if it is too intense. The potatoes will cook in about an hour or so, depending on the heat.

Don't forget to count how many you put in; it's easy to lose a couple in the embers!

VEGETABLE KEBABS

Use a green stick to spear alternate slices of marinated (see page 139) peppers, mushrooms, cherry tomatoes, apple chunks, red onions, courgettes, etc.

Support the skewer over glowing embers, turning occasionally. Eat when well cooked.

BARBECUE BURGERS

Prepare burgers in advance (see page 183) and cook slowly on a grill over hot embers.

BAKED APPLES

Use larger cooking apples, e.g. Bramleys. Core the apple, add a filling of dried fruit and chopped nuts mixed in a little syrup, or invent your own. Seal in foil and place on the ash for about 10-15 minutes.

BREADSTICK TWISTS

Form a thick dough by mixing together flour and water. Add raisins and sultanas if you like. Make a snake-like roll of the dough and twist this snake like fashion on a thick green stick. Support it over glowing embers turning occasionally until the outside turns golden brown.

CHOCOLATE BANANAS

Cut a slit lengthways in the banana and insert some pieces of fairly traded vegan chocolate. Wrap the whole lot in foil and place in the embers. Eat once the chocolate has melted.

Catering for Larger Numbers

Potlucks and fireside cooking are great for smaller numbers of people, but aren't really efficient for groups of more than 20 or so. The logistics of cooking for larger social gatherings such as small community festivals, permaculture convergences or street parties can seem intimidating, but really it's just about good organisation. Food Not Bombs is an all-volunteer global movement that shares free healthy vegan meals at events as a way of highlighting issues around poverty, social injustice and military expenditure. Each chapter collects surplus food that would otherwise go to waste from grocery stores, bakeries and markets, as well as donations from local farmers, then prepares community meals that are served for free to anyone who is hungry. The following guidelines on catering for larger events are adapted from the *Food Not Bombs Handbook*, which can be obtained from www.foodnotbombs.net and the *Anarchist Teapot's Guide to Feeding the Masses*.[42]

Equipment

In general, the equipment you will need includes:

- 2-3 very large pots. 20-40 litre (5-10 gallon) pans and extra large mixing bowls etc. can be obtained from catering suppliers, bought second hand (try eBay) or borrowed from community centres, churches, etc. Avoid aluminium pans – these tend to be cheaper but will leach toxic aluminium into the food, which is not good, go for stainless steel where possible.
- 2-3 heavy cast iron skillets
- Several large bowls for mixing and serving
- Large kitchen spoons for mixing and serving
- 2-3 large, good quality vegetable knives for chopping
- Several cutting boards. Wooden ones are fine, but UK food hygiene requirements involve colour coded hard plastic chopping boards in order to avoid cross-contamination – green for salad vegetables, brown for root vegetables and white for bread. Badly scratched chopping boards should be discarded.
- 1 bread box with lid and attached pair of tongs for self-service
- 1 coffee urn with spout for serving hot liquids
- Cool boxes for keeping perishables plus lots of food grade plastic tubs and boxes for storage
- Propane stove and gas bottles
- 2-3 portable tables. Used as work surfaces for prep and cooking areas, plus for washing up area. Folding tables bought from hardware stores, etc. will not be

sturdy enough to hold large quantities of food. Anarchist Teapot uses army surplus trestle tables with folding legs. An interior door (with the handle removed) supported between a pair of wooden sawhorses is a great improvised solution!

- Large plastic water containers
- 2 large plastic bowls for washing up and rinsing
- First aid kit
- Fire blanket
- Tea towels for holding hot things or covering food, but not for drying, as these can be a vector for cross-contamination. Better to let things dry in the air.
- Separate bins for food (compostable), recyclable and non-recyclable waste
- Personal eating utensils (plates, bowls, cups, spoons, knives, forks, napkins, etc.). This last item involves an on-going debate around environmental appropriateness – enamel plates are expensive and will tend to disappear. Second hand china plates are relatively cheap and reusable, but easily cracked or broken, and also generate a lot of washing up which can add another layer to the logistics of organisation. Disposable plates generate waste and are part of the 'consume and throw away' mentality of modern society, but may be the best option in this situation. If opting for disposable plates, choose paper over plastic or styrofoam, which can at least be composted afterwards. It's also a good idea to encourage participants to bring their own utensils of course!
- Marquee or other temporary shelter

Tips on Cooking for the Masses!

Cooking for 100 people is generally not much different than cooking for ten, although this is not always true. Spices, herbs and salt in particular should not just be multiplied when increasing the quantities in a recipe. Much less is usually needed in most dishes, so let your taste buds be your guide. The same is true of preparation and cooking times, the larger the volume, the more time you should allow. For example, potatoes usually boil in about 20 minutes. But 50kg (110lb) of potatoes will take a lot longer – first you need to bring a huge pan of water to the boil, then the actual cooking will take longer too, around 1½ hours or so. Increase efficiency by doing as much preparation (cutting up veg, etc.) in advance. Soup is one dish that lends itself easily to cooking on site. Upon arrival, set a large pot of water to boil, and while it heats start chopping and adding vegetables, stock and seasoning. Once the vegetables begin to soften, remove half the soup and serve it.

With the remaining half, add more water, seasoning and stock and keep cooking. This can go on indefinitely and become a never-ending pot of soup.

Bear in mind that large quantities of food in a pan will burn much more easily due to the weight. Try to use pans with large, heavy bottoms for anything that's not just water or really liquidy. Whenever sautéing, ensure that you are stirring constantly from the bottom up and evenly all round. Turn down the heat as soon as things start sizzling, and turn up again only when you add liquid, which should be as soon as things start sticking to the bottom of the pan. If the food does burn at the bottom, swear a lot and stop scraping, as this will simply mix the burnt bits throughout the food, which will ruin the flavour. If it's nearly ready simply turn it off, or else transfer to a new pan leaving the burnt bit behind. If a recipe calls for veg and pulses to be cooked in a sauce, it makes sense to cook them both separately then add them to the sauce. This saves time and is less likely to burn.

Sourcing Ingredients

If bulk buying check out cash and carries and wholesale suppliers, or local markets. You should be able to get discount bulk buying accounts with food suppliers. Try to source supplies as local to the event you are catering for. Check local organic suppliers, although sometimes it makes more sense to get locally grown non-organic veg rather than organic but imported veg. Ask around for a nice farmer or where the local farmers' market is, and check food guide directories on the web.

UK wholefood suppliers include Suma[43] (deliver all over UK), Lembas[44] (deliver within 80 mile radius of Sheffield), Infinity Foods[45] (deliver in the south east), Essential[46] (deliver in the south west) and Green City[47] (deliver in Scotland).

Loads of food is discarded by wholesale suppliers, markets and supermarkets that is still perfectly usable. If you do decide to try and get food that has been chucked out to cook with, you'll need to be flexible in your menu planning according to what's available, and make sure that people you are feeding are OK about eating 'waste' food. A lot of restaurants throw out food every day; it might be worth approaching them saying that you are a community cooking group and would appreciate any leftovers. You don't have to take everything they offer you!

Food Handling and Safety

Bear in mind health and safety concerns when handling, preparing or storing food. The following are a few good practice guidelines, but it is also advisable for anybody involved in preparing food to attend a food hygiene course.

- Always wash your hands when handling food. Have a dedicated hand washing area (a sink or bowl) and use a bacterial soap.
- Don't use tea towels when soggy and dirty – avoid altogether or wash often.
- Food needs to be kept at the correct temperature. Hot food should be served at 70°C and cold food should have been stored, covered, at 5°C. Lukewarm food breeds bacteria and bugs.
- Don't leave food to be served sitting around for too long and ensure it is covered. Store all foods off the ground (even indoors); a pallet will do this if you are outdoors. Don't leave packaged food uncovered or exposed.
- Surfaces used for food preparation and serving should be wipe-able, i.e. gloss painted wood, hard plastic, stainless steel, or covered with a stiff plastic table cloth.
- Use utensils when serving food, i.e. not serving with your hands or allowing people to serve themselves with their hands.
- Be aware of health and safety, i.e. don't block paths and gangways, leave knives lying around, watch out for trip hazards, etc.

Sample Menus from *The Anarchist Teapot*

Breakfast: Tea, coffee, herbal tea, two or three different types of cereals, soya milk, dried fruit, bread and spreads.

Lunches: (usually simpler than dinner due to time constraints): Tea, coffee, herbal tea; Spaghetti Bolognese with green salad; Filling soups with bread and spreads (Carrot and coriander, leek and potato, minestrone, golden lentil soup, vegetable and coconut); Chilli wraps with salad; Salads, dips and rolls/jacket potatoes if possible; Tabbouleh and green salad and pitta.

Dinners: (usually main dish, side dish and 1 or 2 salads): Tea, coffee, herbal tea; Potato Provençal (olive, red wine and tomato sauce) with garlic bread and side salads; Mild curry with couscous, pickles, cucumber salad and tomato and onion salad; Armenian beans and nuts with new potatoes and side salads; Creamy pasta with garlic bread, toasted seeds and side salads; Vegan bangers and mash and cider sauce with side salads...

The following recipes are from the *Food Not Bombs Handbook*:

TOSSED SALAD

Wash all vegetables and chop into bite-sized pieces. (For ease of tossing and transporting, use 110 litre (30 gallon) plastic food storage bags, but be sure to double them to be on the safe side.)

Use additional vegetables which might be on hand, such as broccoli, cauliflower, onions, zucchini, beets, mushrooms, spinach, sprouts, apples, raisins, sunflower seeds, cooked whole beans (such as chickpeas, kidney beans, green peas), etc.

Hint: Use a smaller salad bowl for serving and only dress the salad in that bowl. Keep the rest on ice or refrigerated. Salad will keep overnight if undressed.

Makes: 100 servings

Need: very large mixing bowl, smaller serving bowl

Prep time: 2-3 hours

8 heads lettuce, torn

4.5kg (10lbs) carrots, chopped

3 heads celery, chopped

2.5-4.5kg (5-10lbs) tomatoes, chopped

2 heads red cabbage, shredded

2.5kg (5lbs) green pepper, chopped

2.5kg (5lbs) cucumbers, sliced

TAHINI SALAD DRESSING

Place half ingredients in blender and blend until smooth. Add more water, lemon, or apple juice, as necessary, to make a thick, creamy dressing. Repeat.

Makes: 100 servings

Need: blender

Prep time: 15 minutes

8 cups tahini

12 lemons, juice of

2 cups nutritional yeast

2tbsp toasted sesame oil

12 garlic cloves

4 cups water

Apple juice (optional)

MISO SOUP

Makes: 100 servings

Need: 22 litre (20qt.)
or 27 litre (24qt.)
sauce pot

Prep time: 40 minutes

Cooking time: 1 hour

¼ cup oil

2 heads fresh garlic, diced

2tbsp thyme

2tbsp basil

15-19 litres (4-5 gallons)
water

1kg (2lbs) miso

Optional:

1tsp hot oil or cayenne
pepper

2 cups arame (sea
vegetable)

1 head cabbage, shredded

2.5kg (5lb) tofu, cubed

4 cups scallions, chopped

Heat your favourite oil in the bottom of a soup pot. Sauté diced garlic and spices for 30 seconds. Add water and any combination of optional ingredients. Bring to a boil. Remove from heat.

Draw off 1.1-2.2 litres (1-2 quarts) of broth and, in a large mixing bowl, mix with miso paste (miso varies in strength so use about 1-1.3kg (2-3 pounds)).

When all the miso is smoothly mixed into the broth, return it to the vegetables, stir and serve.

Note: Do not boil the miso; it kills the beneficial microorganisms.

YELLOW PEA SOUP

Heat oil in the bottom of soup pot. Sauté garlic for 30 seconds, then add onions and herbs. Sauté until onions start to brown on edges.

Add peas and stir until heated and coated with oil and spices; then add water, barley, salt, and pepper. Bring to a boil.

Add chopped vegetables. Bring to a second boil, then reduce heat to low and cover. Stir occasionally. Simmer for 45 minutes or until peas are cooked to desired softness.

The soup can simmer for as long as you like, as long as you keep adding additional water. Serve hot.

Note: This soup can be made with any bean substituted for the yellow peas; such as black beans, lentils, split peas, etc. or any combination. For the grain, barley works best, but rice, whole oats, and wheat berries, or another wholegrain will work just as well.

Makes: 100 servings

Need: 22 litre (20qt.) soup pot

Prep time: 1 hour

Cooking time: 1 hour +

½ cup safflower oil

2 heads garlic, diced

5 onions, chopped

2tsp thyme

2tsp basil

2tsp oregano

11 litres (3 gallons) water

12 cups yellow peas

4 cups barley

3tbsp sea salt

1tbsp black pepper

10 potatoes, cubed

1kg (2lbs) carrots, chopped

2 heads celery, chopped

POTATO SOUP

Makes: 100 servings

Need: 22 litre (20qt.) soup
    pot

Prep time: 1 hour

Cooking time: 1 hour +

½ cup safflower oil

2 heads garlic, diced

12 onions, chopped

2tsp thyme

2tsp basil

2tsp oregano

13 litres (3 gallons) water

9kg (10 lbs) potatoes, cubed

3-4 tbsp sea salt

2tbsp white pepper

1.8kg (4 lbs) carrots,
    chopped

Heat oil in the bottom of soup pot. Sauté garlic for 30 seconds, then add onions and herbs. Sauté until onions start to brown on edges.

Add water, potatoes, carrots, salt, and pepper. Bring to a boil. Then reduce heat to low and cover. Simmer for 35 minutes or until potatoes are soft.

Ladle some soup into a blender and blend until smooth. (Be careful to hold lid onto blender very tightly; the soup is very hot and will burn you if it splashes onto you.) Blend about half of the soup. Leave some chunks of potato.

Add ½-1 cup of dill and make this Potato Dill soup. Serve hot.

TOMATO SAUCE WITH VEGETABLES

Heat oil in bottom of heavy, 27 litre (24qt.) pot. Add garlic and sauté for 30 seconds. Add onions and herbs and sauté until onions are clear. Add tomatoes, bay leaves, salt, and pepper.

Chop any vegetables you have on hand, especially broccoli, green peppers, beets, carrots, mushrooms, eggplant, etc. and add to the sauce. Cover and simmer on medium low heat for at least 1 hour, stirring occasionally. Add salt, if needed.

Serve over rice, pasta, bread, or use as a base for vegetarian chilli.

Makes: 100 servings

Need: 27 litre (24qt.) pot with lid

Prep time: 1 hours

Cooking time: 1 hour +

1 cup olive oil

1 head garlic, diced

10 onions, chopped

10 (15oz) tomatoes, canned

9kg (10 lbs) assorted vegetables, chopped finely

3tbsp oregano

2tbsp basil

2tbsp thyme

3 bay leaves

2tbsp sea salt

2tbsp black pepper

FRUIT SALAD

Makes: 100 servings.

Need: large mixing bowl, small serving bowl, plastic storage buckets with lids.

Prep time: 60-90 minutes

100 pieces assorted fruit (such as: apples, oranges, pears, peaches, bananas, pineapples, berries, raisins, etc.)

20 lemons, juice of

Cut fruit into bite-sized pieces. In a large mixing bowl, mix fruit together with lemon juice, coating all pieces. The lemon juice helps retard the browning, which occurs when fruit is exposed to the air.

Store in plastic 'tofu' buckets with tight fitting lids and refrigerate, if possible.

Serve in small portions using the small serving bowl. Great with granola, shredded coconut, or ice cream.

Join the Permaculture Plot

Out in the garden, down on the allotment
New ideas and ways are starting to ferment
The old ways are changing; the time has come at last
Soon unsustainability will be a thing of the past...

EARTHCARE! PEOPLECARE! FAIR SHARES!
Join the permaculture plot!

They say this earth of ours is running out of oil
But all of our needs can be met from the soil
Hot beds, deep beds, no dig mulches and worms
Let's create a future for our kids with the techniques we can learn!

EARTHCARE! PEOPLECARE! FAIR SHARES!
Join the permaculture plot!

There's plenty of land for all of us to share
Although seedlings and communities both need a lot of care
But don't worry, just get those seeds into the ground
Permaculture (r)evolution, let's green our sad towns!

EARTHCARE! PEOPLECARE! FAIR SHARES!
Join the permaculture plot! Right now! Today!

Acknowledgements

Creating this book has been something of an epic journey for me. It seems so long ago that I was invited to write a vegan recipe book for Permanent Publications, that somewhere along the line grew into something rather bigger. So first off I'd like to thank Maddy and Tim Harland for both the opportunity and for sticking with it, as well as giving me a free hand to develop the ideas that had been swirling around in my head. I'd also like to thank Tony Rollison, Rozie Apps, Emma Postill and all the creative team at Permanent Publications for all their work behind the scenes and for turning my manuscript and drawings into a work of true beauty.

My own journey began much further back however, with long nature walks with my granddad George Collins when I was very small, catching and studying big (well they seemed big to me at 5 years of age) stripey garden spiders in jam jars (we always let them go afterwards...) and watching woodland ants for hours on end as they teemed around building and maintaining their nests in nearby Hockley Woods in Essex. These early memories instilled in me a sense of earth care, and a fascination for observing the natural world, while my mum Hazel's strong ethics of social justice and respect for other people made sure I was brought up to have a lifelong empathy with the values of people care and fair shares.

I enjoyed my school days during the 1970s, but my abiding memory is that most of the formal lesson time seemed to be about learning how to fit in, get good marks and curtail the excesses of imagination and day-dreaming that I seemed to be prone to. Notable exceptions were my English teacher Ken Dawson (who apparently was married to an Italian anarchist and allowed us to swear in class 'provided it was for a good reason') and my art teacher Tom Davidson, both of whom nurtured and helped me to believe in my own creative abilities as a writer and illustrator.

Leaving school in 1977 coincided with two significant life events; becoming vegetarian and discovering punk rock – a band called Crass taught me that there could be more to the latter than three chord thrash, funny haircuts and safety pins, and more to the 'anarchy' espoused by The Sex Pistols than swearing on tea-time TV. Steve Ignorant, Eve Libertine, Penny Rimbaud and Gee Vaucher introduced me to the idea that 'There is no authority but yourself' (not too dissimilar from the 'prime directive' of permaculture; 'take responsibility for our own existence and that of our children'), and remain good friends, continuing to host my permaculture courses at their Dial House home in Essex to this day.

By the early 1980s I'd begun to realise that the dairy industry had as much (if not more) involvement in animal cruelty as the meat industry, but it was through meeting a young woman who became a lifelong friend called Seema Kapoor at a protest in 1984 that I finally joined the dots and became vegan myself. I quickly recognised however, that it is as easy to lead an unsustainable, unaccountable vegan lifestyle based on imported, fossil fuel hungry convenience foods as it is to live as an unsustainable and unaccountable omnivore. I was pleased therefore to discover the Movement for Compassionate Living, an organisation set up in 1985 to promote 'ecological veganism' through their magazine 'New Leaves', from which I've had permission to adapt some of the recipes that appear in this book thanks to Alan and Elaine Garrett; and the late Kathleen Jannaway's seminal pamphlet 'Abundant Living in the Coming Age of the Tree' that hugely influenced my thinking with its vision of a future tree rather than oil based culture. Kathleen and the MCL's ideas were in fact very similar to those of permaculture, and reading Graham Bell's book *The Permaculture Garden* was for me the 'light bulb moment' that led me to attend an introductory weekend in south London with the late Carl Smith and his partner Nicci Del Rio in 1995, and a full Permaculture Design Course with north London based Naturewise a year or so later.

I've met a whole host of amazing people involved in permaculture who have shared their knowledge, wisdom, inspiration and support, as well as many other wonderful friends and fellow travellers. I can't possibly name them all, but just a few of them are: Ron Bates, Mark Warner, Kamil Pachalko, Sherry Fuller, Steve Jordan and everyone involved in Southend in Transition, Nicole Freris, James Taylor, Claire White, Marianne Cadbury, Crispin Mayfield, Cath Sunderland, Alpay Torgut, Thelma Riley, Taylor Rourke and all the Naturewise crew; Adrian Leaman at Wholewoods; Claire Joy, Ru Litherland, Brian Kelly, Marlene Barrett and all at OrganicLea; Antonio Scotti and Stella Strega of Permacultura Espana; Rob Squires, Jan Mulreany, Stef Geyer, Ed Sears, Tomas Remiarz, Andy Goldring, Suzi High, Joe Atkinson, Debbie Jones, Harriet Walsh, Dom Marsh and all the trustees and staff of the Permaculture Association past, present and future; Ian 'Tolly' Tolhurst, Peter White, David Graham and Jenny Hall at the Vegan Organic Network; Tom Hodgkinson, Merlyn Peter, Andy Langford, Duncan Law, Sarah Cannon and all at Transition Town Brixton; Aranya, Mike Feingold, Bryn Thomas, Sarah Pugh, Klaudia Van Goole, Angus Soutar, Judith Hannah, Brigit Strawbridge, Rootsman Rak, Sinisia and all at Ekosense in Croatia, Sid and Zillah, William Faith, Monica Richards, Geoff Bruce, Crispin Bixler, Scott Horton and all my friends Across The Pond; Rob Hopkins, Hannah Thorogood, Patrick Whitefield, Martin Crawford, Chris Evans, Looby Macnamara, Jo Barker,

Steve Reed, Chrissy Mitchell, Peace Ravenwood, Carol Hunt, Simon and Vicky Lacey, Nicole Vosper, Amanda Baker, Andy and Cath and all at Footprint Workers Co-Op, Malcolm at Housmans, Jon Active, Steve the Vegan Warrior; all of my course students and participants, as well as co-teachers and course hosts, and to anyone else I've forgotten to include – you know who you are, and that I appreciate you!

My biggest thanks of all of course go to my wonderful wife Debby for all of her love and support, and to my children, Chloe, Jen, Jack and Rowan. May your journeys through your lives be as wonderful as mine have been.

Further Reading

By no means a comprehensive list. Note that not all of the titles below are 100% vegan friendly. They do however all contain useful information that you can adapt to your own circumstances. As with any books or ideas, make your own mind up, take what is useful and disregard the rest...

Permaculture

The Earth Care Manual, Patrick Whitefield, Permanent Publications, 2003.

The Earth Users Guide to Permaculture, Rosemary Morrow, Permanent Publications, 2006.

Permaculture a Beginners Guide, Graham Burnett, Spiralseed, 2001.

Permaculture a Designers Manual, Bill Mollison, Tagari, 1988.

Permaculture: Principles and Pathways Beyond Sustainability, David Holmgren, Permanent Publications, 2011.

The Permaculture Way, Graham Bell, Permanent Publications, 2004.

Veganism

Animal Liberation, Peter Singer, Thorsons, 1991.

Compassion: The Ultimate Ethic, Victoria Moran, Thorsons, 1985.

Food for a Future, Jon Wynne Tyson, Thorsons, 1986.

Food: Need Greed and Myopia, Geoffrey Yates, Earthright, 1986.

Why Vegan? Kath Clements, Heretic Books, 1985.

Zone 00 – Personal Health and Well-being

Eat More Raw, Steve Charter, Permanent Publications, 2004.

People and Permaculture, Looby Macnamara, Permanent Publications, 2012.

Becoming Vegan: Comprehensive Edition: The Complete Reference on Plant-based Nutrition, Brenda Davis, Vesanto Melina, Book Pub Co, 2013.

Becoming Vegan: Express Edition: The Everyday Guide to Plant-based Nutrition, Brenda Davis, Vesanto Melina, Book Pub Co, 2013.

The Revolution of Everyday Life, Raoul Vaneigem, Rebel Press, 1983.

The Seven Habits of Highly Effective People, Stephen Covey, Franklin Covey, 1989.

Zone 0 – The Permaculture Home and Kitchen

Eco-house Manual: A Guide to Making Environmentally Friendly Improvements to Your Home, Nigel Griffiths, Haynes, 2007.

How to Store Your Garden Produce, Piers Warren, Green Books, 2008.

Our Ecological Footprint, Wackernagel and Rees, New Society Publishers, 1998.

Jams and Preserves, Good Housekeeping, 1973.

Saving the Planet Without Costing the Earth, Donnachadh McCarthy, Fusion Press, 2004.

The Sprouter's Handbook, Edward Cairney, Argyl Books, 2011.

Zone 1 – Designing the Permaculture Garden

Edible Perennial Gardening: Growing Successful Polycultures in Small Spaces, Anni Kelsey, Permanent Publications, 2014.

Designing and Maintaining Your Edible Landscape Naturally, Robert Kourick, Permanent Publications, 2004.

Gaia's Garden, Tony Hemmenway, Chelsea Green, 2009.

Permaculture Design: A Step-by-Step Guide, Aranya, Permanent Publications, 2012.

The Permaculture Garden, Graham Bell, Permanent Publications, 2004.

The Vegetable Gardener's Guide to Permaculture, Christopher Shein, Timber Press, 2013.

Zone 2 – Growing Your Own

Companion Planting, Gertrud Franck, Thorsons, 1983.

The Encyclopedia of Organic Gardening, Geoff Hamilton, DK Publishers, 1991.

Growing Green, Jenny Hall and Ian Tolhurst, Growing Green International, 2009.

Grow Your Own Vegetables, Joy Larkcom, Frances Lincoln, 2002.

Mycellium Running, Paul Stamets, 10 Speed Press, 2005.

Teaming with Microbes: The Organic Gardener's Guide to the Soil Food Web, Jeff Lowenfels, Timber Press, 2010.

Veganic Gardening, Kenneth Dalziel O'Brien, Thorsons, 1986.

Zone 3 – Maincrops and Staples

Local Food: How to Make it Happen in Your Community, Tamzin Pinkerton, Transition Books, 2009.

Plants for a Future, Ken Fern, Permanent Publications, 2011.

Shopped, Joanna Blythman, Harper Collins, 2011.

The Tassajara Bread Book, Edward Espe Brown, Shambhala, 2011.

The One Straw Revolution, Masanobu Fukuoka, NYRB, 2009.

What's Wrong with Supermarkets? Lucy Michaels, Corporate Watch, 2004.

Zone 4 – Towards a Tree Based Culture

Abundant Living in the Coming Age of the Tree, Kathleen Jannaway, Movement for Compassionate Living, 1991.

Creating a Forest Garden, Martin Crawford, Green Books, 2010.

Community Orchards Handbook, Angela King & Sue Clifford, Common Ground, 2010.

Forest Gardening, Robert Hart, Green Books, 1996.

Restoration Agriculture, Mark Shepard, Acres USA, 2013.

Tree Crops: A Permanent Agriculture, J Russell Smith, Conservation Classics, 1987.

Woodlands: A Practical Handbook, Elizabeth Agate, British Trust for Conservation Volunteers, 2002.

The Woodland Way: A Permaculture Approach to Sustainable Woodland Management, Ben Law, Permanent Publications, 2013.

Zone 5 – Walking on the Wild Side

Food for Free, Richard Mabey, Collins, 1989.

Letting in the Wild Edges, Glennie Kindred, Permanent Publications, 2013.

How to Read the Landscape, Patrick Whitefield, Permanent Publications, 2014.

Sharing Nature with Children, Joseph Kornell, Dawn Publishing, 1999.

Wild, Jay Griffiths, Penguin, 2008.

The Power of Community

A Consensus Handbook, Seeds For Change, 2013.

Do It Yourself: A Handbook for Changing Our World, Trapese Collective, Pluto Press, 2007.

Feeding the Masses: A Guide to Mass Vegan Catering, Anarchist Teapot Mobile Kitchen, Ecoaction, 2009.

Hungry for Peace, Keith McHenry, Food Not Bombs, 2012.

The Transition Companion, Rob Hopkins, Transition Books, 2011.

Toolbox for Sustainable City Living, Scott Kellog and Stacey Pettigrew, Southend Press, 2008.

Some of My Favourite Cookbooks (apart from this one...)

Another Dinner Is Possible, Isy and Mike, Active Press, 2010.

Soy Not Oi!, The Hippycore Crew, Active Press, 2005.

The Tassajara Cookbook, Edward Espe Brown, Shambhala, 2011.

Vegan Cooking, Eva Batt, Thorsons, 1985.

You Can Have Your Permaculture and Eat it Too, Robin Clayfield, Earthcare Education, 2013.

Some Other Essential Resources

Agroforestry Research Trust (for rare and unusual trees and plants for forest gardeners) www.agroforestry.co.uk

Beans and Herbs (Vegan organic vegetable and herb seeds) www.beansandherbs.co.uk

Cool Temperate Nursery (for fruit trees, including 'own rootstock' apples) www.cooltemperate.co.uk

Movement for Compassionate Living the Vegan Way (pioneers of ecological veganism, publish *New Leaves* magazine and Kathleen Jannaway's 'Abundant Living in the Coming Age of the Tree' (free download available)) www.mclveganway.org.uk

Permaculture Activist magazine www.permacultureactivist.net

Permaculture Association (Britain) www.permaculture.org

Permaculture LAND (visit working permaculture projects around the UK) www.permaculture.org.uk/land

Plants for a Future www.pfaf.org

Permaculture magazine www.permaculture.co.uk

Spiralseed (vegan permaculture and other courses and workshops) www.spiralseed.co.uk

Tamar Organics (extensive range of organic vegetable seeds for the home and professional grower) www.tamarorganics.co.uk

The Real Seed Catalogue (grain seeds for home growers, including quinoa) www.realseeds.co.uk

Vegan Organic Network www.veganorganic.net

Vegan Society www.vegansociety.com

References

1. www.pfaf.org
2. www.viva.org.uk/
   what-we-do/slaughter/
   slaughter-farmed-animals-uk
3. The Vegan Society
   www.vegansociety.com
4. www.thelandmagazine.org.uk/sites/
   default/files/can_britain_feed_itself.pdf
5. www.mclveganway.org.uk
6. http://spiralseed.co.uk/
   forest-gardening-in-the-city/
7. www.idler.co.uk
8. www.schnews.org.uk
9. www.indymedia.org.uk
10. www.corporatewatch.org
11. www.wikileaks.org
12. www.yesmagazine.org/issues/
    new-stories/the-great-turning
13. http://footprint.wwf.org.uk/
14. www.bestfootforward.com/
    resources/ecological-footprint
15. www.annforfungi.co.uk
16. *Wild Fermentation*, Sandor Ellix Katz,
    Chelsea Green Publishing, 2003.
17. *The Art of Fermentation*, Sandor Ellix
    Katz, Chelsea Green Publishing,
    2012.
18. *The Earth Care Manual*, Patrick
    Whitefield, Permanent Publications,
    2003.
19. *Permaculture Design: A Step-By-Step
    Guide*, Permanent Publications, 2012.
20. *Gaia's Garden*, Toby Hemenway,
    Chelsea Green Publishing, 2009.
21. www.growingcommunities.org
22. Graham Bell – 'The Sustainable
    Success of Permaculture', from *A
    Future For The Land*, Resurgence
    Books, ed. Philip Conford, 1992

23. www.corporatewatch.org/?lid=252
24. www.theguardian.com/
    lifeandstyle/2009/feb/19/
    national-trust-allotments
25. 'Growing Your Own – the Pros and
    Cons' – article by Peter Harper, date
    unknown.
26. www.tolhurstorganic.co.uk
27. www.growingcommunities.org
28. www.eapples.co.uk
29. http://archive.babymilkaction.org/
    resources/yqsanswered/yqanestle07.
    html
30. http://cerealdisease.cfans.
    umn.edu/files/2012/10/
    NEW-2011-RJA-Crops-that-feed-
    the-world-4-barley-Newton.pdf
31. www.ucsusa.org/publications/
    ask/2012/reforestation.html
32. http://crapes.wordpress.com/
33. www.cooltemperate.co.uk
34. www.naturalbeekeepingtrust.org
35. www.brogdale.org
36. *Food For Free*, Richard Mabey,
    Harper Collins, 1989.
37. www.activedistributionshop.org
38. www.internationaltreefoundation.org
39. www.leafforlife.org/PDFS/english/
    Leafconm.pdf
40. www.topofthecrops.org.uk
41. http://southendsoup.wordpress.com/
42. www.eco-action.org/teapot/
43. www.suma.co.uk
44. www.lembas.co.uk
45. www.infinityfoods.co.uk
46. www.essential-trading.co.uk
47. www.greencity.co.uk

Enjoyed this book?
You might like these

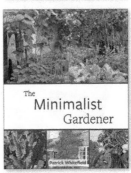

Get 15% off any of our other books above with
discount code: **VEGAN-BOOK**
Just visit **www.green-shopping.co.uk**

Our titles cover: permaculture, home & garden, green
building, food & drink, sustainable technology,
woodlands, community, wellbeing and so much more

See our full range of books here:

www.permanentpublications.co.uk

Subscribe to a better world

Vegan Arancini

Future Care
REDEFINING THE THIRD PERMACULTURE ETHIC

permaculture
Revealing Nature's Intelligence

Each issue of *Permaculture Magazine International* is hand crafted, sharing practical, innovative solutions, money saving ideas and global perspectives from a grassroots movement in over 170 countries

Print subscribers receive FREE digital access to our complete 25 years of back issues plus bonus content

To subscribe call 01730 823 311 or visit:

www.permaculture.co.uk

See our North American specific edition at: **https://permaculturemag.org**